COOKING
SMART

Also by Sharon Tyler Herbst

Breads
Food Lover's Companion
The Joy of Cookies
Simply Sensational Desserts

COOKING SMART

*Recipes, Tips, and Techniques
for Really Using the Time-Saving,
Work-Saving Gadgets in Your Kitchen
to Create Delicious Food*

Sharon Tyler Herbst

HarperCollins*Publishers*

HarperCollins books may be purchased for educational, business, or sales promotional use. For information, please call or write: Special Markets Department, HarperCollins Publishers, Inc., 10 East 53rd Street, New York, NY 10022. Telephone: (212) 207-7528; Fax: (212) 207-7222.

FIRST EDITION

Library of Congress Cataloging-in-Publication Data
Herbst, Sharon Tyler.
    Cooking smart: recipes, tips, and techniques for really using the time-saving, work-saving gadgets in your kitchen to create delicious food/by Sharon Tyler Herbst.—1st ed.
        p.   cm.
    Includes index.
    ISBN 0-06-016117-5
    1. Cookery.   I. Title.
TX714.H467   1991   90-56347
641.5—dc20

92 93 94 95 96 DT/RRD 10 9 8 7 6 5 4 3 2 1

Dedicated with love to Kay and Wayne Tyler (Mom and Dad) for instilling in me a love for food, a respect for words, and the belief that I can accomplish anything I set my heart and mind to.

CONTENTS

ACKNOWLEDGMENTS

No book gets written without plenty of behind-the-scenes people contributing their talent and support. My warm and affectionate thanks go to:

Ron Herbst—my husband, my hero, my best friend—who's always there to brainstorm with, taste my experiments, fix computer glitches, share in my ups and downs, and make me unbelievably happy.

Tia Leslie, my beautiful sister, for her loving support throughout the years, and for encouraging me to keep going when I thought I couldn't write another word or test another recipe.

Leslie Bloom, a dear friend with an infectious sense of adventure, for her creative input, cheerful support, and unanswering certainty that I can do almost anything.

Glenn Miwa, one of my favorite people in the world, for sharing with me his talent and flair for cooking, and for the many fun-filled hours we spent discussing our favorite subject—food.

Fred Hill, my wonderful, creative literary agent and the man who came up with the idea for this book, for his faith in me, his continual encouragement, and unstinting support.

Susan Friedland—my talented editor and guiding light at HarperCollins—who from the start has been a tough taskmaster and great enthusiast for *Cooking Smart*, for her vision in bringing this book together.

Susan Derecskey, my meticulous copy editor, for her gentle suggestions and fine-tuned edits, all of which made *Cooking Smart* a better book than I could have hoped for.

All the talented HarperCollins people who worked so hard on the artwork, layout, proofing, and the dozens of other tasks it took to create this book in its final form. I salute you!

And all my family members and friends for their encouragement and enthusiasm for this latest tome, and for sharing their knowledge and adding to mine.

COOKING
SMART

Cooking Smart

. . . .

I was born at noon on Thanksgiving Day and have been having a love affair with food ever since. I love everything about it. The way it looks, the way it cooks, the smell and feel and texture of it, and mostly how it brings friends and family together for convivial conversation and good times. Many years ago, I told a friend who complimented me on my cooking that I'd be perfectly happy locked away in a kitchen with stacks of ingredients so I could experiment on recipes to my heart's content. Little did I know that a few years later I would become a food writer and get my wish. Making food my career, however, hasn't cooled my ardor for it in any way.

> Food is a subject of conversation more spiritually refreshing even than the weather, for the number of possible remarks about the weather is limited, whereas of food you can talk on and on and on.
> —A. A. Milne

What has changed since my early days of cooking is the amount of effort I put into working with food. There once was a time when I'd spend a week planning a dinner party and at least two days cooking intricate dishes for an elaborate six-course meal. Happily, those days are long gone. Now my personal style of cooking—both for everyday and entertaining—is much more relaxed and free-flowing, more in tune with today's active lifestyles. I'm no longer the zealot who believed that everything had to be done by hand to reflect quality. Thank heavens!

Just exactly what prompted this move away from labor-intensive cooking? Well, times have changed, my life is busier, and the years have made me smarter. That's not to say that I don't still spend time in the kitchen. I do. But I don't spend it doing tasks that can more quickly and efficiently be handled by my kitchen cast of supporting players including the food processor, blender, electric mixer, and microwave oven. On the contrary, now I gladly accept the help of whatever kitchen aid that might assist me in creating wonderful meals with minimal effort.

This comfortable, easy, and relatively effortless style of cooking is tailor-made for anyone who wants hasslefree meals without compromising on quality and flavor. As you'll see in the following pages, the recipes still reflect my passion for food. I haven't relinquished one jot of the freshness, eye-appeal, and lively flavors that make it so enticing. But by efficiently incorporating the use of labor-saving kitchen appliances, the pleasure of cooking is accentuated, its angst is eliminated. Just as the famous Johnny Mercer song says: "Accentuate the positive; eliminate the negative."

Mind you, I don't suggest employing these electronic wonders just for the sake of using them. But if doing so saves time or is more efficient, and the end result is just as wonderful as it would be if hours were spent in preparation, why not? It's the smart thing to do. The ultimate goal is still the same: to create delicious food in the shortest time with the least amount of effort. In short, to make life easier by making smart use of modern kitchen contrivances.

Whether your kitchen appliances rank as countertop clutter or labor-saving helpmates comes down to whether or not you use them. It's also important to put them to work in tandem with each other. For instance, polenta can be burbling away in the microwave oven while you use the food processor to cut the salad vegetables and blend the salad dressing. At the same time, a stovetop or electric skillet can be used to sauté chicken and the blender to puree tomatoes and basil for an almost instant sauce. Tandem cooking at its best!

Personally, there are times when I don't mind a dish taking a long time to cook—as long as I don't have to pay much attention to it. While that dish is busy baking in the oven or stewing on the stovetop, I can do other things. Whether it's finishing the rest of the dinner or snuggling up with a good book depends on my mood and the circumstances.

Most of the following recipes were developed with convenience in mind. Because I personally don't like last-minute hassle, many of them can be prepared to a certain point and finished later. Whether that point is an hour or a couple of days ahead of time depends on the dish and the cook. Many dishes can be completely prepared in advance and refrigerated, to be cooked or reheated just before serving. Others can be frozen, to be pulled out for those times when you have neither the time nor the inclination to cook.

You'll save time in the long run if you read through a recipe before beginning to cook. This will give you a sense of the dish—both for the preparation sequence and for the ingredients and equipment necessary to make it. In the best of all possible worlds, you should measure and set out the ingredients for the recipe, in the order in which they'll be used.

None of the recipes in this book require hard-to-find ingredients or special skills to create. They've all been developed with attention to a balance of contrasting yet complementary flavors, textures, and colors. Where appropriate, I employed the cooking-smart philosophy of making wise use of time-saving appliances. My main purpose, however, was for the food to be absolutely wonderful, and to look as good as it tastes. Of course, taste is intensely subjective, but I hope you'll find favorites in the succeeding pages that will become a regular part of your recipe repertoire.

Here then, for your enjoyment, is my contribution toward giving you a little more time for yourself. I hope the philosophy celebrated in the following pages will start you on the road to a new kitchen lifestyle that will become a regular part of your everyday cooking. My sincere wish is that these recipes bring you pleasure and satisfaction—both in the making and in the eating. Cooking is one of the most positive personal statements you can make. It should be an adventure, not a chore. And, as my dear, late friend Bert Greene once said, "Food, like love, must never be a joyless experience."

COOK SMARTER, NOT HARDER—PUT THOSE APPLIANCES TO WORK FOR YOU!

The philosophy of smart cooking is based on the use of labor-saving kitchen appliances to create delicious food in the shortest time with the least amount of effort. In the following recipes, the machines are used only where appropriate, without compromising on quality or flavor. Following is a brief description of the main appliances used in the application of the smart-cooking principle.

✦✦✦✦✦ Microwave Oven ✦✦✦

About 75 percent of American households today have at least one microwave oven. Generally speaking, people's attitudes toward the microwave are either mystified, skeptical, or zealous. I was somewhere between the first two— either skeptical or mystical, depending on how you look at it. Before writing this book, I used my microwave for such menial tasks as reheating foods and melting chocolate and butter. That's no longer true. I've since discovered that the microwave oven cooks many other things well. I now use it for everything from cooking fish and vegetables to rising bread. Mind you, I don't employ the microwave just for the sake of using it. But it's certainly become a strong supporting player in my kitchen's cast of characters.

How do microwave ovens work? On the simplest terms, they convert electric energy into microwave energy—short, high-frequency electromagnetic waves, similar to those emitted by ordinary daylight and radio waves. This energy makes food molecules vibrate at an incredibly fast rate, creating the friction that heats and cooks the food. Microwaves travel so extraordinarily fast—and cook food so quickly—because they're so short. Attracted to the fat, moisture, and sugar content in food, the waves cook from the outside in and only penetrate food to a depth of about 1½ to 2 inches. The center of the food is generally cooked by heat conduction.

There are dozens of microwave ovens on the market today. They vary greatly in size, wattage, and features. Some are simple three-speed models, others have an electronic touchpad that looks like it's right out of NASA's mission control. Some microwave ovens have a rack or shelf, which allows more than one dish to be cooked at a time. Others have turntables that rotate the food, for even cooking. Portable turntables may be purchased for microwave ovens without one.

Besides the power and size of a microwave oven, there are many other factors that affect how fast food cooks in it. For example, electric currents vary from house to house, and voltage fluctuations are common in many areas during periods of peak consumption. Unlike some other cooking methods, using a different size or shape container can also make a noticeable difference in how long it takes to cook a dish in the microwave. Likewise, you can't increase a recipe and expect it to cook in the same time—two potatoes can take almost twice as long to cook as one. And if you're cooking more than one dish at a time (possible with ovens equipped with a rack), the cooking takes longer because the volume of food is greater. The bottom line is that small amounts of food cook faster than large amounts.

Other characteristics that affect how a microwave cooks food are: shape (thin pieces cook faster than thick), fat and/or bone distribution, density, starting temperature, and the amount of moisture, sugar, and fat the food contains. Foods with low-moisture and/or high-fat or high-sugar content cook faster. With many recipes, there's a standing time after the dish is removed from the microwave oven. These extra few minutes allow heat conduction to finish the job of cooking. As you can see, there are many variables with microwave cooking. It's therefore very important that you watch the food carefully, checking it at the minimum time suggested in a recipe.

Nonmetal containers are used in microwave ovens because microwaves pass through them (unlike metal, which deflects the waves). The waves cook the food from all directions (top, bottom, and sides) at once. The fact that the waves pass through glass and ceramics means that the containers stay relatively cool even though the food they contain becomes quite hot. With long cooking periods, however, the food can heat the dish, so caution is the by-word when removing it from the microwave oven.

Almost any glass or ceramic dish can be used in the microwave oven.

Avoid those with metallic designs or glazes, which will deflect the waves. Many containers are labeled "Suitable for Microwave" or "Microwave Oven Safe." If you're unsure of your container, conduct the following test for microwave safety: *Place eight ounces of cool water in a one-cup glass measure. Set it in the microwave next to or in the center of the dish in question. Microwave on* HIGH *for one minute. If the dish remains cool, it's suitable for microwave cooking.*

Some foods can also be cooked on microwavesafe paper plates or paper towels. There's concern that recycled paper towels contain minuscule specks of metal (which could generate sparks and a subsequent fire), so it's a good idea to avoid those for microwave use. Various plastic containers can be used, as well, but be cautious. Unless they're specifically made for microwave use, plastic containers may warp or melt during prolonged cooking.

Plastic wrap makes a good cover for many containers. Just be sure to use a brand labeled "microwavable." There is some concern that at high temperatures the plasticizers in some plastic wraps could migrate to food in contact with the wrap. Though so far there's no conclusive proof of toxicity, why take a chance? Avoid the problem by not allowing the wrap to touch the food during prolonged cooking where heat gets very high. When an airtight plastic-wrapped container is removed from the oven, the wrap often collapses onto the food. This problem can be avoided simply by poking a tiny hole in the center of the plastic wrap after it's stretched tight over the container. Or, the dish can be vented by turning back a corner of the plastic to allow some of the steam to escape while the food is cooking. When removing plastic wrap from a dish, always fold back the side away from you first, to avoid the escaping scalding-hot steam.

Wax paper, which allows some of the steam to escape during cooking, can be used for a loose-fitting cover. Microwavesafe paper towels are good for covering foods that spatter, thereby avoiding messy clean-up. And, of course, dishes with covers are also good choices.

This is not a microwave cookbook. I do, however, recommend the microwave oven where I've found it to be more efficient. If a dish requires several additions and a lot of stirring—which would mean the hassle of opening and closing the microwave oven door many times—you won't find a microwave method for it. That simply wouldn't be time- or energy-efficient. And where I give a microwave method, I always offer a conventional alternative for those who either don't own a microwave or don't want to use it. My recipes were tested in full-size, 625 to 700 watt microwave ovens. If your oven has less wattage (the owner's manual will tell you), increase the cooking time by about 15 percent. Check your manual for the time-adjustment guide tailored to your oven.

◆◆◆◆◆ Convection Oven   ◆◆◆

Though they've been used since the 1950s in professional kitchens, convection ovens for the home cook have only been available for about 15 years. Very simply, this type of oven has a fan that provides the continuous circulation of hot air. This constantly moving heated air blows over the food, cooking it more evenly and up to a third faster (even when the oven's crowded) than in a conventional oven. Because it's so heat-efficient, a convection oven's heat may be lowered by 25° to 50°F. when cooking many foods. The convection oven saves both time and energy.

Because they heat up so fast, convection ovens usually require little or no preheating. Their hot-air circulation makes them particularly suited for foods like baked goods and roasted and broiled meats and fish. Unlike microwave ovens, convection ovens require no special cookware or major adjustments in cooking time or technique.

The majority of home convection ovens are electric countertop models, most of them about the size of a standard to large microwave. There are also built-in models in varying styles—all convection, convection-thermal (conventional), and convection-microwave. Some two-oven built-in units offer a convection-microwave oven on top and a thermal oven on the bottom. The convection-microwave combinations, which also come in countertop models, combine convection heat and microwave power, either simultaneously or alternatingly. At this writing, they don't, however, have broiling units.

Your owner's manual will give exact recommendations for adapting recipes for the convection oven. Although I haven't given convection-oven times in the recipes in this book, the rule of thumb is that temperatures for meats and fish can be lowered by 25°F. and roasting time decreased by 25 to 30 percent. For baked goods, which can easily overbrown, decrease the oven temperature by 50° to 75°F. but keep the baking time about the same.

◆◆◆◆◆ Food Processor   ◆◆

Though it's hard for some of us to remember what it was like to do without a food processor, it has been part of the modern *batterie de cuisine* only since the early 1970s. Like the Statue of Liberty, this modern-day wonder came to us from France. It has since revolutionized many of America's home kitchens.

The multifunctional food processor is versatile, and it is fast. The speed with which it can chop, dice, slice, shred, grind, and puree most food is a boon to today's busy cook. The larger machines even have the muscle to knead hefty batches of bread dough.

All food processors consist of a clear, sturdy plastic workbowl that sits on a motorized drive-shaft. When the machine is on, the shaft spins at high speed, turning the attachment connected to it. The cover of the bowl has a vertical feed tube through which foods can be added (food can also be placed directly in the bowl). A pusher that fits inside the feed tube is used both to push food into the machine and as a spatter shield for liquid mixtures. Most pushers have a tiny hole in the bottom through which a liquid can enter the work bowl in a fine drizzle—a method used in making mayonnaise and other emulsions. Except for the base, all food processor parts are dishwasher safe.

Food processor models vary widely in power and capacity. Some of the smaller versions only hold two cups of chopped food, whereas the larger models can take up to sixteen. The size of the feed tube can also vary. Some food processors have an expanded feed tube that's almost a third larger than standard. These large tubes can hold whole items like tomatoes, potatoes, or onions. I find myself buying certain vegetables just the right size to fit into the feed tube.

Most full-size processors now come with four standard tools: a metal blade (used for chopping, mixing, and pureeing), a shredding disk, a slicing disk, and a plastic blade for kneading dough. Optional attachments include a range of slicers (from super-thin 1mm to extra-thick 8mm), finer shredders, juicers, pasta makers, French-fry cutters, julienne disks, and even a special whisk (or beaters) designed to beat egg whites and cream. Options vary according to the manufacturer.

There are also two compact versions of the food processor, both designed to handle small amounts of food better than their larger kin. One is the miniature food processor or miniprocessor, which has interchangeable blades that can chop, slice, and shred. The other is the minichopper-grinder, specially designed to chop very small amounts of food, as well as grind grains and coffee beans. It cannot shred or slice, however.

Even if you own a miniprocessor, there are times when it simply makes more sense to chop something small, like a clove of garlic, by hand. Taking into consideration set-up and clean-up time for the processor, the manual method is often faster and easier. On the other hand, a standard food processor can chop a bunch of parsley and the workbowl can be rinsed in a matter of seconds.

There are certain tasks the food processor just can't do. Whipping potatoes is one—the processor's high speed turns the potatoes into a gluey glob. No processor is able to cut geometrical shapes like cubes or wedges. And without special attachments, it can't beat air into mixtures like egg whites. Standard and larger processors also can't grind coffee beans or spices.

This isn't a course in food-processor cookery, but there are a couple of hints I'd like to pass along. Technique makes all the difference when working with the food processor. When using the metal blades, for instance, using quick on/off pulses of power can make all the difference when chopping some foods. This method keeps the food bouncing around in the workbowl in the blade's path. It can keep chopped onions from becoming onion puree or nuts from turning into nut butter.

When using the slicing or shredding disks, the amount of pressure you apply to the pusher is also important. Use gentle but steady pressure. Soft foods like cucumbers require less pressure than dense foods like potatoes.

When processing liquid mixtures, be careful not to overfill the bowl (your owner's manual will tell you how much is too much). If you do, the liquid can leak out between the metal blade and the shaft, as well as at the rim of the bowl.

The sturdy plastic blade is designed to be able to mix and knead dough. It's stubby blades do a great job of kneading and churning the dough around the workbowl. Bread recipes in this book give food-processor kneading in-structions. The metal blade can also be used for the kneading process, though its sharp edges cut the dough—which is okay, but not really desirable for elastic yeast doughs.

In the following recipes, I use the food processor for most of the chopping and slicing (unless it's easier or more logical to do it by hand). When there's a dish that requires many foods to be cut, always start with the driest and least odoriferous food first. For instance, you might chop mushrooms, then zucchini, then green peppers, and finally onions—with a simple paper-towel wipe-out between vegetables. As you chop or slice them, transfer the vege-tables to individual sheets of wax paper or paper plates to save time on clean-up. Vegetables of similar texture, like apples and crisp pears, can be chopped together. When slicing several vegetables for one dish, it's not necessary to remove them from the workbowl as they're sliced unless you plan to cook them separately.

Food processors have become a mainstay in many cooks' kitchens. I could —but wouldn't want to—live without one. My last suggestion is that you reserve a spot for it on your countertop. The food processor is the workhorse of the kitchen, and having it readily available is the only way you'll use it for everyday cooking.

♦♦♦♦♦ Blender ♦♦♦

With the advent of the food processor, the blender has taken a nosedive down the popularity scale. Not in my kitchen, though. While I use the food proces-sor for chopping and slicing, I still use the blender to puree, liquefy, and blend a wide variety of mixtures. Its tall, narrow, leakproof container makes it better for liquid mixtures than the food processor. And nothing can replace the blender for making silky-smooth purees, soups, and sauces, or for whipping up frothy drinks—from breakfast shakes to frozen daiquiris. The small base of the container also allows you to chop or pulverize small amounts of food that might get lost in large food processor models.

The blender cannot shred or slice foods. And, because its container is tall and narrow, air can't get to the food, making it impossible for the blender to whip foods such as egg whites and cream. But then, neither can a food processor without a special attachment.

There are many different blender models on the market today. Some have only three speeds—low, medium, and high—while others have as many as eighteen. Some have electronic keypad controls, others a dial, others push buttons. Standard blender containers hold five cups. Some manufacturers offer one-cup jars that can be attached to the blade housing. These containers have screw-on tops and are good for chopping small amounts of food and blending salad dressings.

Blenders are simple machines to operate, but there are a few rules that should be followed. Before turning on the motor, always cover the blender, placing your hand on the lid to prevent it from popping off in case it's not firmly seated. If pieces of food become lodged in the blades, stop the machine and use a narrow rubber spatula to move the food. Make sure the blades have come to a complete stop before doing so. If a mixture is so thick that it won't move, adding a little liquid will help. Both liquid and dry ingredients can be added through the removable center insert in the lid. Be careful not to tax the motor with heavy ingredients or too much volume. If the machine begins to labor, increase the speed. If that doesn't help, stop the machine and remove half the ingredients, blending the food in two batches. When blending hot mixtures, always begin at low speed and gradually increase to high. Make sure the blades have stopped completely before removing the blender jar from the motor base. Follow the manufacturer's directions on the care and cleaning of your blender.

If you don't already have one, do you need a blender? Probably not if you own a food processor, and don't make a lot of blender drinks or purees. On the other hand, I've yet to find a food processor that will make as smooth a puree as the blender.

✦✦✦✦✦ Immersion Blender

The immersion blender is relatively new in home kitchens. But thank heavens it's finally available! This new-kid-on-the-block is a long, narrow, hand-held blender with rotary blades at one end. These tiny blades do a great job of blending and pureeing both small and large amounts of food. Some models have accessories such as a strainer, blending bowl, spatula, whisk attachment, and a beaker in which to mix drinks. The latter makes it possible to use the immersion blender to whip cream and beat egg whites. The newer models have variable speeds for optimum control.

The biggest attraction of the immersion blender is that it is portable and can be put right into a pot of soup, a bowl of cooked potatoes or other food, a glass, a pitcher, or a beaker—in short, almost any container. This means you can cook, then mix, puree, or blend the food right in the same container. Which, of course, means there's a big bonus with this appliance—minimum clean-up. If you're blending right in the pan, remove it from the heat first. And if your immersion blender has variable speeds, always begin at low speed, gradually increasing to high. With the single-speed models, safeguard your hand from hot spatters by wearing an oven mitt.

Immersion blenders can be cleaned by holding the blade part under running water. If the surface is oily, use a little soap. Always unplug the blender before rinsing, and never submerge it. Follow the manufacturer's instructions that come with your particular model.

Do you need an immersion blender? In my opinion, it's a small investment for a relatively large return in convenience and time saved. If you have a standard blender and a handheld mixer, you might not need this appliance, but once you have it, you'll never want to give it up.

♦♦♦♦♦ Electric Mixers ♦♦♦

Electric mixers have been part of the home kitchen for as long as most of us can remember. They come in two basic styles—stationary (stand) and portable (handheld). Stationary mixers have more powerful motors and therefore can handle heavier mixing jobs. They also take up more counter space. These machines range widely in size, power, and features. Some models are so lightweight that they move around on the countertop when mixing a heavy batter. Other models are so heavy-duty that they can easily handle several pounds of bread dough without moving a millimeter.

Some mixers feature two standard beaters and come with two mixing bowls, small and large. Most of the heavy-duty machines only have one large bowl and are equipped with a flat, paddle-style beater for mixing, plus a balloon wire whisk for whipping. Most stationary mixers also come with dough hooks (a single hook with the larger machines). The capacity for the small bowls is about two quarts; the standard large bowl ranges from three to four quarts, depending on the brand. The large, heavy-duty machines offer bowls ranging in capacity from five to seven quarts.

In addition to the standard beaters and dough hooks, manufacturers offer a wide assortment of attachments, including blenders, citrus juicers, ice crushers, slicer-shredders, grain/coffee mills, pasta makers, sausage stuffers, potato peelers, can openers, meat grinders, splash shields, and pouring funnels.

Mixers excel at beating, mixing, and kneading large amounts of food, such as egg whites, whipping cream, batter, and bread dough. Whether or not you want to use the countertop space for this appliance depends on how you cook. A combination of the food processor, blender (immersion or standard), and portable mixer can handle more kitchen chores than the standard mixer alone—and in about the same collective counterspace. If you're a bread baker, however, you'll probably want one of the heavy-duty mixers for kneading larger batches than is possible in a food processor.

◆◆◆◆◆ Portable (Handheld) Mixers ◆◆◆◆◆◆◆◆◆◆◆◆◆◆◆◆◆◆◆◆◆◆◆◆◆◆◆◆◆◆◆◆◆◆◆◆◆

Portable mixers can be used almost anywhere within the reach of their cord. Their reduced size is due in part to a small motor, which also limits these machines to lighter tasks than their larger relatives. But size almost makes the portable mixer easy to store.

Portable mixers vary greatly in power and speed selections. Some lightweight models bog down when beating a very thick batter. Many, however, have almost as much muscle as the smallest of the stationary mixers. Some of these high-powered models are even equipped with dough hooks. Like the immersion blender, portable mixers can do their job right in a pan, making clean-up a breeze.

When choosing a portable mixer, look for one that's well-balanced and sturdy (weighing two to three pounds). Some models have stands, which gives the mixer the versatility of being used both ways. Many manufacturers offer attachments like bowls and the already mentioned dough hooks.

Portable mixers are lightweight, adaptable, and require little storage space. On the other hand, they must be held, which some cooks find tiring, and which means that the cook can't be doing other things while using this appliance.

Rise-and-Shine Breakfasts

. . . .

Breakfasts differ greatly around the world, in both content and form. Americans are, perhaps, the most eclectic in their taste, and can be found starting the day with anything from coffee to leftover pizza. Most of us, however, prefer more traditional American favorites like cereals (cold or hot), fresh fruit and juices, pancakes and waffles, meats (sausage and bacon being the favorites), eggs in ever imaginable guise, muffins, biscuits, doughnuts, toast, or coffeecake.

In Japan, on the other hand, salads, grilled fish, and rice are the norm, while the Chinese are happier with a bowl of noodles or dim sum. Scandinavians favor herring or other fish, cheese, and hearty rye or whole-grain breads. The classic Parisian morning begins simply—with *café au lait* and a croissant—while the British believe in jump-starting the day with huge breakfasts of porridge, eggs, sausage, kippered herring, bread, and pots of jam.

One of my most memorable morning meals was Sunday brunch at the Meadowood Resort in the Napa Valley. My husband Ron and I sat on the terrace overlooking velvety green croquet courts, while the late morning sun filtered through the branches of a giant weeping willow. Gentle strains of baroque music played in the background as we sipped champagne and enjoyed perfectly crisp croissants topped with shirred eggs and chèvre. Heaven!

Needless to say, I don't (much to my regret) start all my days in such a luxurious, storybook way. Weekdays are hectic and—like so many other Americans—I often make do with a cup of coffee and a muffin, having neither the time nor the inclination for more. Truth be known, I'm one of those people who doesn't want to even think about food until at least 10 A.M.

On the other hand, weekend breakfast—or brunch, as it's called if the morning is late—is my favorite meal of the day. And I'm not alone. Weekend brunch is one of the most popular forms of dining in America today. And it's fast becoming a favorite time for entertaining, as well. People love the leisurely pace and the indulgence of eating something a little more special than usual. Special-occasion brunches might also include sipping something a little spirited like champagne, Mariachi Marys, or Sparkling Fruit Smoothies.

Because I treasure my weekend morning repasts, I definitely don't want last-minute hassle. So I do as much preparation as possible ahead of time. For example, some dishes—like Pastry Cordon Bleu, Mapled Ham Bread Pudding with Maple Cream, and Baked Apples with Walnut–Sausage Stuffing—can be completely assembled the night before and baked in the morning. And others—like Minted Melon Cup and Morning Blues—need no cooking at all; they can be made ahead and refrigerated for an early wake-up call.

There's no reason not to have hasslefree fresh-from-the-oven breads in the morning, either. The ingredients for coffeecakes, muffins, or pancakes can be measured out and combined the night before. If you're making the Rise-and-Shine Sunflower Muffins, for instance, you can combine the dry ingredients in one bowl and the liquid ingredients in another (refrigerating the latter). Even grease the muffin cups so they'll be ready to go. The next morning, all you have to do is combine the two mixtures and pop the muffins-to-be in the oven.

The result of this smart planning and advance preparation, of course, is that the cook has more time to relax in the sun and read the paper along with everyone else.

Another way to prevent morning aggravation is to have the right equipment. The one piece of cookware that can make the difference between ease and frustration for the morning cook is a skillet. A good heavy pan with a nonstick coating is a smart investment. A heavy skillet won't warp, and it will hold and conduct heat more efficiently. Nonstick coatings are a boon for cooking eggs—even the tricky omelet. And, of course, the nonstick finish means that you'll need less oil for frying.

I've included several recipes for delicious breakfast breads in this chapter, but don't overlook the Bread Basket chapter (pages 234–255). Several of those offerings—like Piña Colada Bread (page 239) and Baked Hushpuppies (page 240)—are wonderful with breakfast or brunch.

The recipes that follow are for some of my favorite morning foods. All are user friendly, and many are make-ahead dishes that can be pulled out of the refrigerator in the morning for baking. That way, the cook can sleep in and begin the day on tranquil terms.

SPICY MEXICAN MOCHA

*Makes 4 (8-ounce) or
5 (6-ounce) servings*

This aromatic, slightly sweet concoction is just as good after dinner or to warm body and spirit on a cold winter day as it is for breakfast. The recipe doubles easily so you can serve it for breakfast and have an encore that evening. Or pour the refrigerated mocha into the blender, add 2 ice cubes for every cup, and have an icy Spicy Mexican Mocha.

⅓ **cup instant coffee**
⅓ **cup unsweetened cocoa**
⅔ **cup packed light or dark brown sugar**
¼ **teaspoon ground cinnamon**
¼ **teaspoon ground allspice**
⅛ **teaspoon ground cloves**
⅛ **teaspoon salt**
4 **cups lowfat milk**
1 **tablespoon pure vanilla extract**
3 **teaspoons unsweetened cocoa mixed with 5 teaspoons confectioners' sugar for garnish (optional)**
   cinnamon sticks for garnish (optional)

1. In a medium saucepan, use a whisk to combine the coffee, cocoa, brown sugar, cinnamon, allspice, cloves, and salt. Gradually whisk in 1 cup milk, then the remaining 3 cups milk. If possible, cover and refrigerate at least 1 hour; may be refrigerated overnight.

2. Just before serving, heat the mocha over low heat, stirring often, until it's steaming and hot. Do not boil. Remove from heat and add vanilla. Whisk until frothy.

3. Pour into cups or mugs. If desired, dust with cocoa-sugar mixture and use cinnamon sticks for stirrers.

4. Cover and refrigerate leftover mocha for up to 5 days. Reheat over low heat or serve cold (see recipe headnote).

SPARKLING FRUIT SMOOTHIES

Makes 2 servings

Tailor this drink to your personal taste, using your favorite yogurt and fresh fruit (peeling it, if necessary) and perhaps adding a flavoring like cinnamon or vanilla. You might even want to use a flavored sparkling water, and champagne is festive for special occasions or Sunday brunches.

1 cup plain or fruit-flavored yogurt
1½ to 2 cups chopped fresh fruit
    pinch freshly grated nutmeg
    about ⅔ cup ice-cold champagne, sparkling water, or ginger ale
    sprigs mint or fruit slices for garnish (optional)

1. Combine the yogurt, fruit, and nutmeg in a blender; process until smooth.

2. Pour into glasses, filling ¾ full. Top off with champagne, sparkling water, or ginger ale. Gently stir to combine. Garnish with mint sprigs or fruit slices, if desired.

. . . .

MARIACHI MARYS

Makes 6 (8-ounce) servings

One taste of this snappy sipper and you might just feel like doing the Mexican hat dance! If your palate isn't tuned into heat, use half regular and half spicy tomato juice. This drink gets better if made a couple of days in advance.

1 large lime
    about ¼ cup coarse salt (optional)
6 tiny cherry tomatoes
4½ cups ice-cold Spicy Hot V 8 or spicy tomato juice
1½ cups tequila
⅓ cup fresh lime juice
½ teaspoon chili powder
    salt and freshly ground pepper

1. Cut lime in half; cut each half into quarters. Set 6 lime wedges aside. If desired, salt the rims of 6 tall 10- to 12-ounce glasses. Use the remaining lime wedges to moisten the rim of each glass. Place coarse salt in a saucer; dip each glass in salt. Place glasses in freezer until ready to use.

2. Use a long toothpick (preferably colored) to spear a tomato, then a lime wedge. The tomato should sit atop the lime. Set aside until ready to garnish drinks. (May be made ahead, covered, and refrigerated.

3. In a large pitcher, combine the juice, tequila, lime juice, chili powder, and salt and pepper to taste, stirring to mix well. If desired, cover and refrigerate for up to 3 days.

4. To serve, fill 6 glasses halfway with ice cubes; pour in Mariachi Marys. Top with tomato-lime garnish and serve.

♦**VARIATION: Virgin Mariachi Marys:** Substitute 1½ cups (12 ounces) lime-flavored sparkling water for the tequila. Add and stir gently just before serving.

. . . .

MINTED MELON CUP

Makes 8 servings

Garnish this refreshing breakfast fruit compote with mint sprigs and edible nasturtium blossoms from your garden or from a specialty produce market. Wait for fresh mint to make this—dried mint just doesn't create the same magic. This recipe is so versatile that it can also be served as a salad and dessert (Spiced Melon Coupe, page 259).

¾ **cup chopped fresh mint leaves**
 3 **(3-inch) cinnamon sticks, broken in half**
15 **allspice berries**
15 **cloves**
 3 **cups fresh orange juice**
½ **cup sugar**
    about 4½ tablespoons finely julienned lemon zest (3 large lemons)
 6 **cups mixed melon balls, such as cantaloupe, honeydew, Persian, or watermelon**
 8 **sprigs fresh mint**
 8 **nasturtium blossoms (optional)**

Clement Freud, a British politician born in 1924, wrote in *Freud on Food* that "Breakfast is a notoriously difficult meal to serve with a flourish."

1. Combine the mint and spices in the center of a three-layered, 6-inch circle of cheesecloth. Bring the edges of the cheesecloth up to center; tie securely with string. Place the bag in a medium saucepan and add the orange juice, sugar, and lemon zest. Bring to a boil. Reduce heat; simmer, uncovered, for 40 minutes.

2. Remove the bag of spices. Transfer the sauce into a shallow 2-quart dish; refrigerate or freeze until cool.

3. Add the melon, stirring to coat with sauce. Cover and refrigerate 12 to 24 hours, stirring occasionally.

4. To serve, spoon melon balls into stemmed glasses or glass bowls; drizzle with some of the sauce, including lemon zest. Garnish with fresh mint sprigs and, if desired, nasturtium blossoms.

. . . .

MORNING BLUES

. . . .

Makes 4 servings

Guaranteed to chase the morning grumps away, these maple-kissed blueberries are sure to please. Choose berries that are firm, uniform in size, and a silver-frosted indigo blue. Discard shriveled or moldy berries, and remove any stems. Wash them only when ready to use, then blot off excess moisture with paper towels.

Don't think of these berries as only for breakfast—they're absolutely perfect as a light finale for almost any summer meal.

Maple Cream (page 298)
3 cups fresh blueberries, washed and dried (about 1½ pints)
1 tablespoon finely grated orange zest
⅛ teaspoon finely grated nutmeg

1. Make Maple Cream and refrigerate until ready to use.

2. In a medium bowl, combine the blueberries, orange zest, and nutmeg. Cover and refrigerate until ready to use, up to 24 hours.

♦ TIP ♦

To retard bruising and spoilage in berries, always store them in a single layer. A jelly-roll pan or other large edged pan works nicely. Cover the berries lightly with wax paper and refrigerate for up to 2 days.

3. Remove berries from refrigerator 30 minutes before serving. To serve, spoon berries into 4 stemmed glasses or glass bowls. Top with Maple Cream as desired. Sprinkle with nutmeg.

♦**VARIATION: Peaches and Cream Blues:** Substitute 1½ cups chopped, peeled peaches for the blueberries.

. . . .

RISE-AND-SHINE SUNFLOWER MUFFINS

Makes 12 muffins

Sunflower seeds, orange juice, and orange zest in these light muffins shout "Good morning!" to even the groggiest heads. You can use dry-roasted sunflower seeds for this recipe; if you use salted seeds, decrease the salt to ½ teaspoon. Serve the muffins hot from the oven spread with a flavored butter.

¼ **cup finely chopped toasted sunflower seeds**
 2 **cups all-purpose flour**
 2 **teaspoons baking powder**
½ **teaspoon baking soda**
¾ **teaspoon salt**
 3 **tablespoons sugar**
  about ½ cup whole toasted sunflower seeds
 2 **large eggs, separated, at room temperature**
¼ **cup vegetable oil**
 1 **cup fresh orange juice, at room temperature**
 1 **tablespoon finely grated orange zest**
¼ **teaspoon cream of tartar**
  Sunflower-seed Butter (page 304) or Citrus–Honey Butter (page 308)

  1. Preheat oven to 400°F.
  2. Generously grease 12 muffin cups (2¾ inches across

◆ TIP ◆

Reheat leftover muffins by slicing them into 4 to 5 thin slices and toasting.

top; ½ cup). Sprinkle 1 teaspoon chopped sunflower seeds over bottom and sides of each cup; set aside.

3. In a large bowl, stir together the flour, baking powder, baking soda, salt, sugar, and ⅓ cup whole sunflower seeds; set aside.

4. In a medium bowl, lightly beat the egg yolks. Stir in the oil, orange juice, and orange zest. Stir into the flour mixture just until dry ingredients are moistened; set aside.

5. In the small bowl of the electric mixer, beat egg whites with cream of tartar until stiff but not dry. Stir about 3 tablespoons of the whites into batter to loosen it; gently fold in remaining egg whites.

6. Spoon batter into prepared muffin cups, filling ⅔ to ¾ full. Sprinkle tops of muffins with the remaining whole sunflower seeds.

7. Bake 25 to 30 minutes, or until a wooden pick inserted in the center of a muffin comes out clean. Serve hot with Sunflower-seed Butter or Citrus–Honey Butter.

◆**NOTE:** Stirring muffin butter too vigorously creates tough muffins with pointed, peaked tops.

. . . .

ORANGE-HAZELNUT SCONES

Makes 12 scones

I love these scones drizzled with blackberry honey, but a light caress of butter is really the only embellishment they need. They're wonderful accompanied simply by thick rashers of apple-smoked bacon and steaming cups of French-roast coffee.

A delightful surprise about these scones is that, during the summer months when berries are plentiful, they make marvelous shortcakes. Split the scones and make a double-decker dessert with layers of fresh raspberries and

Frangelico-scented whipped cream. I think the phrase that most aptly describes the result of this union is "To die for!"

  2 **large eggs**
  ¼ **cup heavy whipping cream, at room temperature**
  ¼ **cup Frangelico or other hazelnut-flavored liqueur or orange juice, at room temperature**
  ½ **teaspoon pure vanilla extract**
    about 3½ tablespoons finely grated orange zest (1 large orange)
  2 **cups all-purpose flour**
  ¼ **cup sugar**
2½ **teaspoons baking powder**
  ½ **teaspoon baking soda**
  ½ **teaspoon salt**
  8 **tablespoons (1 stick) cold butter, cut into 8 pieces**
  ½ **cup coarsely chopped hazelnuts**
  1 **tablespoon Frangelico or orange juice**
  2 **tablespoons finely chopped hazelnuts**

♦ TIP ♦
Use the food processor to make quick work of chopping nuts. Place about 1 cup of whole nuts in food-processor workbowl fitted with the metal blade. Process, using quick on/off pulses, until nuts are desired texture. Be careful not to overprocess.

1. Preheat oven to 425°F. Grease a large baking sheet; set aside.

2. In a small bowl, lightly beat the eggs. Stir in the cream, the ¼ cup liqueur, vanilla, and orange zest; set aside.

3. In a large bowl, combine the flour, sugar, baking powder, baking soda, and salt. Use a pastry cutter or 2 knives to cut in butter until mixture resembles coarse crumbs. Add the liquid mixture and coarsely chopped nuts, stirring only until dry ingredients are moistened.

Food Processor Method: Place the flour, sugar, baking powder, baking soda, and salt in the food-processor workbowl fitted with the metal blade; process 15 seconds. Add butter; process in quick on/off pulses until mixture resembles coarse crumbs. With the machine running, add the liquid mixture, then the nuts. Process only until dry ingredients are moistened. If dough is overprocessed, scones will be tough.

4. Turn the dough out onto a generously floured work surface; gently press dough until it holds together. Divide in half. With floured hands, pat each half into a circle about ½ inch thick. Cut each circle into 6 wedges with a floured knife. Use a metal spatula to place the wedges 2 inches apart on the prepared baking sheet. Brush tops of scones with 1 tablespoon liqueur or orange juice; sprinkle with finely chopped nuts. Bake 12 to 15 minutes, or until golden brown.

. . . .

GINGERBREAD PANCAKES

Makes 12 to 16 pancakes

Had I but a penny in the world, thou shouldst have it for gingerbread.
—WILLIAM SHAKESPEARE,
Love's Labour's Lost

Accompany these light pancakes with Molasses Butter (page 308), Whipped Ginger Cream (page 298), or lemon honey butter (page 308). What a way to start the day!

1   cup all-purpose flour
1   teaspoon baking powder
½   teaspoon ground ginger
¼   teaspoon ground cinnamon
¼   teaspoon ground allspice
2   eggs, separated, at room temperature
2   tablespoons unsulphured molasses
1   tablespoon vegetable oil
2   tablespoons packed light or dark brown sugar
¾   cup half-and-half, at room temperature
1   teaspoon pure vanilla extract
1   teaspoon finely grated lemon zest
2   teaspoons minced crystallized ginger (optional)
¼   teaspoon salt

1. Lightly oil a large griddle or skillet; set aside.

2. In a large bowl, stir together the flour, baking powder, ginger, cinnamon, and allspice; set aside.

3. In a medium bowl or 2-cup glass measure, lightly beat egg yolks. Stir in molasses, oil, brown sugar, half-and-half, vanilla, lemon zest, and, if desired, crystallized ginger. Set aside.

4. Preheat the oiled griddle or skillet over medium heat until a drop of water dances across surface; heat electric griddle or skillet to 425°F. In the small bowl of an electric mixer, beat the egg whites and salt together until stiff but not dry.

5. Stir the liquid mixture into the flour mixture just until dry ingredients are moistened. Gently fold in egg whites.

6. Use a ¼- or ⅓-cup measuring cup to pour the batter onto preheated griddle. Cook until golden brown underneath and bubbles begin to break through to surface. Turn and cook second side until golden brown.

♦ VARIATION: **Whole-wheat Gingerbread Pancakes:** Substitute ½ cup whole wheat flour for ½ cup of the all-purpose flour; add 2 tablespoons wheat germ.

. . . .

♦ TIP ♦

Store brown sugar in a thick plastic bag in a cool, dry place. If sugar begins to harden, add a wedge of apple to the bag. Let stand for 1 to 2 days or until the sugar softens. Or put a cup of brown sugar in a covered dish and microwave on HIGH for 30 to 60 seconds.

✦✦✦✦✦✦✦✦✦✦✦✦✦✦✦✦ ALL ABOUT EGGS ✦✦✦✦✦✦✦✦✦✦✦✦✦✦✦✦✦✦

WHICH CAME FIRST?   Legends about eggs have abounded throughout the ages. The early Phoenicians thought that a primeval egg split open to form heaven and earth; Egyptians believed that their god *Ptah* created the egg from the sun and the moon; and American Indians thought that the Great Spirit burst forth from a giant golden egg to create the world. In all of the early legends the chicken is never mentioned as the creator.

GRADING EGGS   Most hens' eggs on the market today have been classified according to quality and size under USDA standards. In descending order, egg grades are AA, A, and B, the classification being determined by both exterior and interior quality. The factors determining exterior quality include the soundness, cleanliness, shape, and texture of the shell. Interior quality is judged by candling, so-named because in days gone by an egg was held up in front of a candle to see inside. Today, candling is more likely to be accomplished electrically, with the eggs moving and rotating on rollers over high-intensity lights. The interior quality is determined by the size of the air cell (the empty space between the white and shell at the large end of the egg, which is smaller in high-quality eggs), the proportion and density of the white, and whether or not the yolk is firm and free of defects. In high-quality eggs, both the white and yolk stand higher, and the white spreads less than in lower-grade eggs.

EGG SIZES   Eggs come in the following sizes based on their minimum weight per dozen: jumbo (30 ounces), extra large (27 ounces), large (24 ounces), medium (21 ounces), small (18 ounces), and peewee (15 ounces). The recipes in this book are based on large eggs.

THE SHELL   An eggshell's color is determined by the breed of hen that laid it and has nothing to do with either taste or nutritive value.

WHAT'S INSIDE   A large egg contains only about 75 calories. The egg white is an excellent source of protein and riboflavin. The yolk is a good source of protein, iron, vitamins A and D, choline, and phosphorus. It also contains all of the fat, which is the component that helps thicken sauces. The color of the yolk depends entirely on the hen's diet. Hens fed on alfalfa, grass, and yellow corn lay eggs with darker yolks than wheat-fed hens. The thick, cordlike strands of egg white that anchor the yolk to the shell membrane so that it stays centered are called chalazae (kuh-LAY-zee). The more prominent the chalazae, the fresher the egg. Chalazae do not affect the egg in any way; some custard recipes call for straining to remove them for esthetic reasons. Blood spots on egg yolks are the result of a natural occurrence, such as a blood vessel rupturing on the surface. They do not indicate that the egg is fertile, nor do they affect flavor. Contrary to popular belief, fertile eggs—expensive because of high production costs—are no more nutritious than those that are nonfertile. They contain a small amount of male hormone and do not keep as well as other eggs.

CHOLESTEROL IN EGGS   The hen's egg has long been bedeviled by its high cholesterol content (about 213 milligrams for a large egg), which is contained entirely in the yolk. Since the American Heart Association recommends that adult cholesterol consumption be no more than 300 milligrams of cholesterol a day, strict cholesterol watchers have had to drastically reduce their egg consumption or else eat the whites only. However, modern feeding techniques have now produced some low-cholesterol eggs that breeders claim contain from 150 to 200 milligrams of cholesterol (depending on the chicken's breeding and feed, as well as the method of cholesterol analysis), and 55 milligrams of sodium (compared to 70 milligrams in a regular egg). Such eggs are presently available only on a limited basis.

STORING EGGS   Eggs must always be refrigerated. When stored at room temperature, they lose more quality in one day than in a week in the refrigerator. Eggs should be stored in the carton in which they came; transferring them to the egg container in the refrigerator door exposes them to odors, which they easily absorb, and potential damage. They should always be stored large-end up and never be placed near odoriferous foods such as onions. The best flavor and cooking quality will be realized in eggs used within a week. They can, however, be refrigerated for up to three weeks, providing the shells are intact. Eggs with cracked shells should be used as soon as possible and only in foods that are to be well cooked. Hard-cooked eggs should be refrigerated no more than a week.

SAVING LEFTOVER YOLKS AND WHITES   Leftover yolks can be covered with cold water and refrigerated, tightly covered, for up to three days. They can be frozen but only with the addition of ⅛ teaspoon salt or 1½ teaspoons sugar or corn syrup per ¼ cup of yolks. Whether you add salt or sugar depends on how the yolks will be used when thawed. Tightly-covered egg whites can be refrigerated for up to a week; frozen for up to six months. An easy way to freeze whites is to place one in each section of an ice-cube tray. Freeze, then pop the egg-white squares out into a freezer-weight plastic bag. Frozen egg yolks and whites should be thawed overnight in the refrigerator before being used.

OTHER EGG FORMS   Eggs are available in other forms including powdered and frozen (whole or separated). Commercially frozen egg products are generally pasteurized and some contain stabilizing ingredients. A liquid product labeled "imitation eggs" is sold in cartons. This product is usually a blend of egg whites, food starch, corn oil, skim-milk powder, artificial coloring, and a plethora of additives. It contains no cholesterol but each serving is almost as high in sodium as a real egg. Imitation eggs can be scrambled and also used in many recipes calling for whole eggs.

BLACK-BEAN BREAKFAST BURRITOS

Makes 6 servings

This is a company-special dish perfect for breakfast, brunch, or even a midnight supper. You can do almost everything the night before—make the relish and salsa, wrap the tortillas in foil, mix the eggs, and grate the cheese. That way, it's a cinch to make the burritos the next morning with little or no effort, and you come off looking like a real winner.

Serve breakfast burritos with the nicely browned chorizo or other sausage and Mariachi Marys (page 16) for a south-of-the-border start to your day.

    Black Bean Relish (page 287; optional)
    Avocado Salsa (page 286; optional)
  6 flour tortillas (8- to 10-inches in diameter)
12 large eggs
    about 1 cup sour cream
½ teaspoon chili powder
    salt and freshly ground pepper
½ cup canned chopped mild green chilies (4-ounce can)
  1 cup cooked black turtle beans, well drained
  3 tablespoons vegetable oil
¾ cup grated jalapeño Jack (3 ounces)
¾ cup grated cheddar (3 ounces)
  6 sprigs cilantro

1. If you're planning to serve the Black Bean Relish and Avocado Salsa, make them the night before.

2. Preheat oven to 250°F.

3. Wrap tortillas airtight in foil. Place in oven to heat while cooking eggs. If desired, heat dinner plates at the same time.

4. In a deep medium bowl, combine the eggs, 3 tablespoons of the sour cream, the chili powder, and salt and pepper to taste. Beat until well combined but not foamy. Stir in the green chilies and black beans; set aside.

5. In a large skillet, heat oil over medium-low heat. Pour in egg mixture. Use a rubber spatula to slowly stir eggs, scraping the bottom and sides of skillet. Cook just until eggs begin to firm. Stir in cheese. Cook, stirring constantly, until eggs are almost set. Immediately remove from heat.

♦ TIP ♦

The secret to successfully scrambling eggs is slow cooking. A rubber spatula does a good job of moving the eggs. Don't worry about melting the rubber—the heat is (or should be) too low to damage it. Always remove scrambled eggs from the burner a minute before you think they're done because the residual heat will continue to cook them.

6. Place 1 tortilla in the center of each warm plate. Spoon a sixth of the scrambled eggs onto the center of each tortilla. Roll tortilla to enclose filling; fold right and left sides toward center, then finish rolling. Or simply roll the tortilla into a cigar shape.

7. Top each burrito with a dollop of sour cream and garnish with a sprig of cilantro. If desired, spoon about ¼ cup each of the Black Bean Relish and Avocado Salsa alongside each burrito.

♦**NOTE:** A nice touch for any meal is to heat the plates. It's particularly important here because you have to do some quick assembly at the last minute, and you don't want the eggs to get cold. Simply stack the plates and put them in the oven with the tortillas.

. . . .

BAKED EGGS ICE HOUSE

Makes 4 servings

This recipe comes from Denver's Mocha Cafe, compliments of owners Carol Wheeler and Susan Black. I knew I had to have it when my husband pointed out that I was humming as I was eating it—the sign (in Sharon parlance) of a sure winner. Ice House was the name of Carol and Susan's first restaurant, in Telluride, Colorado.

All the components (even the eggs) for this simple one-dish breakfast can be prepared the night before for easy assembly at breakfasttime. The English muffins and bacon should be done extremely crisp so they retain some texture in the finished dish.

Baked Eggs Ice House is an extremely versatile dish. You can substitute ham or smoked salmon for the bacon, finely chopped tomatoes for the green chilies, gouda or

♦ TIP ♦

Gather recipe ingredients the night before for a speedily assembled breakfast the next morning.

jarlsberg for the Monterey Jack and cheddar . . . well, you see what I mean. Serve this dish with Minted Melon Cup (page 17), and you're sure to see a lot of smiles at the breakfast or brunch table.

  8 **large eggs**
  2 **tablespoons white vinegar (optional)**
  ¼ **cup grated cheddar**
  ¼ **cup grated Monterey Jack**
  4 **English muffins, split and toasted until crisp**
 12 **strips bacon, fried until very crisp**
  ½ **cup canned chopped mild green chilies (4-ounce can)**
  1 **cup heavy whipping cream, at room temperature**
      salt and freshly ground pepper
      about 2 tablespoons finely chopped chives (optional)

1. Fill a large, shallow bowl with ice water; set aside. Lightly oil a deep nonreactive skillet, sauté pan, or large saucepan. Add 2 to 3 inches of water. If desired, add 2 tablespoons vinegar per quart of water. Bring water to a boil; reduce heat to keep water simmering.

2. Break each egg into a small cup or dish. Hold the dish close to water's surface and slip each egg into simmering water. Depending on the size of the pan, cook up to 4 eggs at a time without crowding. Simmer eggs, uncovered, 3 minutes. To test, use a slotted spoon to lift each egg from water and press with your fingertip. The white should be firm, the yolk soft. Transfer poached eggs to the bowl of ice water. Cover and refrigerate for up to 2 days.

3. In a small bowl, combine the cheeses; set aside.

4. Preheat oven to 400°F. Lightly oil 4 individual ovenproof bowls, about 5 inches in diameter.

5. Break a toasted English muffin into bite-size pieces; place in the bottom of a bowl. Crumble 3 slices crisp bacon over the muffin; sprinkle with 2 tablespoons green chilies. Use a slotted spoon to remove 2 poached eggs from the cold water; place on top of the chilies. Pour ¼ cup cream over eggs; salt and pepper to taste. Sprinkle with about 2 tablespoons cheese. Repeat for the remaining 3 servings.

O f course, the finest way to know that the egg you plan to eat is a fresh one is to own the hen that makes the egg.
—M. F. K. FISHER

6. Bake 8 to 10 minutes, or until cream is bubbly and cheese is completely melted. If desired, sprinkle each serving with chives. Serve hot.

SALMONELLA AND EGGS

Raw eggs have been linked to an increase in cases of *Salmonella enteritidis*, mainly in the Northeastern and Mid-Atlantic states. Most of the outbreaks have occurred at the institutional food service level (restaurants, nursing homes, banquets, etc.) as a result of improper handling of eggs. Such abuses include lack of refrigeration, inadequate cooking or cooling after cooking, inadequate reheating or holding temperatures, inappropriate use of raw eggs, and excessive holding time between preparation processes.

The salmonella in eggs is found most prevalently on the shell and in the yolk. As with most bacteria, salmonella finds it difficult to multiply in the egg white because the white contains antibacterial substances and lacks the nutrients needed to induce growth.

If you live in an area where salmonella-infected eggs are a problem, there are several ways to protect yourself. First of all, use fresh, uncracked eggs, and always keep them refrigerated. Any bacteria will multiply rapidly if the food is held between 40° and 140°F. for more than an hour. Only use recipes that require temperatures that will kill bacteria, or that contain acidic ingredients that will reduce bacteria or inhibit its growth, or that have additional built-in safety factors such as low-water, or high-sugar, or high-alkaline content.

Pasteurization—which kills salmonella—occurs when eggs are cooked at 140°F. for 3½ minutes. Since egg whites coagulate between 144° and 149°F., and yolks between 149° and 158°F., any method of cooking eggs in which the white is thoroughly set and the yolk has begun to thicken or gel is sufficient to kill most salmonella. Cooking eggs over gentle heat for a longer time allows for even heat penetration, bringing the yolk to a thickened (not hard) stage.

According to the Egg Nutrition Center in Washington, D.C., the chances of contamination from eggs is 1 out of 10,000 in the Northeastern and Mid-Atlantic states. Factoring this out over the rest of the United States raises the odds to 1 in millions. Being an informed consumer is only smart, so if you have a question regarding the safety of eggs in your area, check with your local health department.

APRICOT-CRANBERRY COFFEECAKE

Makes 8 to 12 servings

Crowned with cranberry streusel, this sweetly tart bread is moist, fragrant, and festive. It is every bit as wonderful with afternoon tea or after-dinner coffee as it is for breakfast. It also makes a luscious homemade gift for holidays or special occasions.

CRANBERRY STREUSEL TOPPING

⅓ cup whole fresh or unthawed frozen cranberries
¼ cup all-purpose flour
¼ cup firmly packed brown sugar
3 tablespoons walnut pieces
1 tablespoon butter

COFFEECAKE

3 cups all-purpose flour
2 teaspoons baking powder
1 teaspoon baking soda
1 teaspoon salt
½ teaspoon ground cinnamon
½ teaspoon ground allspice
⅛ teaspoon ground cloves
¾ cup finely chopped dried apricots (about 6 ounces)
1 cup coarsely chopped fresh cranberries or unthawed frozen cranberries (1 heaping cup whole berries)
2 large eggs, at room temperature
4 tablespoons butter, melted
½ cup sugar
1¼ cups canned apricot nectar (10 ounces)
1 cup chopped walnuts
12 whole cranberries for garnish

   1. Combine all the streusel topping ingredients in a food-processor workbowl fitted with the metal blade. Process, using quick on/off pulses, just until cranberries are coarsely chopped and mixture is combined. Place in refrigerator.
   2. Preheat oven to 350°F. Generously grease a 9-inch springform pan; set aside.
   3. In a large mixing bowl, combine the flour, baking

powder, baking soda, salt, cinnamon, allspice, and cloves. Stir to combine. Stir in the apricots and cranberries; set aside.

4. In a medium bowl, lightly beat the eggs. Stir in the butter, sugar, and apricot nectar. Gradually add to the flour mixture, stirring just until the dry ingredients are moistened. Stir in the walnuts.

5. Turn into prepared pan; smooth top. Sprinkle with cranberry streusel. Arrange whole cranberries around outer edge of batter, 1 inch from pan. Bake 65 to 75 minutes, or until a wooden pick inserted in the center comes out clean.

6. Let stand in pan 10 minutes. Run a thin knife around inside edge of pan; release spring and remove side of pan. Set coffeecake, still on the pan bottom, on a rack to cool for 20 minutes. Use 2 large metal spatulas to carefully transfer coffeecake from pan bottom to serving plate or leave coffeecake on pan bottom and place on serving plate. Serve warm or at room temperature.

7. Wrap leftovers in plastic wrap and store at room temperature for up to 5 days. Or wrap and refrigerate for up to 10 days; double-wrap and freeze up to 6 months.

♦**NOTE:** Use the food processor to chop both the cranberries and apricots. If using frozen cranberries, chop them while they're still hard. To make chopping the apricots easier, add about 2 tablespoons of the sugar called for in the recipe—it will keep the fruit from sticking to the blade. Or use kitchen shears to snip the apricots into small pieces, dipping scissors in hot water to keep them from sticking.

. . . .

> My wife and I tried to breakfast together, but we had to stop or our marriage would have been wrecked.
>
> —WINSTON CHURCHILL

PASTRY CORDON BLEU

Makes 8 to 10 servings

This simple but sophisticated dish features cheese and smoked ham, crisply upholstered in puff pastry. Not to worry—the puff pastry is storebought, which makes this dish as easy as it is beautiful. Almost any kind of cheese that melts nicely will work: cambazola (a cross of Camembert and Gorgonzola), Monterey Jack, Gruyère, Brie, or

Gouda, just to name a few. Whether you use mustard or chutney depends on your personal taste and the cheese you use.

Pastry Cordon Bleu can be prepared up to two days ahead and refrigerated, or frozen and baked just before serving. The fact that it can also be served with soup or salad makes this dish a real favorite in my recipe repertoire.

 2 sheets frozen puff pastry, thawed but still cold (1-pound package)
 1 egg mixed with 1 teaspoon water for glaze
12 ounces cambazola or Brie, softened and rind removed, or about 8 ounces thinly sliced Gruyère or Monterey Jack
 8 to 12 ounces thinly sliced smoked ham
    about 2 tablespoons sweet and hot or Dijon mustard or about ⅓ cup chutney with any large pieces of fruit finely chopped (optional)

1. Remove 1 pastry sheet from package; refrigerate remaining sheet. On a lightly floured work surface, roll out pastry to a 12-inch square; cut into 9 (4 x 4-inch) squares, by cutting 3 strips each way.

2. Brush the egg glaze over a ½-inch border of each square. Divide half the cheese among the pastry squares (spread soft cheese, tear firm cheeses) to fit within the border. Top with half the ham, dividing evenly among pastry squares. If desired, spread ham with a thin layer of mustard or chutney.

3. Fold pastry squares diagonally in half to form triangles. Firmly press edges together with the tines (tips only) of a fork to seal. Brush tops of pastries with egg glaze. Place 2 inches apart on an ungreased baking sheet. Cover with foil or plastic wrap. Refrigerate until ready to bake (up to 2 days) or wrap airtight and freeze up to 1 month. Repeat with the second sheet of puff pastry and the remaining ham and cheese.

4. Preheat oven to 400°F. when ready to bake.

5. If pastries have been frozen, let stand at room temperature for about 20 minutes. Refrigerated pastries may be placed directly in the oven. Bake 20 to 25 minutes, or until pastries are puffed and golden brown. Serve hot.

6. Reheat baked pastries in a 350°F. oven for about 10 minutes, or until crisp and warmed through.

． ． ． ． ． ． ． ． ． ． ．

POLENTA HASH

Makes 6 to 8 servings

This dish was inspired by one of the best and certainly one of the most creative cooks I know—Glenn Miwa. Prepare the polenta the day before so it gets very firm. Chop the vegetables ahead of time and refrigerate them in individual plastic bags. That way, twenty minutes of preparation the next morning and breakfast is ready! I must confess, though, that at my house, Polenta Hash is just as often served for dinner with a salad as it is for breakfast with eggs.

My personal preference is to use half sweet and half hot Italian sausage, but you can use all of one or the other, if you prefer. This recipe can be converted easily into a vegetarian dish by omitting the sausage and substituting an additional cup each of corn kernels and chopped vegetables. Either way, it's a winner.

  3 **cups homemade chicken stock or canned chicken broth**
  1 **medium clove garlic, minced**
  ¼ **teaspoon cayenne**
1½ **cups polenta or coarse yellow cornmeal**
  1 **cup grated Asiago or Parmesan (8 ounces)**
  1 **tablespoon minced fresh oregano or 1 teaspoon dried oregano**
     salt and freshly ground pepper
  1 **pound Italian sausage, ½ pound *each* sweet and hot sausage**
  2 **medium onions, chopped**
  1 **large green bell pepper, seeded and chopped**
  1 **large red bell pepper, seeded and chopped**
     about 2 tablespoons olive oil (optional)
  1 **cup fresh or thawed frozen corn kernels (1 large ear of corn)**

1. In a large saucepan over high heat, bring the stock, garlic, and cayenne to a full rolling boil. Whisking rapidly, gradually add polenta. When polenta is incorporated, reduce heat to low. Cook, stirring occasionally, about 5 minutes, or until mixture is very thick and pulls away from side of pan. This is extremely important because if the polenta doesn't cook long enough, it won't set firmly enough to be sautéed.

Microwave Method: In a 2-quart casserole, combine the stock, garlic, cayenne, and polenta. Microwave on HIGH for 3 minutes. Stir mixture, making sure no cornmeal is clinging to the bottom or sides of dish. Cover and continue to cook on HIGH another 6 minutes, stirring after 3 minutes, or until polenta is very thick and pulls away from side of dish.

2. While the polenta is cooking, generously oil a 13 x 9-inch baking pan; set aside.

3. Remove polenta from stovetop or microwave oven; stir in ½ cup of the grated cheese and the oregano. Salt and pepper to taste. Turn into prepared pan. Use a rubber spatula or wooden spoon to smooth the surface and push polenta into corners. Let cool to room temperature. Cover with foil or plastic wrap and refrigerate overnight.

4. Squeeze sausage out of casings into a very large skillet. Cook over medium-high heat, crumbling sausage as it cooks, until well browned. Use a slotted spoon to transfer sausage to a medium bowl; set aside.

5. Add onions to sausage drippings in skillet; cook 3 minutes over medium-high heat. Add peppers; sauté 3 minutes, or until crisp-tender. Use a slotted spoon to transfer to bowl of sausage.

6. While vegetables are sautéing, cut polenta into ½-inch cubes, cutting 12 strips lengthwise and 18 strips crosswise. If necessary, add enough olive oil to drippings to make 2 tablespoons. If not using a nonstick pan, additional oil may be necessary to prevent polenta from sticking.

7. Add polenta cubes to skillet. Cook over medium-high heat, using a pancake turner to gently toss cubes, until polenta begins to brown. If necessary, add additional

oil to prevent polenta from sticking. Add the corn, reserved sausage, onions, and peppers. Cook until warmed
through. Stir in the remaining ½ cup cheese; salt and pepper to taste. Serve hot.

. . . .

MAPLED HAM BREAD PUDDING WITH MAPLE CREAM

Makes 8 to 10 servings

This breakfast version of the classic dessert is accented
with ham and maple syrup. Besides its country-good flavor, one of the nicest features of this dish is that it can be
assembled the night before for morning baking. Use a
light-textured bread, preferably with a soft crust so it
won't have to be trimmed.

Eggs, milk, bread, and ham make this a one-dish breakfast. Accompany it with Minted Melon Cup (page 17)
and—for those with hearty appetites—hash browns.

  1 **loaf (1 pound) brioche or other egg-enriched bread**
  5 **large eggs**
4¼ **cups milk (whole or lowfat)**
 ¾ **cup pure maple syrup**
1½ **teaspoons pure vanilla extract**
 ½ **teaspoon freshly grated nutmeg**
 ½ **teaspoon salt**
  8 **ounces smoked ham, cut into ¼-inch cubes (about
     1¾ cups cubed ham)**
     Maple Cream (page 298)

  1. Butter a 13 x 9-inch baking pan; set aside.

  2. If bread crust is fairly soft, trimming it isn't necessary. Cut bread into ½-inch slices; set aside.

  3. In a large bowl or a 2-quart pitcher, lightly beat the
eggs. Add the milk, ½ cup of the maple syrup, the vanilla,
nutmeg, and salt; stir to combine. Set aside.

  4. Arrange half the bread slices over the bottom of prepared pan, tearing bread as necessary to fit. Sprinkle with
half the ham. Repeat layers. Pour or ladle egg mixture
over bread. Let stand 15 minutes or cover and refrigerate

♦ TIP ♦
Before measuring syrupy sweeteners, such as honey, molasses, corn syrup, and so on, oil the measuring cup. Every drop of the syrup will easily slip out.

up to 24 hours. (If refrigerated, let stand at room temperature 45 to 60 minutes before baking.)

5. Preheat oven to 350°F. when ready to bake.

6. Just before baking, drizzle surface of pudding with remaining ¼ cup maple syrup. Bake 50 to 60 minutes, or until a dinner knife inserted in the center comes out almost clean.

7. While pudding is baking, prepare the Maple Cream. Serve pudding hot from the oven, accompanied by the Maple Cream.

. . . .

BAKED APPLES WITH WALNUT-SAUSAGE STUFFING

Makes 6 servings

If you use the Chicken–Apple Sausage (page 229), make it at least three hours ahead of time so the flavors can develop. The apples can be stuffed the day before for easy baking the next morning. Two tablespoons of "red-hots" (cinnamon candies) stirred into the stuffing mixture add a touch of fun that kids of all ages will love. Pair this dish with Gingerbread Pancakes (page 22).

½ **cup Lyle's Golden Syrup or ¼ cup** *each* **honey and dark corn syrup**

6 **large baking apples, such as Cortland, Northern Spy, Rome Beauty, Winesap, or York Imperial**

⅓ **recipe Chicken–Apple Sausage or ½ pound commercial bulk sausage**

¾ **cup chopped toasted walnuts**

3 **tablespoons currants**

2 **tablespoons apple or cranapple juice**

¼ **teaspoon ground cinnamon**

3 **tablespoons finely chopped cranberries, about ¼ cup whole berries (optional)**
   salt and freshly ground pepper
   Golden Cream (page 298; optional)

1. Preheat oven to 375°F. Lightly oil a 13 x 9-inch baking pan; set aside. In a 2-cup glass measuring cup, combine the golden syrup with 1 cup water; set aside.

2. Wash apples and cut ¼ to ⅜ inch off the top. Use a grapefruit spoon or knife to scoop out each apple, leaving a ¾-inch shell. Finely chop ½ to 1 cup apple (½ cup if using Chicken–Apple Sausage, 1 cup if using commercial bulk sausage).

3. In a medium bowl, combine the chopped apple, sausage, ½ cup of the walnuts, the currants, apple juice, cinnamon, and cranberries, if desired. Salt and pepper to taste. Spoon into apple cavities, mounding on top if necessary.

4. Arrange stuffed apples in prepared pan. Drizzle about 1 teaspoon water-syrup mixture over each apple. Pour remaining mixture around base of apples. Apples may be covered and refrigerated overnight at this point. (If apples are refrigerated, let stand at room temperature 1 hour before baking.)

5. Cover with foil and bake 30 minutes. Remove foil. Spoon 1 teaspoon of the liquid in the pan over each apple. Divide remaining walnuts evenly over apples. Increase heat to 400°F. Bake, uncovered, 15 more minutes. If desired, spoon a little of the remaining pan liquid over each apple and serve warm with Golden Cream.

. . . .

◆ ◆ ◆

◆ ◆ ◆

Appeteasers

. . . .

Graham Greene once said, "There's a charm in improvised eating which a regular meal lacks." The renowned novelist's words speak to the eclectic contents of this chapter—improvisational food designed to please a variety of culinary whims. You'll find nibbles, sandwiches, and snack breads, and savory tempters to serve with drinks before dinner.

Appetite teasers are not at all new, of course. As with so many good ideas, they've been enjoyed throughout the ages. Each country has its own version. The Italians have *antipasti,* the Germans *Vorspeisen,* while in Russia *zakuski* are the tradition. Hawaiians serve *pupus* before a meal, the Spanish, *tapas,* and the French, *hors d'oeuvres.*

I can remember the day when I couldn't give a dinner party without serving a formal first course. Thank goodness, home entertaining has evolved into a more relaxed, free-flowing style that's much more in tune with today's active lifestyles. Now I whet my guest's appetites with flavorful bites that tease their tastebuds to the point of readiness for the main event. Brandied Brie Snaps with Creamy Herbed Brie, Mushroom Stroganoff Strudelettes, Chinese Chicken Puffs, or Savory Shortbread Sticks keep everyone happily nibbling in the living room while I'm finishing the rest of the meal in the kitchen.

If I feel the occasion absolutely demands a more formal first course, I'm more likely to choose something elegant yet understated, such as soup or pasta. Silky Brie–Apple Bisque (page 80) and Icy Spicy Avgolemono (page 84) are two starters that never fail to elicit raves. The same is true of Fenneled Farfalle with Toasted Pine Nuts (page 127) or the Saffron-buttered Spätzle (page 124).

This chapter also offers a selection of snacks—little nibbles for munching on between or before meals. Pita Crisps, Italian Sausage Snack Bread, and Twice-Tomato Bruschetta will all stop the hunger gap. If you want something more substantial—closer to a light meal—try the Smoked Corn and Chorizo Burritos or Pan Bagnat, a French Riviera–style pressed sandwich.

You'll find that many of the following dishes can be made at least a day ahead of time. Others can be done in stages so that much of the preparation can be done in advance. Some are finger foods, easily eaten while sitting or standing. Others require a small plate and fork. If you're among the multitudes who love unstructured dining, don't forget that a tempting selection of appeteasers can easily make a meal!

. . . .

DILLED SMOKED TROUT BRANDADE WITH CORNICHONS

Makes about 2 cups

The French word *brandade* (brahn-DAHD) is derived from *brandir* (to brandish with a cane). It refers to the fact that this preparation is beaten until smooth—originally with a wooden spoon, later in a mortar with a pestle, and today with the food processor. Cornichons, usually imported from France, are tiny, wonderfully crisp pickles made with very young gherkins.

Contrary to its sophisticated flavor, this spread goes together quickly and easily. Serve it with Pumpernickel Crostini (page 45) to accompany before-dinner drinks.

    4 cornichons
    3 small cloves garlic
    ¼ cup, loosely packed, fresh dill
    3 small smoked trout, skinned and boned (about 6 ounces
       each)
    ½ cup Crème Fraîche (page 301) or heavy whipping cream
    5 tablespoons butter, softened
  1½ tablespoons fresh lime juice
    ⅛ teaspoon cayenne
       salt and freshly ground pepper

1. Prepare one of the cornichons for a garnish by cutting it in thin slices from the tip to within ¼ inch of stem end. Wrap in plastic wrap and refrigerate until ready to garnish brandade.

2. In a food-processor workbowl fitted with the metal blade, process the remaining 3 cornichons, using on/off pulses, until finely chopped. Transfer to a small plate;

S atisfy your hearts with food and wine, for therein is courage and strength.

—HOMER

set aside. Wipe out food-processor workbowl with paper towels. Replace metal blade. With machine running, drop garlic cloves one by one through feed tube. Process until garlic is chopped and clinging to sides of bowl. Scrape garlic down from sides of workbowl. Add the dill and trout; process until finely chopped. Add Crème Fraîche, butter, lime juice, and cayenne. Process until mixture is well blended. Stir in chopped cornichons. Salt and pepper to taste.

To Prepare by Hand: Finely chop remaining 3 cornichons; set aside. Mince garlic and dill. Combine with trout in a medium bowl; use a fork or pestle to mash trout. Add Crème Fraîche, butter, lime juice, and cayenne; mix until well blended and fairly smooth. Salt and pepper to taste.

3. Turn brandade into a serving bowl, mounding high in center. May be covered and refrigerated for up to 3 days. Just before serving, spread out the sliced cornichon to form a fan and place it in the center of the brandade.

◆◆◆◆◆◆◆◆◆◆◆◆◆◆◆◆◆ ABOUT BUTTER ◆◆◆◆◆◆◆◆◆◆◆◆◆◆◆◆◆

Unsalted butter was used in testing all the recipes in this book not just because of its creamery-sweet flavor but because it gives the cook more control over the end product. If you are using salted butter or margarine, slightly decrease the amount of salt called for in a recipe.

Unsalted butter is labeled as such. It's sometimes erroneously referred to as "sweet" butter; packages labeled "sweet cream butter" contain salted butter. Because unsalted butter contains absolutely no salt, which acts as a preservative, it's more perishable than salted butter. It should be stored in the refrigerator for no more than 2 weeks. It can be placed in a plastic bag and frozen for up to 6 months.

◆◆◆

SMOKED SALMON TARTARE

Makes 6 appetizer servings

This dish was originally created for my mother, Kay Tyler, an avid fan of smoked salmon. It's so easy and delicious, however, that it's become a fairly regular event in the Herbst household. Buy smoked salmon ends and trimmings—they're much less expensive, and perfect for this dish. Serve Smoked Salmon Tartare with Herbed Pumpernickel Crostini made with dill (page 46) and iced vodka for a winning start for dinner parties.

1 pound smoked salmon, finely chopped (about 5 cups)
1 to 1½ tablespoons olive oil
1 tablespoon fresh lime juice
1 tablespoon vodka
2 tablespoons capers, rinsed and drained
2 tablespoons minced shallots
1½ tablespoons finely chopped fresh dill or 1½ teaspoons dried dillweed
    salt and freshly ground pepper
4 to 6 red-leaf lettuce leaves
1 slice lime for garnish
    Herbed Pumpernickel Crostini (page 46)

1. In a medium bowl, combine salmon, oil, lime juice, and vodka; blend well. Stir in capers, shallots, and dill. Salt and pepper to taste.

2. Cover and refrigerate for at least 3 hours. Taste and adjust seasonings, if necessary. For lime garnish, cut slice once from outer edge to center. Twist slice to form an S.

3. To serve, line center of a large serving plate with lettuce leaves. Mound tartare in center of leaves; top with lime twist. Arrange Pumpernickel Crostini around the tartare.

. . . .

CREAMY HERBED BRIE

Makes about 2½ cups

Fragrant and flavorful, this creamy mélange has many uses. It can be served with Pumpernickel Crostini (page 45) or piped into Belgian endive leaves for an appetizer, or spread on a sandwich to complement everything from chicken to ham, or dolloped atop hot vegetables.

2 medium garlic cloves
  about ½ cup chopped chives
¼ cup packed parsley or watercress leaves or
  2 tablespoons *each*
2 tablespoons packed basil leaves
8 ounces Brie, rind removed, softened
8 ounces cream cheese, softened
2 ounces blue cheese, softened
2 tablespoons sour cream
1 tablespoon balsamic vinegar
½ teaspoon freshly ground pepper
  salt

1. With the machine running, drop the cloves of garlic one by one into the food-processor workbowl fitted with the metal blade; process until garlic is chopped and clinging to sides of bowl. Scrape down sides of bowl. Add the chives, parsley, and basil; process until minced, about 20 seconds. Or mince ingredients by hand.

2. In an electric mixer bowl, beat the Brie, cream cheese, and blue cheese until perfectly smooth. Add the sour cream, vinegar, and pepper. Begin at low speed, gradually increasing to high, beating until mixture is smooth and fluffy. Add herb mixture; beat to combine. Salt to taste.

3. Spoon or pipe into a glass serving dish. May be covered and refrigerated for up to 5 days. Let stand at room temperature 30 to 60 minutes before serving as a spread.

. . . .

SUNDRIED TOMATO TORTA WITH MINT PESTO

Makes about 10 servings

This impressive-looking appetizer will have your guests thinking you spent hours in the kitchen—and what's wrong with a little culinary deception? It's great for entertaining because it has to be made the day before. The red and green colors make it perfect for the Christmas season, but you might have difficulty locating mint in the winter. In that case, substitute basil, which is now hothouse-grown year-round. Serve the torta with fresh or toasted bread. Use leftovers as a sandwich spread, topped with thin slices of smoked ham, chicken, or turkey.

1 cup firmly packed mint leaves
½ cup shelled green pistachio nuts
1 tablespoon fresh lime juice
   about ⅔ cup olive oil
   salt and freshly ground pepper
1 cup sundried tomatoes, commercial or homemade (page 289)
3 medium cloves Roasted Garlic (page 309)
1 teaspoon Hungarian paprika
¼ teaspoon cayenne pepper
¾ pound butter
12 ounces cream cheese, softened
2 sundried tomatoes, julienned, for garnish
   sprig mint for garnish

1. Line a 4-cup, smooth-sided mold with plastic wrap. Allow enough plastic wrap to drape over sides to cover top of mold when completed. Set aside.

2. In a food-processor workbowl fitted with the metal blade or in a blender, combine the mint leaves, pistachios, lime juice, and 2 tablespoons of the olive oil. Process until pureed, scraping sides of container as necessary. Mixture should have a fairly smooth spreading consistency. If necessary, add additional oil, a tablespoon at a time, and process until desired consistency is reached. Turn mixture into a medium bowl. Salt and pepper to taste; set aside.

3. Rinse food processor workbowl and blade, or blender jar and dry. If sundried tomatoes are oil-packed, drain and reserve oil. Combine the tomatoes, garlic, pa-

prika, cayenne, and 2 tablespoons olive oil or reserved tomato oil in food processor or blender. Process until pureed, scraping sides of container as necessary. Mixture should have a fairly smooth spreading consistency. If necessary, add additional oil, a tablespoon at a time, and process until desired consistency is reached. Turn mixture into a medium bowl. Salt and pepper to taste; set aside.

4. In the large bowl of an electric mixer, beat the butter and cream cheese until perfectly smooth.

5. Spread ⅛ of the cheese mixture over the bottom of prepared mold. The layer should be even and completely cover the bottom. Spread cheese with ⅓ of the tomato mixture, spreading evenly to edges of mold. The third layer will be another ⅛ of the cheese mixture; the fourth, ⅓ of the mint pesto. Repeat layers, finishing with cheese.

6. Bring up the plastic wrap that's hanging over the edges and cover top of mold. Rap mold firmly on countertop several times to settle contents. Refrigerate 24 hours.

7. To serve, fold back plastic wrap on top and invert mold onto a serving plate. Let stand at room temperature for 30 minutes. Remove plastic wrap. Garnish top of torta with julienned sundried tomatoes and a mint sprig. Leftover torta can be covered and refrigerated for 5 days.

> There is no love sincerer than the love of food.
> —GEORGE BERNARD SHAW

PUMPERNICKEL CROSTINI

Makes about 40 Crostini

Great served with cocktails before dinner, either alone or as a foil for pâté, Smoked Salmon Tartare (page 42), Dilled Trout Brandade (page 40), or Creamy Herbed Brie (page 43). A French baguette can be substituted for the pumpernickel, if you prefer.

8 **tablespoons (1 stick) butter, softened**
¼ **teaspoon freshly ground pepper**
   salt
1 **oblong (10-inch) loaf pumpernickel, cut into ¼-inch slices**

1. Preheat oven to 300°F. In a medium bowl, combine the butter and pepper; add salt to taste. Spread a thin layer over one side of pumpernickel slices.

2. Place slices, buttered side up, on ungreased baking sheets. Bake 20 to 30 minutes, or until crisp. Cool to room temperature before serving.

3. Store in a tightly sealed plastic bag at room temperature for up to 3 days, refrigerate for 1 week, or freeze for 6 months. Recrisp at 300°F. for 5 to 10 minutes.

♦**VARIATIONS: Parmesan Pumpernickel Crostini:** Add ½ cup grated parmesan to butter mixture.

Herbed Pumpernickel Crostini: Add 1½ teaspoons minced fresh herbs or ½ teaspoon crushed dried herbs to the butter.

. . . .

PITA CRISPS

Makes 12 dozen crisps

Serve these crisp wedges as an accompaniment to soups or salads or as a scoop with your favorite dip. Try one of the savory compound butters (pages 304–307) to add a delicious difference to your pita crisps.

6 pita breads (about 7 inches in diameter)
    about 6 tablespoons butter or savory compound butter,
    softened
    salt and freshly ground pepper

1. Preheat oven to 350°F. Lightly oil 2 large baking sheets.

2. Use a pointed knife to separate pitas horizontally, so you have 2 rounds from each pita. Spread each round with butter, and salt and pepper to taste.

3. Stack 3 or 4 pita rounds at a time. Using a large, sharp knife, cut each stack into 12 wedges. Repeat with remaining pitas.

4. Arrange pita wedges on prepared baking sheets. Bake 8 to 10 minutes, or until golden brown. Halfway through baking time, rotate baking sheets.

5. Remove from oven; cool on paper towels. Store cooled chips in tightly sealed plastic bags for up to 5 days. If necessary, recrisp in 350°F. oven for 5 minutes.

. . . .

♦ TIP ♦

All ovens have hot spots. For more even baking, rotate baking sheets or pans front to back and top to bottom halfway through the baking time. If you're using 2 shelves at once, make sure they're at least 6 inches apart. Always leave plenty of space between pans on the same shelf for proper air circulation.

OVEN-FRIED TORTILLA CHIPS

. . . .

Makes about 12 dozen chips

Make homemade tortilla chips without the mess of frying. They disappear so fast that I keep both my ovens going and make huge amounts of these crispy pleasers at one time. Corn tortillas take slightly longer than flour tortillas to crisp, but both are delicious. You can personalize the chips by sprinkling with your favorite topping, such as chili powder, grated cheese, finely chopped herbs, curry powder, salt—the list is endless. If you like to dip your chips, try Jalapeño Aioli (page 288) or Cucumber–Corn Salsa (page 285).

12 flour or corn tortillas (8 to 10 inches in diameter)
   about ½ cup olive or vegetable oil
   chili powder (optional)
   salt

1. Preheat oven to 350°F. Lightly oil at least 2 large baking sheets, depending on your oven space.

2. Lightly brush oil on one side of tortillas. Stack 3 or 4 tortillas at a time. Using a large, sharp knife, cut each stack into 12 wedges. For tortilla strips, cut tortillas in half. Turn and cut crosswise into ¾-inch strips. Repeat with remaining tortillas.

3. Arrange tortilla wedges or strips on prepared baking sheets. If desired, sprinkle with chili powder and salt. Bake flour tortillas about 5 minutes, or until golden-brown around edges and crisp; corn tortillas, 10 minutes, or until crisp. Halfway through baking time, rotate baking sheets from top to bottom and front to back.

4. Remove from oven; cool on paper towels. Store cooled chips in tightly sealed plastic bags for up to 5 days. If necessary, recrisp in 350°F. oven for 5 minutes.

. . . .

OVEN-FRIED SWEET POTATO CHIPS

Makes 4 servings

The main thing to remember about this recipe—unless you want to slice the potatoes by hand—is to buy potatoes that will fit vertically into your food processor tube. Regular baking potatoes can be substituted for sweet potatoes.

This recipe can easily be doubled. The actual number of servings is a matter of willpower. I guarantee you can't eat just one!

1 **pound sweet potatoes, scrubbed**
3 **to 4 tablespoons olive or canola oil**
    salt and freshly ground pepper (optional)

1. Fit food processor with the 2-mm slicing blade. If necessary, cut potatoes in half horizontally to fit processor's feed tube. Slice potatoes into rounds. Slicing may also be done by hand.

2. Put potatoes in a colander; rinse well under running water. Place slices in a large bowl; fill with cold water and add 6 ice cubes. Let stand 30 minutes. Drain; repeat process for a total soaking time of 1 hour. Spread potato slices out on 2 to 3 layers of paper towels. Blot well; potatoes should be dry.

3. Preheat oven to 400°F. Lightly brush 2 to 3 large baking sheets with oil.

4. Arrange potato slices in a single layer on baking sheets (some overlapping edges are okay). Lightly brush tops of slices with oil; salt and pepper, if desired.

5. Bake 15 to 20 minutes, or until golden brown, reversing baking sheets top to bottom and front to back halfway through baking time. Cool 5 minutes; potatoes will crisp as they cool. Serve immediately.

♦**NOTE:** To make crisp potato strips from leftovers, scrape out baked-potato skins and brush them with olive oil. Use scissors to cut the skins into strips, then sprinkle with salt, pepper, and a little chili powder. Bake at 400°F. until crispy, about 10 minutes. Great for snacks, appetizers, or chopped and sprinkled over soups and salads.

♦**VARIATIONS: Regular Potato Chips:** Substitute baking potatoes for sweet potatoes.

Smoked Potato Chips: At least 1 hour before grilling, soak 2 cups wood chips in water to cover. When ready, light fire in outdoor grill according to manufacturer's directions. Just before grilling, sprinkle wood chips over heat source (briquettes, lava rock, etc.). After baking potato chips, transfer them (still on the baking sheets) to the grill. Cover grill; smoke 3 to 5 minutes, depending on desired degree of smoky flavor.

Spicy Oven-fried Potato Chips: Stir ¼ teaspoon each cayenne and chili powder into oil before brushing over potatoes.

Herbed Oven-fried Potato Chips: Stir ½ teaspoon each dried oregano, basil, and crushed rosemary into oil. Let stand 1 hour before brushing over potatoes.

Garlic Potato Chips: Add 2 large cloves garlic, crushed, to oil. Let stand 1 hour before brushing over potatoes.

'Tis the potato that's the queen of the garden.
—IRISH SAYING

SAVORY SHORTBREAD STICKS

Makes 32 sticks

These melt-in-your-mouth appetizers are both easy and quick to make. Use a pair of kitchen shears to snip the tomatoes into tiny pieces. If you don't have roasted garlic on hand, substitute a crushed small clove of fresh garlic.

½ **pound butter, softened**
2 **medium cloves Roasted Garlic (page 309), pulp squeezed from skins**
1 **tablespoon finely chopped fresh oregano or 1 teaspoon dried oregano**
¾ **teaspoon salt**
½ **teaspoon freshly ground pepper**
2 **cups all-purpose flour**
8 **sundried tomatoes, commercial or homemade (page 289), finely chopped (about 2 tablespoons)**
1 **tablespoon olive oil**
 additional salt and freshly ground pepper

1. Preheat oven to 350°F. Set aside an ungreased 13 x 9-inch baking pan.

2. In a food-processor workbowl fitted with the metal blade or in a large electric mixer bowl, process the butter, garlic, oregano, salt, and pepper until thoroughly combined. If necessary, scrape down sides of bowl.

3. Add flour and tomatoes. Process with on/off pulses just until mixture resembles coarse crumbs. If using an electric mixer, beat at lowest speed until flour is incorporated.

4. Turn mixture into baking pan. Use the back of a tablespoon or your fingers to press dough evenly over bottom of pan. Dampen the spoon or your fingers with cold water if dough begins to stick. Drizzle dough with olive oil. Use back of a spoon to smooth over surface. Sprinkle with salt and pepper to taste.

5. Bake 25 to 30 minutes, or until shortbread begins to pull away from sides of pan.

6. Cut while warm into 32 fingers about 1 x 3 inches long, cutting 8 strips lengthwise and 4 strips crosswise. Cool in pan. Store in an airtight container.

◆**NOTE:** To quickly soften a stick of cold butter cut it into ½-inch slices and place on a microwavesafe plate. Microwave on DEFROST (30% power) until soft, 30 to 60 seconds.

. . . .

BRANDIED BRIE SNAPS

Makes about 8 dozen crackers

The perfect accompaniment for Brie–Apple Bisque (page 80), these crispy crackers are just as wonderful served all by themselves, with cocktails or wine, or as a salad partner. If you'd prefer not to use brandy, substitute milk.

⅔ **cup toasted walnuts**
1½ **cups all-purpose flour**
½ **teaspoon salt**
½ **teaspoon freshly ground pepper**
5 **tablespoons cold butter or margarine, cut into 8 pieces**
8 **ounces very cold Brie, rind removed, cheese cut into ½-inch chunks**
2 **to 3 tablespoons brandy**
about 1½ teaspoons coarse salt (optional)

1. Grind the nuts in blender. In a medium bowl, combine the nuts, flour, salt, and pepper. Use a pastry blender or 2 knives to cut in the butter and cheese until mixture resembles coarse crumbs. Sprinkle 2 tablespoons brandy over mixture, mixing lightly with a fork just until mixture begins to hold together.
Food-Processor Method: In a workbowl fitted with the metal blade, use on/off pulses to finely grind the nuts. Add the flour, salt, and pepper; process a few seconds to combine. Add the butter and cheese; use on/off pulses to

process until mixture resembles coarse crumbs. Add 2 tablespoons of the brandy; process just until mixture holds together. If necessary, add remaining brandy to hold dough together. Do not overprocess or dough will become tough.

2. Turn dough out onto a work surface; divide in half. Form each half into a log about 9 inches long and 2 inches in diameter. Wrap each log in plastic wrap; refrigerate 6 hours or until very firm.

3. Preheat oven to 375°F.

4. Remove logs from refrigerator one at a time. Cut each log into ⅜-inch slices. Place 1 inch apart on ungreased baking sheets. If desired, sprinkle dough rounds lightly with coarse salt.

5. Bake 10 to 15 minutes, or until golden brown, reversing baking sheets top to bottom and front to back halfway through baking time. Cool to room temperature before serving. Store in an airtight container for up to 1 week. Recrisp at 350°F. for 5 minutes.

♦**NOTE:** Use an oven thermometer for accurate oven temperatures. Preheat oven at least 15 minutes before beginning to bake.

. . . .

TWICE-TOMATO BRUSCHETTA

Makes 6 servings

This warm, fragrant bread can be served as an appetizer or as a soup or salad accompaniment—or simply when you want to snack on something wonderful.

12 (½-inch) slices French or Italian bread
⅓ to ½ cup olive oil
2½ to 3 tablespoons finely chopped sundried tomatoes, commercial or homemade (page 289)
1½ teaspoons minced fresh rosemary or ½ teaspoon minced dried rosemary
6 to 8 large cloves Roasted Garlic (page 309)
3 large tomatoes, seeded and thinly sliced
   salt and freshly ground pepper
   about ⅓ cup grated Parmesan

1. Place rack 4 inches from broiling element; preheat broiler.

2. Place bread slices on a large baking sheet. Broil until golden brown on both sides. Remove. Leave broiler on.

3. In a small saucepan, combine the oil, sundried tomatoes, and rosemary. Cook over low heat for 10 minutes.

Microwave Method: Combine the oil, sundried tomatoes, and rosemary in a 1-cup glass measure. Cover with plastic wrap; microwave on HIGH for 1 minute. Let stand 5 minutes.

4. Squeeze garlic from skins into a small bowl. Use a fork to mash, blending in 2 to 3 teaspoons of the flavored oil.

5. Spread a thin layer of garlic over one side of each slice of toast. Top with a single layer of tomato slices; salt and pepper to taste. Sprinkle lightly with Parmesan.

6. Return to oven; broil 1 to 3 minutes, or until cheese begins to brown. Serve immediately.

ITALIAN SAUSAGE SNACK BREAD

Makes 8 servings

Studded with bits of Italian sausage and sundried tomatoes, this rosemary-scented quick bread is baked in a skillet to give it an especially crisp crust. Serve it warm as a snack or the perfect companion for hearty soups and crisp green salads.

½ pound sweet or hot Italian sausage, or ¼ pound *each*
1 large clove garlic, minced
1⅔ cups all-purpose flour
⅓ cup fine yellow cornmeal
2 teaspoons baking powder
1 teaspoon salt
½ teaspoon freshly ground pepper
1 large egg
   about ½ cup olive oil
¾ cup milk, at room temperature
1½ teaspoons finely chopped fresh rosemary or ½ teaspoon dried rosemary, crushed
⅓ cup finely chopped sundried tomatoes, commercial or homemade (page 289)
½ cup freshly grated Parmesan

1. Heat a heavy 10-inch ovenproof skillet over medium-high heat. Squeeze sausage out of casings into skillet. Cook until nicely browned, finely crumbling the sausage as it cooks. Add garlic for the last 2 minutes. Use a slotted spoon to transfer sausage and garlic to a medium bowl; set aside.

2. Drain all but 1½ tablespoons sausage drippings from skillet. If there isn't enough fat add olive oil to equal 1½ tablespoons.

3. Place skillet in oven. Turn oven to 400°F.

4. In a large bowl, combine the flour, cornmeal, baking powder, salt, and pepper.

5. Add the egg and ½ cup olive oil to sausage; lightly mix to break up egg. Stir in milk, rosemary, and sundried tomatoes. Add to flour mixture, stirring only until dry ingredients are moistened.

6. Remove heated skillet from oven. Rotate so fat evenly coats sides and bottom. Turn batter into hot skillet.

Working quickly, use a large spoon to spread batter evenly over bottom of skillet. Sprinkle Parmesan over surface.

7. Bake for 15 to 20 minutes, or until golden brown. Let stand in skillet 5 minutes. If necessary, run a knife around edge to loosen bread. Cut into 8 wedges. Serve warm.

8. Wrap leftovers in foil and refrigerate up to 5 days. Reheat in foil in a 300°F. oven for 10 minutes.

. . . .

STILTON SPIRALS

Makes 32 pastry spirals

Four ingredients are all it takes to create these savory crisps. Served hot, Stilton Spirals are a good accompaniment to the icy-cold Peppered Pear Soup (page 78). I also serve them—hot or at room temperature—before dinner with drinks. They're light enough to stave off hunger pangs without ruining your appetite.

If you don't have the time to make your own puff pastry, be a smart cook and buy it. Prepared puff pastry is available in most supermarkets (usually frozen) or in specialty food shops. Thaw frozen puff pastry about 10 minutes at room temperature. It should still be cold when you begin to roll it out.

For busy times, make these crisps up to six weeks ahead of time and freeze them, unbaked. Then all you have to do is pop them in the oven—adding two or three minutes to their baking time.

4 **ounces Stilton, softened**
2 **tablespoons butter, softened**
2 **tablespoons finely chopped chives**
1 **puff pastry sheet, thawed if frozen (about 9½-inches square)**

1. Preheat oven to 400°F. Lightly grease 2 large baking sheets; set aside.

2. In a small bowl, combine the Stilton, butter, and chives until soft and creamy; set aside.

♦ TIP ♦

Use vegetable shortening or unsalted butter to grease baking pans. Salted butter may cause baked goods to stick to pans; it will cause overbrowning at temperatures over 400°F.

◆ TIP ◆

Freeze individual foods, such as pastries, cookies, or appetizers, by placing them on a baking sheet, freezing until hard, then wrapping in a plastic freezer bag or heavy-duty foil. Foods may be frozen either before or after baking or cooking. Some foods must be defrosted before heating; others can be heated frozen. Follow individual recipe directions.

3. Place puff pastry sheet on a lightly floured work surface. Spread half the cheese mixture to within ½ inch of edges. Fold dough in half to form a rectangle. Roll rectangle out to 8 x 14 inches. Spread with remaining cheese mixture, going all the way to edges.

4. Using a floured knife, cut rectangle crosswise into 4 sections, 3½ inches each; cut each section lengthwise into 1-inch strips, 32 in all. Dip knife in flour between cuts to keep pastry from sticking. Holding each strip at both ends, twist in opposite directions twice, making a spiral. Arrange spirals 1½ inches apart on prepared baking sheets. Lightly press ends onto baking sheet to secure.

5. Bake 10 to 12 minutes, or until deep golden-brown. Reverse baking sheets, top to bottom, halfway through baking time. Serve immediately. Wrap leftover Stilton Spirals in an airtight bag; refrigerate up to 1 week. To freeze, double-wrap in a plastic bag, then aluminum foil. To recrisp, place on baking sheet and heat at 400°F. for 3 to 5 minutes.

. . . .

FENNELED FOCACCIA WITH ROASTED GARLIC

Makes 4 to 6 servings

The main differences between this Italian flatbread (pronounced foh-CAH-chee-ah) and its city cousin, pizza, are that the flavoring ingredients are generally kneaded into the dough (rather than adorning the top) and that the dough is richer in olive oil. And, while pizza is usually considered a meal, focaccia is more likely to be eaten as a snack or accompaniment to soups or salads.

When making focaccia be careful not to add too much flour to the dough; it should be quite soft and pliable. Using quick-rising yeast and letting the dough rise in the microwave means that you can make, bake, and enjoy focaccia in about an hour.

1 (¼-ounce) package quick-rising or active dry yeast
  (1 scant tablespoon)
½ teaspoon sugar
¾ cup warm water (100°F.)
2 to 2½ cups bread flour or all-purpose flour
1½ teaspoons fennel seeds
1 teaspoon salt
½ teaspoon ground pepper
¼ cup plus 2 tablespoons olive oil
  about 1½ tablespoons yellow cornmeal
4 to 5 medium cloves Roasted Garlic (page 309)
2 tablespoons chopped fennel greens

1. In a 1-cup measure, dissolve the yeast and sugar in warm water. Let proof until foamy, about 5 minutes. Turn mixture into either the large bowl of an electric mixer or a food-processor workbowl fitted with the plastic kneading blade or metal blade.

Electric Mixer or Manual Method: Add 2 cups of the flour, the fennel seeds, salt, pepper, and ¼ cup oil to the yeast. Use electric mixer fitted with beater(s) to beat at medium speed for 2 minutes (or beat 200 vigorous strokes by hand). Change to dough hook(s) (or turn dough out onto a lightly floured surface). Add only enough remaining flour to make a very soft dough. Knead dough with the dough hook(s) or by hand for 6 to 8 minutes, or until smooth and elastic, adding only enough flour to prevent sticking. Form dough into ball; return to mixing bowl.

Food-Processor Method: Add 2 cups of the flour, the fennel seeds, salt, pepper, and ¼ cup oil to the yeast. Process until the mixture holds together, about 1 minute. Scrape down sides of bowl; process 1 minute more. Dough should be elastic and soft, but not sticky. If necessary, add a small amount of additional flour and process 30 seconds, or until flour is incorporated. Turn dough out onto a lightly floured work surface; knead about 1 minute, or until smooth and elastic.

2. Form dough into ball; place in a lightly oiled medium bowl. Cover bowl with a slightly damp towel; set in a warm place free from drafts. Let rise until doubled in bulk, about 1 hour (about 40 minutes for quick-rising yeast).

Microwave Method: Cover with damp towel; microwave on LOW (10% power) for 10 minutes, rotating bowl halfway through. Let rest in microwave oven 5 minutes. Repeat for 5 to 10 minutes, or until doubled in bulk.

3. Use the finger-poke method (page 247) to test if dough has risen sufficiently. Punch dough down; knead 30 seconds to expel excess air. Cover and set aside 5 minutes to relax gluten.

4. Preheat oven to 450°F. Generously rub a 15 x 10-inch jelly roll pan with olive oil; sprinkle lightly and evenly with cornmeal.

5. Press the garlic out of the skin. In a small bowl, mash the pulp. Blend in the remaining 2 tablespoons olive oil, a little at a time; set aside.

6. Press dough evenly over bottom of prepared pan. Brush with garlicky olive oil; sprinkle with chopped fennel greens. Bake 15 to 20 minutes, or until golden brown. Remove from oven; use kitchen shears to cut focaccia into 10 5 x 3-inch pieces, cutting 2 strips lengthwise and 5 strips crosswise. Serve warm or at room temperature.

♦**VARIATIONS: Roasted Garlic Focaccia:** Add 10 to 15 mashed cloves Roasted Garlic (page 309) while kneading. Before baking, brush focaccia with 2 tablespoons olive oil; sprinkle lightly with coarse salt or sesame seeds.

Sundried Tomato Focaccia: Add ½ cup finely chopped sundried tomatoes, commercial or homemade (page 289) while kneading. Before baking, brush focaccia with 2 tablespoons olive oil, sprinkle lightly with coarse salt.

Cheese Focaccia: Press dough into pan and brush with 1 tablespoon olive oil. Stud surface with about 1 cup tiny cubes provolone. Press into dough.

Herbed Focaccia: Omit fennel seeds. Add ⅓ cup minced fresh herbs, such as basil, oregano, or rosemary during kneading process. Before baking, brush focaccia with 2 tablespoons olive oil. Five minutes before focaccia is done, sprinkle with 2 more tablespoons minced fresh herbs.

. . . .

MUSHROOM STROGANOFF STRUDELETTES

Makes about 4 dozen

These butter-crispy bite-size appetizers freeze beautifully to be baked at the spur of the moment for drop-in guests. They are also wonderful partners for soups and salads. Before you start, see About Phyllo (page 61).

12 **tablespoons (1½ sticks) butter**
 1 **large shallot, minced**
 2 **medium cloves garlic, minced**
1½ **pounds mixed cultivated and wild mushrooms, such as shiitakes, chanterelles, or morels, finely chopped**
 ¼ **cup Madeira or dry sherry**
 1 **cup finely chopped toasted walnuts or pecans**
 ⅓ **cup finely chopped scallions, white and green parts**
 ¼ **cup finely chopped watercress leaves**
 1 **cup sour cream**
 ¼ **teaspoon freshly grated nutmeg**
    salt and freshly ground pepper
12 **(12 x 16-inch) sheets phyllo, thawed if frozen (about 10 ounces)**

  1. In a very large skillet over medium heat, melt 4 tablespoons of the butter. When butter is sizzling, add shallot. Cook, stirring occasionally, until shallot begins to soften, about 5 minutes. Add garlic and mushrooms; cook, stirring often, for 3 minutes. Stir in Madeira and cook, stirring occasionally, until all the liquid has evaporated, about 10 minutes.

  2. Remove from heat. Stir in the walnuts, scallions,

watercress, sour cream, nutmeg, and salt and pepper to taste; set aside.

3. Melt the remaining 8 tablespoons butter; set aside to cool. Unwrap phyllo and place stack of pastry sheets on a large piece of wax paper. To prevent phyllo from drying out, keep it covered with another sheet of wax paper and a damp cloth at all times.

4. Working with one sheet of phyllo at a time, use scissors to cut each sheet lengthwise into strips about 3 inches wide. Working with one strip at a time, fold phyllo in half crosswise. Brush with melted butter. Place a rounded teaspoon of the mushroom mixture at one short end and roll up the phyllo to the midpoint. Fold about ½ inch of both the left and right sides toward the center; continue rolling to form a neat package. Brush all over with melted butter. Place, seam side down, on an ungreased baking sheet. Repeat with remaining filling and phyllo, placing strudelettes 1 inch apart on the baking sheet.

5. Strudelettes may be covered with plastic wrap and refrigerated for up to 2 days or frozen for up to 3 months. (To freeze, place them on a baking sheet, transfer to a plastic bag when hard, and seal airtight. Remove from freezer and place directly on baking sheets when ready to bake.)

6. Preheat oven to 400°F.

7. Remove strudelettes from refrigerator 15 minutes before baking. Bake for 15 minutes (20 minutes, if frozen), or until puffy and golden brown. Serve warm or at room temperature.

. . . .

✦✦✦✦✦✦✦✦✦✦✦✦✦✦✦✦✦✦ ABOUT PHYLLO ✦✦✦✦✦✦✦✦✦✦✦✦✦✦✦✦✦✦✦

Phyllo or *filo* (pronounced FEE-loh), literally "leaf" in Greek, refers to tissue-thin sheets (or leaves) of pastry dough. Packaged fresh and frozen phyllo is readily available—the former in Middle-Eastern markets, the latter in your supermarket's frozen-food section. Fresh phyllo can be stored, tightly wrapped, in the refrigerator for up to one month. Phyllo can be frozen for up to one year. Thaw frozen phyllo in the refrigerator overnight. Once thawed, use phyllo within one week; do not refreeze.

The size of phyllo sheets varies. The frozen phyllo commonly available in supermarkets ranges in size from 12 x 16 inches to 14 x 18 inches. If your phyllo sheets aren't the same size as indicated in the recipe, just cut to size according to the directions.

The most important thing to remember when working with phyllo is to keep it covered; otherwise, it will dry out and become brittle. Have everything ready before you unwrap the phyllo. Place a stack of pastry sheets on a large piece of wax paper. Keep it covered with another sheet of wax paper and a damp cloth at all times. Don't let the damp cloth touch the phyllo itself. Remove one sheet of phyllo at a time.

Use scissors to cut the sheet to the desired size. After it's cut, quickly brush the surface with melted butter or oil to keep it moist and pliable. Tightly wrap any unused phyllo and refrigerate for up to one week.

✦✦✦

PAN BAGNAT

Serves 4 to 6

This popular pressed sandwich can be found everywhere along the French Riviera, from street vendors to bistros to fine restaurants. The traditional *pan bagnat* (pronounced pahn bahn-YAH) contains anchovies, which, since I'm not a fan, have been omitted from my rendition. By all means, personalize your *pan bagnat* by adding thinly sliced ham or smoked chicken, red bell peppers, fresh mushrooms, even anchovies; whatever your heart desires. Accompany it with brie, fresh fruit, and a chilled white Burgundy, and you have the perfect French *pique-nique!*

 1 French baguette or round loaf (1-pound)
   about ½ cup Roasted Garlic Vinaigrette (page 106)
 1 small head Boston or Bibb lettuce
 2 large ripe tomatoes, sliced paper-thin
 1 medium red onion, sliced paper-thin
 1 large green bell pepper, sliced paper-thin
   about 1 cup marinated artichoke hearts, thinly sliced
   (6-ounce jar)
 4 hard-cooked eggs, thinly sliced
 1 cup coarsely chopped watercress leaves
 ½ cup pitted Niçoise, Greek, or Italian olives, cut in half

1. Cut loaf of bread in half horizontally. Pull out some of the soft inside; set aside to make bread crumbs. Generously brush inside of crust shells with vinaigrette.

2. Line bottom half of loaf with layers of lettuce, tomato, onion, green pepper, artichoke, and egg; drizzle with 2 to 3 tablespoons vinaigrette. Sprinkle with watercress and olives; replace top of loaf. Press firmly down on sandwich; wrap tightly in plastic wrap or foil. Place a small cutting board or baking sheet and a 5-pound weight on top of sandwich; refrigerate for 1 hour. Remove weight; refrigerate overnight, or at least 8 hours.

3. Use a serrated knife to cut baguette into 3-inch lengths; round loaf into wedges.

✦✦✦✦✦✦✦✦✦✦ CHILI PEPPERS: TOO HOT TO HANDLE? ✦✦✦✦✦✦✦✦✦✦

Caution is the watchword when working with chili peppers because the seeds and membranes contain oils that can severely irritate skin and eyes (which is why removing those seeds and membranes also greatly decreases a chili's heat). Once you cut the pepper open, don't touch your mouth, nose, or eyes. Wash your hands with soap and water as soon as you're finished handling the peppers. Wearing rubber gloves will protect your hands.

✦✦

SMOKED CORN AND CHORIZO BURRITOS

Makes 6 to 8 servings

These burritos get their smoky nuance from being grilled. For a more intense smoked flavor, use the indirect grilling method which takes longer and gives the burritos more smoke exposure. This is a great recipe for entertaining because the burritos can be made the day ahead, then grilled in minutes.

Chorizo (chor-EE-zoh) is a highly-seasoned, coarsely-ground pork sausage widely used in both Latin American and Spanish cooking. There's a huge quality difference among chorizo so buy it from a butcher you trust. There are also many varieties of canned refried beans available in the market today. The only type I've found that isn't made with lard is called "vegetarian refried beans." Check the label if you're watching saturated fats in your diet.

½ **pound chorizo, crumbled and fried until crisp**
1½ **cups refried beans, homemade or canned (16-ounce can)**
    about ¾ cup fresh corn kernels (1 medium ear corn) or thawed frozen kernels
1 **tablespoon finely chopped jalapeño chili pepper**
8 to 10 **flour tortillas (8 to 10 inches in diameter)**
2 **cups shredded sharp cheddar (about 8 ounces)**
    about ¼ cup olive or canola oil
2 **cups Cucumber–Corn Salsa (page 285) or 2 cups Avocado Salsa (page 286), or 1 cup each**

1. In a medium bowl, combine the sausage, refried beans, corn, and jalapeño. Place ¼ to ⅓ cup of the bean mixture on a third of a tortilla (the side closest to you); sprinkle with a scant ¼ cup shredded cheese. Roll tortilla halfway toward center to enclose filling; fold right and left sides toward center, then finish rolling. The roll should enclose filling completely, but does not need to be tight. Press down lightly on burrito to distribute filling. Lightly brush oil over all exposed areas of tortilla. Repeat with remaining tortillas. Place burritos, seam side down, on baking sheet; cover and refrigerate until ready to grill.

2. One hour before grilling burritos, soak 2 cups wood chips in water to cover. Remove burritos from refrigerator

30 minutes before grilling. Light fire in outdoor grill according to manufacturer's directions. Just before grilling burritos, sprinkle wood chips over heat source (briquettes, lava rock, etc.).

3. Place burritos, seam side down, on grill; cover grill. Cook 1 to 3 minutes per side, depending on whether direct or indirect method is used. Watch carefully, or you'll end up with blackened burritos. Use a spatula to turn burritos carefully to cook second side.

4. Burritos may also be cooked indoors on an ungreased griddle over medium-high heat until deep golden-brown on each side. Prepared in this manner, the burritos won't have a smoky flavor.

5. Serve immediately, accompanied with Cucumber–Corn Salsa or Avocado Salsa.

. . . .

CHINESE CHICKEN PUFFS

Makes 25 puffs

Oyster sauce, a popular oriental seasoning comprised mainly of oysters, brine, and soy sauce, doesn't taste fishy but lends, instead, an exotic flavor when used in discreet amounts. Oyster sauce is available in most large supermarkets and can always be found in Asian markets.

8 ounces skinless and boneless chicken breast, minced (about 1 cup)
3 tablespoons dry sherry
3 tablespoons light soy sauce
2 tablespoons oyster sauce
1½ teaspoons minced fresh gingerroot
1 large clove garlic, minced
½ cup finely chopped scallions, white and green parts
1 puff pastry sheet, thawed if frozen (about 9½ inches square)
1 large egg white mixed with 2 tablespoons water for glaze

1. In a medium skillet over medium heat, combine the chicken, sherry, soy sauce, oyster sauce, ginger, and garlic. Cook for 10 minutes. Add scallions; cook until soft, about 5 minutes. Remove from heat and cool to room temperature. To speed cooling, transfer mixture to a plate.

2. Preheat oven to 400°F.

3. Gently unfold puff pastry sheet. On a lightly floured work surface, roll into a 12½-inch square. Cut square into 25 squares (2½ inches each).

4. Lightly brush squares with egg-white glaze. Place a teaspoon of the cooled chicken mixture in the center of each square. Pull the 4 corners up to the center, pinch together, and twist slightly to make a pyramid. Lightly brush with remaining egg-white glaze.

5. Place pyramids 1½ inches apart on ungreased baking sheet. Bake 10 to 15 minutes, or until puffed and golden. Serve warm or at room temperature.

H ow do they taste?
They taste like more.
—H. L. MENCKEN

Soups for All Reasons

. . . .

An old Spanish proverb has it that "Of soup and love, the first is best." Whether or not you agree, one fact is indisputable—soup is comfort food at its very best. Like love, everything about soup is seductive, from the way it perfumes the air to the way it delivers pleasure from the first to last spoonful.

One of soup's most appealing features is that it's almost always better made a day in advance. The overnight rest in the refrigerator allows the flavors to mingle and develop, giving a deeper character to the soup. Chilling soup also makes it easier to degrease, if necessary, since the fat hardens and can be lifted off the surface.

A smart cook will prepare a double batch of soup and make encore meals of it during the week or freeze it for future pleasure. Soup that begins as the first course of a meal can become a meal in itself another day, paired with cheese and crusty bread.

By far the biggest timesaver when making soups is the food processor. It's indispensable for chopping or slicing vegetables, doing the work in a fraction of the time it would take most of us by hand. If different vegetables go into the pot at different times, chop or slice them separately, transferring each one to a dish as it's cut. Always start with the least messy vegetable. Mushrooms, for example, should be cut and set aside before chopping something moist like onions. Wiping out the workbowl between vegetables is up to you. If it's all going into the same pot anyway, why bother?

Pureeing soup is a snap using the food processor, blender, or immersion blender. In general, the blender will give you the finest puree, with the food processor and immersion blender close behind. When pureeing hot soup, be careful not to get spattered with the scalding liquid. If using a blender, cover it, begin at low speed, and gradually increase to high. Inserting the pusher in a food processor's feed tube will prevent hot liquid from escaping. With both the food processor and blender, it's advisable to puree in batches, filling the container only part full. The easiest way to puree soup is with an immersion blender right in the pan. If you have a multiple-speed model, begin low and gradually increase to high. If yours is a one-speed immersion blender, wear an oven mitt to shield your hand from the hot liquid or keep the blender in the bottom of the mixture and move it slowly.

Though it's true that homemade stock gives soup a richness and depth of flavor hard to match with canned broth, I certainly don't maintain that a good soup can't be made without it. I gave up any stock snobbism I had left when I heard Julia Child say that she often used canned chicken broth and thought it was perfectly fine. There's certainly no argument that the convenience of canned broth is hard to beat.

If using canned broth, be aware of the type you purchase. There's the ready-to-serve type, which is already diluted, and condensed broth. If you buy the latter, be sure to add water according to the label directions to avoid an unpalatably salty soup. If you keep cans of broth in the refrigerator, the fat will congeal; then you can easily lift it off and discard it. Canned broth can be substituted for homemade stock in all the following recipes. Because almost every general cookbook on your shelf has recipes for stock, you won't find any in this book. I opted, instead, to reserve the space for other, more creative offerings.

When making soup, keep in mind that some herbs—like basil—lose much of their flavor and aroma when cooked for more than about 20 minutes. At the end of the cooking time, taste the soup and if it seems a bit lackluster, stir in some chopped fresh herbs shortly before serving.

There's no real advantage to making soup in the microwave. Most soups, in fact, can be completed quicker on the stovetop. Where the microwave shines, however, is in reheating soups right in the bowl. Though it's usually not necessary to cover microwave-heated soup, be sure to stir it after about a minute to distribute the heat. Thick soups—like split pea—often have little explosive bursts while heating. Cover the bowl with plastic wrap to prevent spatters. The length of time for heating soup in the microwave depends on its density and the amount being heated. Individual bowls don't usually take more than two to three minutes.

ORANGE-SPIKED PEANUT-SAUSAGE SOUP

Makes 4 to 6 servings

The peanut (really a legume, not a nut) was so revered by the ancient Peruvians that they buried pots of peanuts with their mummified dead for nourishment in the hereafter. The peanut took a step into everyman's land when peanut butter was developed in 1890. Today there are many peanut butters available on the market, including those with sugar and so-called natural varieties, which contain only peanuts. Any type you choose will be suitable for this versatile soup.

Either a smoked or garlic-flavored sausage works well in this soup—just don't choose one highly seasoned with strong herbs.

4½ tablespoons finely grated orange zest
3 cups homemade chicken stock or canned chicken broth
1 cup fresh orange juice
½ pound carrots, coarsely chopped (about 1½ cups)
1 medium onion, coarsely chopped
1 tablespoon minced gingerroot
⅛ teaspoon cayenne
8 ounces cream cheese, cut into 12 pieces, at room temperature
¾ cup smooth peanut butter
½ pound bulk sausage, browned and very finely crumbled
salt
additional cayenne (optional)

1. Reserve about 2 tablespoons of the orange zest. If necessary, chop zest so it's extremely fine; set aside. In a medium saucepan, combine the chicken stock, orange juice, carrots, onion, remaining orange zest, ginger, and cayenne. Bring to a boil. Reduce heat; cover and simmer 15 minutes.

2. Use blender to puree soup in 2 batches, adding half of the cream cheese and peanut butter to each batch. Or use an immersion blender to puree soup in pan. Begin at low speed, gradually increasing to high.

3. Pour through a medium-fine sieve back into the pan. Stir in sausage; bring to boil. Reduce heat; cover and simmer 15 minutes. Season to taste with salt and, if desired,

♦ TIP ♦

Zest is the outer colored portion of the citrus peel. Freshly grated orange or lemon zest packs a flavor wallop no bottled dried zest can match.

♦ TIP ♦

Make quick work of mincing very fresh gingerroot by pressing it through a garlic press.

additional cayenne. Serve hot. Garnish each serving with a sprinkling of reserved orange zest.

. . . .

ROASTED EGGPLANT PARMIGIANA ZUPPA

Makes 4 to 6 servings

Using all or part Smoked Chicken Broth (page 73) adds a wonderful huskiness to this hearty soup, inspired by the Italian dish. The rice in this recipe is used as a thickener. Brown rice may be substituted for white, but don't use instant rice.

2 pounds eggplant (about 2 medium)
5 to 6 tablespoons olive oil
6 cups homemade chicken stock or canned chicken broth or Smoked Chicken Broth
½ cup long-grain white rice
1 large clove garlic
1 large onion, chopped
1 medium green bell pepper, chopped
1 pound tomatoes, peeled, seeded and chopped, or 1¼ cups canned cut-up peeled tomatoes, drained (14½-ounce can)
1 teaspoon balsamic vinegar
   salt and freshly ground pepper
8 to 12 (⅛-inch) slices mozzarella (about 8 ounces)
4 to 6 tablespoons grated Parmesan

1. Preheat oven to 400°F.

2. Cut the stems from the eggplants. Cut each eggplant in half lengthwise; slice each half lengthwise into 3 pieces. Place eggplant pieces, skin side down, on a large baking sheet. Lightly brush exposed flesh with olive oil. Roast 45

to 55 minutes, or until well browned. Cool to room temperature before peeling.

3. In a large saucepan, combine the peeled eggplant, chicken stock, rice, and garlic. Bring to a boil. Cover and simmer 30 minutes.

4. Meanwhile, heat 2 tablespoons of the oil in a large skillet. Sauté the onion and green pepper over high heat, stirring constantly, until nicely browned. Remove from heat; set aside.

5. In a blender jar, puree the soup in batches, beginning at low speed, gradually increasing to high. Strain back into saucepan, using a rubber spatula to press mixture through strainer.

6. Add the tomatoes, sautéed onion and pepper, and vinegar. Salt and pepper to taste. Cover and simmer 10 minutes.

7. Position rack 8 inches from broiling unit. Preheat broiler.

8. Place soup bowls on a large baking sheet; ladle soup into each bowl. Gently float a single layer of mozzarella (generally two small slices) on surface of soup so cheese doesn't sink. Sprinkle each serving with about 1 tablespoon of Parmesan. Place soup under broiler for 1 to 2 minutes, or until cheese is lightly browned. Serve immediately.

. . . .

♦**TIP:** Use leftover cooked potatoes or rice to thicken soups. For smooth soups, simply add the potatoes or rice before pureeing. Otherwise, combine the rice or potatoes with a little liquid; puree, then stir into the soup.

♦ TIP ♦

Cheeses like Swiss, cheddar, and Monterey Jack are easier to grate—by hand or in the food processor—if they're cold. On the other hand, hard cheeses like Parmesan and Romano must be at room temperature. Hard and semihard cheeses can be grated ahead of time and stored in a plastic bag until ready to use. If the pieces stick together, simply break them up with your fingers.

COMFORTS' TORTILLA SOUP

Makes 6 to 8 servings

This recipe is compliments of my dear friend, Glenn Miwa, owner of Comforts, a popular restaurant in California's Marin County. I'm told that the secret is roasting the tomatoes, which gives them a richer flavor. I make the tortilla strips either the day before or early on the day I want to serve the soup. Glenn used to fry his chips, but he's now using my oven-frying method, a lower-calorie, less labor-intensive process.

The chipotle (chee-POHT-lay) chili pepper is a smoke-dried jalapeño. It's very hot, and has a rich, smoky flavor. Chipotles can be found canned (often in adobo sauce) in Latin American markets and some supermarkets. The amount you use depends on how fireproof your mouth is.

1   recipe Oven-fried Tortilla Chips (page 47), cut into strips
12 plum (Roma) tomatoes
1   tablespoon olive oil
1   large onion, chopped
2   large cloves garlic, minced
1   tablespoon fresh minced oregano or 1 teaspoon dried oregano
¼   cup dry sherry (optional)
½   to 1 chipotle chili pepper, seeded
    about 8 cups homemade chicken stock or canned chicken broth
1   to 2 teaspoons sugar (optional)
    salt and freshly ground pepper
    lime wedges, sour cream, avocado slices, and sprigs of cilantro for garnish

1. Prepare tortilla chips. This may be done a day ahead.
2. Position rack 4 inches from broiling unit. Preheat broiler. Lightly oil a large baking sheet; set aside.
3. Stem tomatoes and cut in half. Arrange, cut side down, on prepared baking sheet. Broil until tomatoes begin to brown, about 10 minutes. Use a spatula to gently turn tomatoes; broil second side.
4. While tomatoes are broiling, heat oil in a large heavy saucepan. Cook onion over medium heat until nicely browned, 10 to 15 minutes. Stir in garlic and oregano;

◆ TIP ◆

Add a touch of freshness to leftover soup by stirring in a tablespoon or two of fresh herbs just before serving. The same amount of wine, sherry, or Madeira can also give a lift to secondhand soup. Add spirits at the beginning when you start reheating the soup.

cook 2 more minutes. Add sherry, if desired, and increase heat to high. Cook, stirring constantly, until sherry reduces to about 1 tablespoon.

5. Remove tomatoes from oven and pull off any blackened bits of skin. Process tomatoes and chipotle in a blender or food processor until pureed.

6. Add tomato puree, 6 cups of the chicken stock, and half the tortilla strips to onions. If tomatoes are not at their peak of flavor, stir in 1 to 2 teaspoons sugar. Bring soup to a boil. Reduce heat and simmer, uncovered, 25 minutes.

7. If desired, soup can be cooled to room temperature, then covered and refrigerated overnight. Since the tortilla strips continue to absorb the liquid while the soup stands, if it's been refrigerated overnight it will probably be necessary to add more broth. Heat the soup first, then add stock or broth until the soup is the consistency you desire. Taste for seasoning.

8. Serve soup hot. Top each serving with a small handful of the remaining tortilla strips, a dollop of sour cream, 1 or 2 slices of avocado, and a sprig of cilantro. Serve lime wedges and any remaining tortilla strips on the side.

♦**NOTE:** Substitute an equal amount of fresh or canned jalapeños and about ½ teaspoon chili powder for chipotles if you can't find them.

. . . .

G obble your food however you might,
Never eat a dish that is trite.
—GREEK PROVERB

SMOKED CHICKEN BROTH

Makes 3 quarts

For my palate, this broth is too intense to sip alone; however, it adds a mysterious undertone to many dishes, including sauces, soups, rice, and stews. In most instances, the smoked chicken will have to be special-ordered from your butcher. You may have a choice of hot- or cold-smoked. The cold-smoking method, which—depending on the processor—can take up to a month, smokes meat at about 90°F. Hot-smoked meats are cured in temperatures ranging between about 100° and 190°F. I prefer cold-

✦ TIP ✦

Hot soup can be degreased either by skimming or by using a grease mop (an inexpensive kitchen utensil that looks like a miniature rag mop made with absorbent white strips).

smoked chicken because it is moister. Either is ready-to-eat without additional preparation.

Smoked chicken meat can be used in many ways including salads, sandwiches, pasta dishes, tacos, and omelets. After you've enjoyed the meat, the bones take the starring role in creating the broth. Adding the skin to the stock pot creates a stronger-flavored broth. I freeze the broth in half-cup portions (each in a reclosable sandwich bag) to add as I please to sauces and other preparations.

bones and skin from 1 large smoked chicken (5 to 6 pounds)
1 medium onion, peeled and cut into 6 pieces
1 large carrot, scrubbed
1 large stalk celery, cut into 4 pieces
3 sprigs parsley
1 bay leaf
10 peppercorns

1. In a large, heavy stockpot or kettle, combine the ingredients with 3 quarts water; bring to a boil. Reduce heat; cover and simmer for 1½ hours.

2. Strain broth; cool to room temperature. Refrigerate 4 hours; skim off any fat. Broth may be refrigerated for up to 5 days, frozen for at least 6 months.

. . . .

CREAMY WILD RICE SOUP

Makes 6 to 8 servings

Nothing is more satisfying on a cold winter night than this wonderful soup. Puffed Wild Rice (page 141) makes a good crunchy garnish. See page 132 for more information on wild rice.

Wild rice is expensive, but the cost is reduced here by the addition of pureed brown rice, which both flavors and thickens the soup. Brown rice is available in regular and quick-cooking forms. Since the latter takes about half the time to prepare, that is what I generally use.

⅔ **cup wild rice (about 4 ounces)**
3 **tablespoons butter**
1 **cup chopped onion**
¾ **cup quick brown rice**
1½ **tablespoons all-purpose flour**
¼ **teaspoon mace**
5½ **cups homemade chicken stock or canned chicken broth**
2 **cups half-and-half or 1 cup *each* half-and-half and heavy whipping cream**
1 **cup dry white wine**
3 **cups sliced mushrooms (about ½ pound)**
salt and freshly ground pepper
1 **cup Puffed Wild Rice, for garnish**

1. Place wild rice in a strainer and rinse well with cold running water. In a medium saucepan, combine rice with 2 cups water; bring to a boil. Reduce heat; cover and simmer, adding additional water if necessary, for 45 to 60 minutes, or until tender. Drain off any excess water; set aside.

Presoak Method: In a medium saucepan, combine the wild rice with 2 cups water. Bring to a boil; cook for 5 minutes. Remove from heat; cover and let stand 1 hour. Drain water. Bring 2 cups water to a boil; add soaked rice. Cover and simmer for 25 to 30 minutes, or until tender.

2. Meanwhile, melt the butter in a large saucepan. Sauté the onion and brown rice over medium-high heat until onion is soft. Stir in the flour, salt, pepper, and mace; cook over medium heat for 2 minutes. Gradually stir in chicken stock; bring to a boil. Cover and simmer 20 minutes, or until rice is tender.

3. Puree the brown rice mixture in the pan, using an immersion blender. Or turn half of the mixture at a time into a blender or food processor and puree. Begin at low speed, gradually increasing to high. Return pureed mixture to pan.

4. Add the half-and-half, wine, and mushrooms. Cook

over medium heat, stirring occasionally, for 10 minutes, or until the mushrooms are tender. Stir in the cooked wild rice. Salt and pepper to taste. Ladle into serving bowls; garnish with Puffed Wild Rice.

✦NOTE: Use the food processor to slice the mushrooms (set them aside until ready to use), then to chop the onions. When the vegetables are done in that order, it's not necessary to wash the workbowl between vegetables.

. . . .

CLAM VELVET

Makes 6 servings

The flavor of this velvety-rich soup belies the ease with which it's made. Serve it with Brandied Brie Snaps (page 51).

4 dozen raw clams, such as littlenecks or cherrystones, shucked
   about 2¼ cups bottled clam juice
½ cup chopped leeks, white part only
1 medium red bell pepper, seeded and chopped
3 medium cloves garlic, peeled
½ teaspoon dried thyme
3 cups half-and-half
3 cups grated Gruyère, Jarlsberg, or other Swiss-style cheese (12 ounces)
2 tablespoons cornstarch
2 tablespoons dry sherry or additional clam juice
   salt and white pepper
2 to 3 tablespoons finely chopped chives
   about 10 chives, cut into 2- to 3-inch lengths, for garnish (optional)

1. Coarsely chop the clams. Save all the liquor, adding enough bottled clam juice to equal 3 cups. Cover and refrigerate chopped clams until ready to use.

2. In a large saucepan, combine clam juice, leeks, red pepper, garlic, and thyme. Bring to a boil, reduce heat, and simmer, uncovered, for 15 minutes.

3. Pour into a blender or food-processor workbowl fitted with the metal blade. Process for 1 minute, or until mixture is smooth. To prevent scalding yourself when using the blender, begin at low speed and gradually increase to high; place the pusher in the feed tube of the food processor.

4. Strain the soup through a fine sieve back into pan. Add the half-and-half and cheese. Cook over medium-low heat, stirring often, until cheese is melted and soup is smooth, about 6 minutes.

5. Place cornstarch in a small bowl. Slowly stir in sherry or additional clam juice, blending until smooth. Gradually stir into soup. Cook, stirring frequently, for 5 minutes, or until soup is velvety thick. Season with salt and pepper to taste. If desired, soup may be made to this point, covered, and set aside for 2 hours at room temperature or overnight in the refrigerator. Reheat over medium-low heat before continuing.

6. Add the clams and chives; cook for 5 minutes. Do not overcook or clams will become tough. If desired, arrange several chives atop each serving for garnish.

◆◆◆◆◆◆◆◆◆◆◆◆◆◆◆◆◆◆◆◆◆ **EYE APPEAL** ◆◆◆◆◆◆◆◆◆◆◆◆◆◆◆◆◆◆◆◆◆

The adage "You eat with your eyes first" is just as true with soups as it is with any other food. For that reason, garnishes are recommended for all of the soups in this chapter. If you don't have the suggested garnish, use another that is intrinsic to the soup. For example, the puffed wild rice garnish for the Creamy Wild Rice Soup can be replaced with several paper-thin slices of mushroom (another ingredient in the soup). For extra eye appeal, present soup in an unusual container. In the summer when tomatoes are abundant, for example, serve Minted Tomato Bisque in huge hollowed-out tomatoes for a showstopping presentation.

◆◆◆

PEPPERED PEAR SOUP

Makes 6 servings

The classic combination of Stilton cheese and pears is updated here with a sassy cold pear soup accompanied by hot Stilton Spirals (page 55). Crystallized ginger and freshly ground black pepper add zip to this slightly sweet starter.

The soup, which takes only minutes to prepare, must stand overnight for the flavors to reach their full development. Though the food processor can be used to puree the ingredients, I find that the texture is never quite as smooth as I like. For that reason, I use the blender. The immersion blender also works well. Heating the soup intensifies the pepper and ginger flavors, and burns off the alcohol as well.

The late harvest Riesling adds a touch of sweetness but you need to be sure that the wine you use has no more than 6 percent residual sugar content (listed on most late harvest Riesling labels). More than that, and you'll have a dessert soup. If you prefer, substitute one of the sweeter Gewürztraminers for the Riesling.

> ◆ TIP ◆
> Grated cheese makes a simple garnish for soup. Or pass cubes of cheese to drop into the soup at table.

6 ripe pears, peeled, cored, and cut into chunks
2 tablespoons fresh lemon juice
4 teaspoons finely chopped crystallized ginger
¼ teaspoon salt
¼ teaspoon freshly ground black pepper
2 cups late harvest Riesling (no more than 6% residual sugar content)
   about ⅓ cup Gingered Crème Fraîche (page 302)
   additional freshly ground black pepper
   Stilton Spirals (optional)

1. In a blender jar or food-processor workbowl fitted with the metal blade, combine the pears, lemon juice, ginger, salt, pepper, and 1 cup of the wine. Or place the ingredients in a deep, medium bowl and use an immersion blender. Process, pushing down pears as necessary, until puree is thick and smooth. With machine running, slowly add the remaining wine. Process to combine.

2. Turn puree into a large saucepan. If the mixture is extremely thick, add ½ cup water. Cook over medium heat, stirring often, until puree comes to a full boil. Stir-

ring constantly, continue cooking for 2 minutes. Cool to room temperature. Cover pan and refrigerate overnight.

3. To serve, ladle cold soup into six glass soup cups, bowls, or icers. Top each serving with a dollop of Gingered Crème Fraîche and a fine sprinkling of pepper. If desired, serve with hot Stilton Spirals.

. . . .

TOMATO-CORN CHOWDER WITH SAFFRON CREAM

. . . .

Makes 6 servings

Scented with saffron, this remarkable chowder is delicious either hot or cold. Serve the soup with Polenta–Cheese Crackers (page 242) as a first course, or accompany it with warm crusty bread and a salad for lunch or dinner.

Saffron Cream:

4 saffron threads
2 teaspoons very hot water
1 cup sour cream
   salt

Chowder:

2 tablespoons olive or vegetable oil
½ cup chopped leeks, white part only
1 medium clove garlic, minced
   about ¼ teaspoon saffron threads (0.2-gram vial)
1 small baking potato, peeled and chopped (about 8 ounces)
1 tablespoon finely grated lemon zest
8 medium ears fresh corn, kernels removed, or about 6 cups frozen corn kernels
⅛ teaspoon cayenne
6 cups homemade chicken stock or canned chicken broth
1 pound fresh tomatoes, peeled, seeded, and coarsely chopped, or 1¼ cups canned cut-up peeled tomatoes, drained (14½-ounce can)
3 tablespoons finely chopped chives
   salt

Chowder breathes reassurance. It steams consolation.
—CLEMENTINE
PADDLEFORD

1. To prepare the saffron cream, combine the saffron threads and hot water in a medium bowl. Let stand for 5 minutes. Add sour cream; stir to blend. Salt to taste. Cover and refrigerate for at least 1 hour before serving, or up to 3 days.

2. To prepare the chowder, heat oil over medium-high heat in a large saucepan. Add the leeks; sauté until soft, about 5 minutes. Add garlic and saffron threads; sauté for 1 more minute.

3. Add potato, lemon zest, 3 cups of the corn kernels, the cayenne, and stock; bring to a boil. Reduce heat and simmer, partly covered, for 30 minutes.

4. Pour soup, in batches if necessary, into a blender or food-processor workbowl fitted with the metal blade. Process for 1 minute, or until pureed. To prevent scalding yourself when using the blender, begin at low speed and gradually increase to high; if using a food processor, place the pusher in the feed tube.

5. Strain soup through a medium-fine sieve back into pan. Use a rubber spatula or wooden spoon to press puree through sieve. Add tomatoes, chives, and remaining corn. Cook over medium heat just until warmed through. Salt to taste. Serve hot. Garnish each serving with a dollop of saffron cream, swirling slightly.

6. To serve cold, do not return pureed soup to heat. After stirring in tomatoes, chives, and remaining corn, immediately transfer soup, uncovered, to refrigerator. Chill at least 4 hours in refrigerator, 2 hours in freezer. Stir occasionally while soup is chilling. Or, chill uncovered for 3 hours, then cover and refrigerate overnight. When ready to serve, garnish each serving with a dollop of saffron cream, swirling slightly.

. . . .

BRIE–APPLE BISQUE

Makes 8 to 10 servings

Besides its luxurious flavor, one of the nicest features of this bisque is that it can be prepared up to two days in advance. The shredded apple garnish, however, should be prepared the day you serve the soup. Brandied Brie Snaps (page 51) are the perfect accompaniment.

4   **tablespoons butter, divided**
1   **medium onion, sliced**
8   **cups homemade chicken stock or canned chicken broth**
2   **pounds apples, unpeeled, cored, and sliced or chopped**
1   **large clove garlic**
1   **star anise**
2   **tablespoons cider vinegar**
1   **pound Brie, rind removed, cut into small pieces, and softened**
1   **cup half-and-half**
    salt and white pepper
1   **large apple, unpeeled, cored, shredded, and tossed with 1 teaspoon lemon juice for garnish (optional)**
    freshly grated nutmeg (optional)

1. Melt 2 tablespoons of the butter in a large skillet. Sauté onion over medium heat until golden-brown.

2. While the onions are cooking, bring chicken broth to a boil in a large pot. Add onion and any butter in which it was cooked, the sliced or chopped apples, garlic, star anise, and vinegar. Return to boil. Reduce heat; cover and simmer 30 minutes. Stir in Brie and half-and-half; cook for an additional 5 minutes.

3. Use blender to puree soup in 2 batches. Or, puree soup in pan with immersion blender. Always begin at low speed, gradually increasing to high. Pour soup through a medium-fine strainer back into pan. Season to taste with salt and pepper. Bisque may be refrigerated at this point and reheated over low heat before serving. Do not return to a boil.

4. If desired, prepare an apple garnish. In a medium skillet over medium heat, melt the remaining 2 tablespoons butter. Add the shredded apples; sauté just until they begin to soften. Remove from heat; cool to room temperature. Apples may be covered and refrigerated for up to 8 hours. Remove from refrigerator 30 minutes before serving. Float about 1 tablespoon shredded apples on top of each serving; sprinkle lightly with nutmeg.

· · · · · · · · · · ·

◆ TIP ◆

Soup makes an elegant first course for any special meal. Choose one that will complement the flavors of the other dishes in the meal, while at the same time providing textural contrast. A creamy bisque, for example, is the perfect prelude for a simple grilled meat with crisply sautéed vegetables. It shouldn't, on the other hand, be served with a rich, creamy entree like beef stroganoff.

MINTED TOMATO BISQUE

Makes 4 servings

This fresh soup is the perfect summertime starter, when the weather is hot and tomatoes and mint are abundant and at their prime. If you don't have full-flavored, vine-ripened tomatoes, use the canned—the flavor will be much better than the gas-ripened tomatoes commonly found in supermarkets. There is, however, no substitute for fresh mint. And keep in mind that the mintiness of the soup will depend on the type of mint used. Peppermint is more pungent than spearmint.

2½ pounds vine-ripened tomatoes, peeled and coarsely chopped, or 3 cups chopped canned tomatoes with juice (28-ounce can)
 1 medium clove garlic, minced
 ½ cup firmly packed fresh mint leaves
 ⅔ cup buttermilk or lowfat sour cream
    salt
 4 small sprigs mint for garnish

The greatest dishes are very simple dishes.
—AUGUSTE ESCOFFIER

1. Combine all the ingredients except the salt and mint sprigs in a blender jar. Or combine the ingredients in a deep, medium bowl and use an immersion blender. Blend at low speed, gradually increasing to high, until mixture is smooth. Strain through a medium sieve into a medium bowl. Cover and refrigerate for at least 4 hours. Place in freezer 30 minutes before serving.

2. Just before serving, salt to taste. Ladle into individual soup cups. Garnish each serving with a small mint sprig.

SMOKED TOMATO SOUP

Makes 6 to 8 servings

This soup was inspired by one I had at Timothy's, a wonderful restaurant in Louisville, Kentucky. Though Timothy served his version hot, I've since discovered that it's equally delicious cold. Since chilling food mutes its flavor, the smoky flavor is less intense. Make a meal out of Smoked Tomato Soup by accompanying it with Twice-Tomato Bruschetta (page 53) or Fenneled Focaccia (page 57).

Be sure to start the Crème Fraîche (page 301) at least a day before you plan to serve the soup. Sour cream can be used as a last-minute substitute.

¾ **cup Crème Fraîche or sour cream**
2 **tablespoons minced chives**
1 **medium onion, chopped**
⅓ **cup long-grain white rice**
2 **tablespoons olive oil**
2 **medium garlic cloves, minced**
3 **cups canned cut-up peeled tomatoes in juice (2 14½-ounce cans)**
8 **cups Smoked Chicken Broth (page 73)**
¼ **teaspoon freshly grated nutmeg**
   salt and freshly ground pepper

1. In a 1-cup glass measuring cup, combine the crème fraîche or sour cream and chives. Cover and refrigerate.

2. In a large saucepan over medium-high heat, sauté the onion and rice in oil until the onion begins to brown, about 5 minutes. Add the garlic and cook 2 minutes more.

3. Add the tomatoes, broth, and nutmeg; bring to a boil. Cover and simmer 30 minutes.

4. In a covered blender jar, puree soup in batches. Begin at low speed, gradually increasing to high. Return to saucepan; salt and pepper to taste. If serving cold, refrigerate 4 to 6 hours, stirring occasionally.

5. Serve hot or cold. Garnish each serving with a dollop of crème fraîche with chives.

ICY SPICY AVGOLEMONO

Makes 4 to 6 servings

The lemony avgolemono (ahv-goh-LEH-moh-noh) is the king of Greek soups. This nontraditional rendition takes three steps away from the classic—the rice is pureed, spices are added, and it's served cold. Having the eggs at room temperature will mean that they'll incorporate more easily with the hot liquid. Making this soup the day before you serve it will allow the flavors to develop. An immersion blender or regular blender works better for pureeing than the food processor. Serve this frosty soup as a starter or with a salad or a sandwich for lunch or a light dinner.

6 cups homemade chicken stock or canned chicken broth
2 tablespoons butter
⅓ cup long-grain white rice
¼ teaspoon freshly grated nutmeg
¼ teaspoon ground allspice
¼ teaspoon cayenne
⅛ teaspoon cinnamon
4 large eggs, at room temperature
¼ cup fresh lemon juice
   salt and freshly ground pepper
4 to 6 slices (⅛-inch) lemon
   additional freshly grated nutmeg

1. In a medium saucepan, combine the stock, butter, rice, nutmeg, allspice, cayenne, and cinnamon. Bring to a boil. Reduce heat; cover and simmer 20 to 30 minutes, or until rice is tender.

2. Put the eggs into a blender jar or a food-processor workbowl fitted with the metal blade. Process until frothy, about 30 seconds. With machine running, add lemon juice, a tablespoon at a time, blending well after each addition.

3. With machine running, add 1 cup of the hot soup, ¼ cup at a time, blending well after each addition.

4. Whisking constantly, slowly pour egg mixture into remaining soup. Cook over medium-low heat, stirring constantly, just until soup is steaming and slightly thickened, about 3 minutes. Overcooking will cause eggs to curdle. Don't worry if that happens: blending the soup in

the following step will make it smooth again.

5. Use the immersion blender to puree soup in pan. Or pour the soup, in batches, into a blender jar or food-processor workbowl fitted with the metal blade. Process for 1 minute, or until pureed. To prevent scalding yourself when using the blender, begin at low speed and gradually increase to high; place the pusher in the feed tube of the food processor.

6. Strain soup through a fine sieve, using the back of a spoon to rub rice through. Cool to room temperature. Cover and refrigerate overnight. Just before serving, salt and pepper to taste. Garnish each serving with a slice of lemon dusted lightly with nutmeg.

. . . .

Salad Days and Dressings

Salads today are no longer relegated to supporting roles alongside entrees. In many guises and all shapes and sizes, salads are in the spotlight as the main dish, and often as the first course. Part of the reason for the enhanced role of salads today is their versatility. They can just as easily feature meat and potatoes as they can noodles and peanuts. They can be light and fruity or hearty and earthy. And salads are no longer simply served cold. Many are at their best at room temperature or warm. The best salads have a dual personality—their textures and flavors complement each other, while creating exciting contrasts at the same time.

> The table is the only place where a man is never bored for the first hour.
> —Anthelme Brillat-Savarin

The good news for salad lovers is the greater availability of a wide variety of greens, vinegars, and oils. There are dozens of lettuce varieties available in markets today. Among the more popular are the butterhead lettuces, such as Boston and Bibb, crisphead lettuces, the most common being iceberg, leaf lettuces like red leaf and oak leaf, and romaine (also known as cos) lettuce. Lettuce growing seasons peak at different times of year, so there's always a large selection. In addition to the many lettuces available there is a wide assortment of delicious and eye-appealing greens (see page 90), as well as cabbage—red, white, and crinkly Chinese—and spinach, both of which add color and flavor to salads.

No salad would be complete without a dressing of some sort. Salad dressings should be exciting and full-flavored. Their main purpose, however, is to showcase the salad, not overpower it. Though the most common salad dressing combination is oil and vinegar, other ingredients can also be used. In Hot Brie Dressing, for example, brie and chicken broth form the base; Chutney Cream Dressing is a blend of cream and chutney.

Though lemon or lime juice are sometimes used, vinegar is still the favorite for salad dressings. Once only distilled white, cider, and red and white wine vinegars were available, but today there's a dazzling array of flavors. There are fruit vinegars, made with many different fruits including blackberries, blueberries, cranberries, lemons, limes, peaches, pears, raspberries, and strawberries. Herb vinegars are also popular; they might be infused with basil, chervil, chives, dill, mint, oregano, rosemary, savory, tarragon, or thyme. There's the yeasty-flavored malt vinegar, and my favorite—balsamic vinegar—made from the Trebbiano grape and traditionally aged in barrels of various woods and sizes for at least ten years.

Oils are just as varied. There is, of course, a wide variety of olive oils (see page 97) and vegetable oils. The very mild canola oil (also known as rapeseed oil) is lower in saturated fats (only about 6 percent) than any other oil, and has more cholesterol-balancing monounsaturated fat than any oil except olive oil. It also has the distinction of containing Omega-3 fatty acids, the wonder polyunsaturated fat reputed to lower both cholesterol and triglycerides. Other vegetable oils commonly used for salads include safflower and corn oil.

Olive and vegetable oils are just the beginning. There are dozens of other oils on the market today including nut oils, made with almonds, hazelnuts, and walnuts; sesame oil (ranging from the pale and light kind to dark Oriental oils with a deep sesame fragrance and flavor); hot-pepper oil, made by steeping hot chili peppers in oil; and oils flavored with foods such as garlic, herbs, mushrooms, and sundried tomatoes.

The presentation of a salad is almost as important as its flavor. One easy way to add color is with edible flowers, available at specialty produce markets and some gourmet markets—and from your garden (if you've not used pesticides). Some of the more popular are chrysanthemums, nasturtiums, daisies, geraniums, lavender blossoms, lilacs, marigolds, violets, and almond, apple, chive, borage, lemon, orange, and squash blossoms. Either use the flowers whole, or scatter the petals on top of the salad. The key when using flowers is subtlety, not cuteness. Edible flowers can be stored, tightly wrapped, in the refrigerator for up to a week.

The following pages present salads for all seasons. Many of the dressings at the end of the chapter are versatile enough to use on a variety of salads and other foods. So have fun, experiment—and may all your salad days be fresh!

. . . .

HOPPIN' JOHN SALAD

Makes 4 servings

Legend has it that if Hoppin' John is eaten on New Year's Day, it will bring good luck for the rest of the year. Personally, I wouldn't start the year off without it. The traditional dish is served hot, but I think you'll find this salad rendition a refreshing change of pace. You can use fresh, dried, or frozen black-eyed peas but not the canned variety, which are often mushy. For a different but equally delicious flavor, substitute the Roasted Garlic Vinaigrette (page 106) for the Honeyed Mustard Vinaigrette. See page 243 for information on tasso.

  3 **cups cooked black-eyed peas, (½ pound dried)**
1½ **cups cooked white rice**
 ⅓ **cup diced green pepper**
 ⅓ **cup diced red pepper**
 ¼ **pound tasso or ham, diced**
 ½ **cup plus 2 tablespoons chopped scallions, white and green parts**
  1 **cup Honeyed Mustard Vinaigrette (page 107)**
    salt and cayenne
    salad greens (optional)

1. In a medium bowl, combine the black-eyed peas, rice, green pepper, red pepper, tasso, ½ cup of the scallions, and the Honeyed Mustard Vinaigrette. Cover and refrigerate 3 hours.

2. Season to taste with salt and cayenne. If desired, serve on a bed of salad greens; garnish with remaining 2 tablespoons scallions. May be covered and refrigerated up to 3 days.

✦✦✦✦✦✦✦✦✦✦✦✦ WASHING AND STORING GREENS ✦✦✦✦✦✦✦✦✦✦✦✦

The general rule when buying lettuce or other greens is to look for those that are crisp and free of blemishes. They should smell fresh, never sour. Greens will last longer if they're washed as soon as you get them home.

The easiest way to clean greens is to put them in a sink or large container full of cold water. Swish the greens around with your hands, then let them stand for a few minutes for the dirt to sink to the bottom. All greens must be thoroughly dried before using or storing. I use a salad spinner (the best $15 investment I ever made). Rather than overload the spinner, do the greens in batches. They can also be blotted dry with paper towels or a cotton dish towel.

Wrap clean greens loosely in paper towels, then put them in a tightly sealed plastic bag. Remove as much air as possible from the bag before sealing it. Greens prepared and stored in this manner can be refrigerated for up to a week.

✦✦✦

✦✦✦✦✦✦✦✦✦✦✦ THERE'S MORE TO GREENS THAN LETTUCE ✦✦✦✦✦✦✦✦✦✦✦

In addition to lettuce, there are many salad greens available today, all of which add their own flavor and color. Among the many greens you're likely to find in markets are:

ARUGULA Dark green leaves with a peppery mustard flavor. Also called rocket.

BELGIAN ENDIVE Tightly packed, cigar-shaped heads of cream-colored, slightly bitter leaves.

CURLY ENDIVE Lacy, dark green leaves with a pale center. Often called chicory.

FRISÉE Pretty, pale green, frilly leaves with a slightly bitter taste. Like young, tender curly endive in appearance.

ESCAROLE Broad, slightly curled, green leaves with a slightly bitter flavor.

DANDELION GREENS Narrow, bright green, jagged-edged leaves with a tangy, slightly bitter flavor.

MÂCHE Small clusters of dark green leaves with a tangy, nutlike flavor. Also called corn salad, lamb's lettuce, and field lettuce.

MUSTARD GREENS Rich, dark green leaves with a pungent mustard flavor. Use only young, tender leaves.

RADICCHIO White-ribbed leaves ranging in color from pink to burgundy red with a slightly bitter flavor.

WATERCRESS Small, dark green leaves with a peppery taste that can range from mild to hot.

WARM MUSHROOM SALAD WITH HOT BRIE DRESSING

Makes 4 servings

Cold greens with warm mushrooms and dressing are a delight. This dish can be served as either a first course or a side dish with simple grilled meats. If your budget is anemic, use all cultivated mushrooms for this recipe—the result will still be delicious.

1 cup Hot Brie Dressing (page 103)

½ pound mixed lettuce greens, such as curly endive, Bibb or Boston lettuce, radicchio, mâche, red-leaf, and romaine lettuce

½ pound cultivated mushrooms

½ pound wild mushrooms, such as shiitakes, chanterelles, porcini, or morels

3 tablespoons vegetable oil

⅛ teaspoon freshly grated nutmeg
salt and pepper

1. Make the Hot Brie Dressing; keep warm in a hot-water bath.

2. Wash and spin-dry the lettuce; tear into bite-size pieces (you will have about 3 cups). Divide among 4 salad plates; cover and refrigerate.

3. Use a food processor fitted with the 6-mm blade to slice the mushrooms. Or use a knife to cut them into ¼-inch slices. You should have 2½ to 3 cups.

4. In a large skillet, heat the oil over medium-high heat. Add the mushrooms and nutmeg; sauté just until mushrooms begin to soften, about 5 minutes. Remove from heat; salt and pepper to taste.

5. Spoon the mushrooms and their juices over salad greens; drizzle with hot dressing. Serve immediately.

♦ TIP ♦

Use the best ingredients you can afford. Any dish can only be as good as the ingredients that go into it.

. . . .

TOMATO-TOMATILLO TOSS

Makes 4 to 6 servings

The tomatillo (toh-mah-TEE-oh) belongs to the same family as the tomato. In fact, it resembles a small green tomato in size, shape, and appearance, except for the thin parchmentlike husk.

¾ **cup Santa Fe Salad Dressing (page 104)**
 3 **large tomatoes, seeded and chopped**
 4 **fresh tomatillos, husked, washed, and chopped**
¾ **cup chopped, peeled jícama**
¼ **cup finely chopped chervil or parsley**
 1 **to 2 tablespoons minced cilantro**
   salad greens (optional)

1. Make Santa Fe Salad Dressing. Refrigerate until ready to use.

2. At least 1 hour and up to 6 hours before serving, combine ½ cup of the salad dressing with the remaining ingredients except the salad greens. Toss to thoroughly coat ingredients with dressing; add more dressing to taste.

3. Cover and refrigerate. Remove from refrigerator 30 minutes before serving. If desired, serve on a bed of salad greens.

♦**NOTE:** Tomatillos look like small green tomatoes in a husk. Unlike tomatoes, however, tomatillos are eaten when still green and quite firm; their texture is crisp and their flavor hints of lemon, apple, and herbs. They can be found in specialty produce stores, Latin-American markets, and some supermarkets. Choose firm fruit with dry, tight-fitting husks. Store in a paper bag in the refrigerator for up to one month.

. . . .

GREEK EGGPLANT SALAD

. . . .

Makes 4 to 6 servings

This colorful salad is hearty enough to be served as a main dish, but it makes a refreshing side dish for roasted or grilled meats as well. Use large capers for this salad if you can find them.

2 pounds eggplant (about 2 medium), unpeeled and cut
   lengthwise into ½-inch slices
   salt
⅔ cup olive or vegetable oil
3½ tablespoons fresh lemon juice
2 tablespoons plus ¼ cup finely chopped fresh mint
1 large clove garlic, minced
½ teaspoon minced lemon zest
   freshly ground pepper
   additional olive oil
2 large tomatoes, seeded and chopped
1 cup chopped green bell pepper (about 1 medium)
1 cup chopped peeled and seeded cucumber (about 1
   medium)
1 cup kalamata olives
⅓ cup capers, rinsed and well drained
1 cup crumbled feta (4 ounces)
½ cup finely chopped parsley
   salad greens (optional)
⅓ cup toasted pine nuts (about 1 ounce)
   sprigs mint (optional)

1. Lay eggplant slices on paper towels; sprinkle with salt. Cover with more paper towels, then a large baking sheet. Weight baking sheet with something heavy—several 1-pound cans, a six-pack of soda, etc. Let eggplant drain 30 minutes.

2. Meanwhile, make the salad dressing. In a 1-cup glass measuring cup or small bowl, combine the oil, lemon juice, 2 tablespoons of the mint, garlic, lemon zest, ½ teaspoon salt, and ¼ teaspoon pepper. Cover and refrigerate until 20 minutes before using.

3. Position rack 5 to 6 inches from broiling unit. Preheat broiler.

4. Thoroughly blot eggplant with paper towels, wiping off excess salt. Arrange eggplant on 1 or 2 large baking sheets. Brush both sides lightly with olive oil.

5. Broil eggplant until surface begins to brown, about 5 minutes. Flip slices and broil the other side until browned. When eggplant is cool enough to handle, peel, if desired, and cut into ½-inch chunks.

6. In a large bowl, combine eggplant, tomatoes, green pepper, cucumber, olives, capers, feta, parsley, and the remaining ¼ cup mint. Add dressing; toss to combine. Cover and refrigerate for at least 2 hours, or up to 8 hours.

7. Remove salad from refrigerator 30 minutes before serving. Toss just before serving. If desired, spoon salad onto a bed of salad greens. Sprinkle top with pine nuts and, if desired, garnish with mint sprigs.

♦ TIP ♦

Never refrigerate tomatoes! Cold temperatures make the flesh of a tomato pulpy and kill the flavor. Store tomatoes at room temperature away from the sun. Unripe fruit can be ripened by placing it in a pierced paper bag with an apple and leaving it for several days at room temperature.

CAPERS

Capers are the buds of the *Capparis spinosa*, a bush native to the Mediterranean and parts of Asia. After the buds are picked, they're usually sundried, then pickled in a vinegar brine. Capers range in size from that of a tiny peppercorn (the petite nonpareil variety from southern France—considered the finest) to some as large as the tip of your little finger (from Italy). Capers generally come in brine but can also be found salted and sold in bulk. Either way, rinse capers before using them to flush away as much salt as possible. Capers lend piquancy to many sauces and condiments; they can also be used as a garnish for meat and vegetable dishes.

AZTEC SALAD

Makes 6 servings

Pineapple, avocado, jícama, and ginger are combined here in a distinctive and refreshing mélange.

I've always served this dish as a salad, but my friend Donna Michaud serves it (without jícama) as a dessert, topped with Spiced Crème Fraîche (page 303).

2 tablespoons fresh lemon juice
2 teaspoons grated fresh gingerroot
¼ teaspoon freshly grated nutmeg
¼ teaspoon salt
3 cups diced fresh pineapple
3 cups diced avocado
2 cups diced peeled jícama
¾ cup mayonnaise
¾ cup Crème Fraîche or sour cream
   salad greens
1 teaspoon paprika

1. In a large bowl, combine the lemon juice, ginger, nutmeg, and salt. Add the pineapple, avocado, and jícama; toss to combine. Cover and refrigerate. One hour before serving, combine mayonnaise, Crème Fraîche, and paprika. Spoon over pineapple mixture; gently combine. Cover and refrigerate until ready to serve.

2. Mound mixture on a bed of greens for each serving; sprinkle with additional paprika, if desired.

✦✦✦✦✦✦✦✦✦✦✦✦✦✦✦✦✦✦✦ **ABOUT JÍCAMA** ✦✦✦✦✦✦✦✦✦✦✦✦✦✦✦✦✦✦✦

Originally from Mexico, jícama is a large, bulbous root vegetable with thin brown skin and crisp flesh; it has a slightly sweet, nutty flavor. Use it instead of celery to add crunch to salads; like celery, it can also be cooked. You can find jícama in most supermarkets today and in Latin-American and Asian markets. Peel it just before using.

✦✦

FAJITA SALAD

Makes 6 servings

This variation on a theme is a meal in itself. Pass small bowls of sour cream, guacamole, chopped cilantro, and salsa for guests to garnish their salads as they please. Warm flour tortillas make the perfect accompaniment. To make sure the meat takes on as much of the marinade's delicious flavor as possible, start the day before.

MARINADE/DRESSING:

1⅓ cups vegetable or olive oil or ⅔ cup *each*
 ⅓ cup plus 1 tablespoon lime juice
 1 medium onion, finely chopped
 2 medium cloves garlic, minced
 1 to 1½ tablespoons finely chopped cilantro
 2 teaspoons chili powder
1½ teaspoons ground cumin
1½ teaspoons dried oregano or 1½ tablespoons finely chopped fresh oregano
 ¾ to 1 teaspoon crushed red pepper

SALAD INGREDIENTS:

1½ pounds flank steak, about ½ inch thick
    salt
 1 small jícama, peeled and chopped
 2 medium tomatoes, seeded and chopped
 2 cups canned pinto beans, rinsed and well drained (15-ounce can)
 2 medium avocados, peeled and chopped
 2 cups coarsely broken Oven-fried Tortilla Chips (page 47), or commercial tortilla chips
1½ cups grated cheddar (about 6 ounces)

1. In a shallow glass or ceramic pan large enough to hold the steak, combine all the marinade ingredients; stir well.

2. Trim all visible fat from the steak. If necessary, pound steak so that it's about ½ inch thick all over. Score steak in a diamond pattern on each side, cutting about ⅛ inch deep.

♦ TIP ♦

The best salad is a study in both contrast and balance of textures, colors, and flavors. Mix crunchy ingredients with those that are soft; tangy flavors with mild or slightly sweet; and bright colors with those more muted. The result will be an eye-pleasing, palate-teasing salad.

3. Dip meat in marinade to coat one side; flip to coat second side. Cover tightly with plastic wrap; refrigerate overnight, or for at least 8 hours (best if marinated 24 hours). Once or twice during marinating time, either turn the steak over, or spoon marinade over surface. Or place the meat and marinade in a large plastic bag, seal tightly, and refrigerate, turning several times.

4. One hour before grilling, soak 2 cups wood chips in water to cover; remove meat from refrigerator. Drain marinade into a small saucepan; cover meat with plastic wrap and leave at room temperature. Bring marinade to a boil; cook 3 minutes. Transfer to a large salad bowl; refrigerate.

5. Light a fire in an outdoor grill. Just before grilling the meat, sprinkle the soaked chips over the heat source. Brush grill lightly with vegetable oil. Grill steak over high heat, 3 to 5 minutes per side. Let stand 10 minutes; carve by cutting diagonally across the grain into thin slices. Cut slices into 1½-inch strips.

6. Remove marinade/dressing from refrigerator. Add any meat juices; whisk to combine. Salt to taste. Add steak; toss to coat with dressing. Add jícama, tomatoes, and beans; toss. Cover and refrigerate for at least 3 and up to 12 hours.

7. Just before serving, add avocados and tortilla chips; toss to combine. Sprinkle cheddar on top.

. . . .

◆◆◆◆◆◆◆◆◆◆◆◆◆◆◆ **ABOUT OLIVE OILS** ◆◆◆◆◆◆◆◆◆◆◆◆◆◆◆

Olive oil is graded according to the degree of acidity. The best olive oil is made from olives that are hand-picked and then cold-pressed (that is, without heat or chemicals), a process that produces a naturally low level of acidity. Extra virgin olive oil, which comes from the first pressing, is only one percent acid. It is considered the finest and fruitiest olive oil and is therefore also the most expensive. It can range from pale champagne to greenish-gold to bright green in color. In general, the deeper the color, the more intense the olive flavor.

After extra virgin, olive oil is classified in ascending order of acidity as superfine, fine, and pure. So-called pure olive oil is extracted with the aid of heat and solvents and blended with virgin oil; it is paler in both color and flavor than the others. The new "light" olive oil contains the exact same number of calories as regular olive oil. The term "light" refers to the lighter color, fragrance, and flavor obtained by an extremely fine filtration process. All of which make this oil better for baking and cooking, where the distinctive flavor of olive oil might be undesirable.

The flavor of olive oil depends on where the olives come from. In general, olive oils from France have a lighter flavor than those from Greece, Italy, and Spain. If you find yourself with an olive oil that's too strongly flavored for your taste, simply dilute it with canola oil, which has virtually no flavor of its own. In the end, as with all food, one's taste in olive oil is purely subjective. Try several and compare—it's the only way to choose a favorite.

◆◆

SWEET POTATO AND SMOKED TURKEY SALAD

Makes 6 servings

I prefer using the darker-skinned sweet potato varieties (often mislabeled as yams), which have an orange flesh that is moister when cooked than the pale-skinned varieties. Their color also makes this salad more visually interesting. Though true yams are hard to find in most markets, they make a delicious substitution for sweet potatoes in this recipe.

1½ **pounds small (6- to 8-ounce) sweet potatoes**
 2 **cups ½-inch cubes smoked turkey**
 1 **cup diced celery**
 1 **cup Orange–Curry Vinaigrette (page 107)**
¾ **cup coarsely chopped toasted walnuts**
¼ **cup finely chopped chervil or Italian parsley**

1. Preheat oven to 400°F.

2. Prick potatoes in several places. Bake just until the potatoes are tender when pierced with a fork. Don't overbake the potatoes or they won't cut nicely. Cool potatoes completely, then peel and cut into ½-inch cubes.

Microwave Method: Prick potatoes in several places. Place in microwave oven on a layer of paper towels. Microwave on HIGH 10 to 13 minutes, or until almost tender when pierced with a fork. Cover with foil; let stand 5 minutes. Cool potatoes completely. Peel and cut into ½-inch cubes.

3. In a large bowl, combine the potatoes, turkey, celery, and 1 cup Orange–Curry Vinaigrette; gently toss. Cover and refrigerate at least 1 hour. Salad can be prepared up to one day ahead. Just before serving, add walnuts and chervil; toss well.

♦NOTE: If you can't find 6- to 8-ounce sweet potatoes, buy the larger size and cut into 6-ounce pieces before baking. The potatoes can be baked a day ahead and refrigerated.

. . . .

SWEET AND HOT POTATO-SAUSAGE SALAD

Makes 6 to 8 servings

I generally use smoked kielbasa in this salad, however, any smoked sausage you like can be used. The added sweetness in the dressing makes a nice contrast to the sausage's smokiness and the chili pepper's heat. For a change of pace, substitute sweet potatoes for white potatoes.

1¼ cups Santa Fe Salad Dressing (page 104)
  2 tablespoons sugar
  2 pounds baking potatoes, scrubbed
  ¾ pound smoked sausage, diced
  1 cup chopped chives or scallions, green parts only

¾ **cup chopped celery**
½ **cup finely chopped red bell pepper**
½ **cup finely chopped watercress**
  salt and freshly ground pepper

1. Make Santa Fe Salad Dressing, adding 2 tablespoons sugar; cover and refrigerate.

2. Cut the potatoes in quarters. In a large pot, cook the potatoes in boiling water until barely tender, about 15 minutes. Put potatoes in a colander; rinse under cold running water. Drain well; cool to room temperature.

3. Sauté sausage until lightly browned. Drain on paper towels.

4. Peel the potatoes and cut into ½-inch chunks. In a large bowl, combine the potatoes with the dressing. Add the sausage, chives, celery, bell pepper, and watercress; toss to combine. Salt and pepper to taste. Cover and refrigerate for up to 36 hours. Let stand at room temperature 1 hour before serving.

. . . .

SPICY ASIAN NOODLE SALAD

*Makes 4 main course or
6 to 8 first course or
side dish servings*

An artful blend of Thai and Chinese inspiration, this salad is flavored with peanuts, ginger, sesame, and smoky-sweet Chinese sausage. Serve it with Quick Chinese Scallion Bread (page 241) for a main course or make it a satisfying starter or side dish.

Lop chong—the most popular Chinese sausage sold in the United States—is a dry, rather hard sausage with a texture similar to pepperoni. It's highly seasoned, a wonderful addition to this dish.

Sesame oil comes in two basic styles. One is light in color and flavor, while the other—commonly known as Oriental sesame oil—has a darker color and a stronger, nuttier flavor and fragrance. The latter can overpower other flavors in a dish, so discretion is advised. Oriental sesame oil is available in Asian markets, as well as the gourmet section of large supermarkets.

1 pound dried Chinese noodles, spaghetti type
¼ cup vegetable oil
¼ cup Oriental sesame oil
⅓ cup light soy sauce
¼ cup smooth peanut butter
¼ cup, packed, light or dark brown sugar
3 tablespoons balsamic or red-wine vinegar
1 tablespoon light unsulphured molasses
2 medium cloves garlic, minced
2 teaspoons minced fresh gingerroot
1 teaspoon crushed red pepper
¾ to 1 cup chopped scallions, white and green parts
⅓ cup chopped cilantro
¾ to 1 pound lop chong or other Chinese sausage, thinly sliced
¼ cup toasted sesame seeds

1. Cook noodles in boiling water just until tender but still firm to the bite. Drain well; turn into a large bowl.

2. In a blender jar or a food-processor workbowl fitted with the metal blade, combine the vegetable oil, sesame oil, soy sauce, peanut butter, brown sugar, vinegar, molasses, garlic, ginger, and crushed red pepper. Process until smooth, about 30 seconds.

3. Pour dressing over warm noodles; toss to combine. Add scallions, cilantro, and sausage. Cover and refrigerate at least 8 hours, or up to 1 day. Toss once or twice during that time.

4. Just before serving, toss noodles again; sprinkle with sesame seeds. May be served chilled or at room temperature.

· · · · · · · · · · ·

CHICKEN CHOW MEIN SALAD WITH GINGER-SOY DRESSING

. . . .

Makes 4 servings

Crunchy chow mein noodles play a starring role in this main-course salad. You'll find the noodles, packed in cans or in cellophane packages, in the Chinese foods section of your supermarket. The salad can be served plain or on a bed of shredded lettuce.

  1 pound skinless and boneless chicken breasts
3½ tablespoons Oriental sesame oil
  ¼ cup red wine vinegar
2½ tablespoons light soy sauce
  1 tablespoon sugar
  2 tablespoons minced fresh gingerroot
  1 large clove garlic, minced
  ⅛ to ¼ teaspoon crushed red pepper
  8 ounces fresh snow peas
  1 cup chopped celery
  1 cup canned sliced water chestnuts, drained, rinsed and blotted dry (8-ounce can)
  1 cup canned, sliced bamboo shoots, drained, rinsed and blotted dry (8-ounce can)
  1 cup fresh mung bean sprouts
  ¾ cup chopped watercress leaves
  ⅓ to ½ cup chopped scallions, white and green parts
  2 tablespoons minced cilantro
  3 cups crisp chow mein noodles (about 5½ ounces)
    sprigs cilantro for garnish (optional)
    shredded red-leaf lettuce (optional)

1. Pound chicken breasts to flatten slightly. Cut into strips, about 2½ inches x ⅜ inches.

2. In a large skillet over medium-high heat, heat 1 tablespoon of the sesame oil. Add the chicken strips. Sauté, stirring often, just until chicken is done through, about 5 minutes.

3. While chicken is sautéing, make dressing. In a large bowl, combine remaining sesame oil, vinegar, soy sauce, sugar, ginger, garlic, and crushed red pepper.

4. Add hot chicken to dressing, tossing to coat. Let cool to room temperature, about 10 minutes.

5. Snap stems off snow peas and use to pull string off top ridge. Slice snow peas on the diagonal in thirds; add to chicken.

6. Add the remaining ingredients except sprigs of cilantro and lettuce. Toss to combine; serve immediately. Or combine all the salad ingredients except the chow mein noodles and garnish; toss. Cover and refrigerate up to 6 hours. Ten minutes before serving, add chow mein noodles and toss. Serve salad on a bed of shredded lettuce leaves and garnish with sprigs of cilantro, if desired.

. . . .

COOL AND CREAMY GREEN PEA SALAD

Makes 6 servings

This makes a great substitute for potato salad with picnic or barbecue fare, such as ribs or chicken. If you can't find fresh basil, fresh mint is a good substitute; parsley will suffice.

   1 cup sour cream
  ¼ cup packed fresh basil leaves, finely chopped
   1 small clove garlic, minced
   1 tablespoon balsamic or red wine vinegar
      salt and cayenne
3½ to 4 cups fresh green peas or thawed frozen petite peas
      (16-ounce package)
   2 small ripe tomatoes, seeded and diced
  ¾ pound bacon, fried until crisp and crumbled

1. In a medium bowl, combine the sour cream, basil, garlic, and vinegar. Season to taste with salt and cayenne. Add the peas, tomatoes, and all but ½ cup bacon. Cover and refrigerate for at least 4 hours, or up to 24 hours.

2. Before serving, sprinkle salad with reserved bacon. May be made up to a day in advance, in which case, reserved bacon should be refrigerated in an airtight jar or plastic bag.

DRESSINGS

HOT BRIE DRESSING

Makes 1 cup

This dressing is one of my favorites. It's one of those versatile concoctions that's just as good drizzled over greens (see Warm Mushroom Salad, page 90) as it is over warm vegetables, or used as a warm dip for crudités. You may want to make a double batch.

⅓ cup homemade chicken stock or canned chicken broth
2 tablespoons olive oil
2 tablespoons white wine vinegar
¼ cup minced leek, white part only
1 large clove garlic, minced
1½ teaspoons Dijon mustard
3 tablespoons heavy whipping cream, at room temperature
8 ounces brie, rind removed, cut into ½-inch chunks, and softened
salt and white pepper

1. In a small saucepan over high heat, combine the chicken stock, oil, vinegar, leeks, garlic, and mustard. Bring to a boil. Reduce heat to low; simmer for 10 minutes. Add cream; stir to combine.

2. Stirring constantly, add 3 or 4 pieces of cheese at a time to the simmering mixture. Stir until cheese is melted before adding more cheese. If dressing begins to bubble, remove from heat for a few seconds. Do not let boil. Remove from heat when cheese is melted and mixture is warmed through.

3. Pour hot dressing into a blender jar or food-processor workbowl fitted with the metal blade (the blender does a better job here). Process for 1 minute. To prevent scalding yourself when using the blender, begin at low speed and gradually increase to high; in the food processor, place the pusher in the feed tube. Salt and pepper to taste.

4. If using dressing within the hour, return to pan and keep warm in a hot-water bath or double boiler. Or cool to room temperature, cover, and refrigerate. Rewarm in a small saucepan over low heat or place dressing in a 2-cup glass measuring cup and microwave on MEDIUM (50% power) for about 2½ minutes, stirring halfway through. The amount of time it takes in the microwave depends on how cold the dressing is to begin with.

. . . .

SANTA FE SALAD DRESSING

Makes about 1¼ cups

This dressing got its appellation from a spicy-hot salad I enjoyed in Santa Fe, New Mexico. I couldn't wangle the recipe from the hostess, but I am pleased with my duplication. This dressing is particularly good on slaws and potato salads, such as the Sweet and Hot Potato–Sausage Salad (page 98). Adjust the amount of cayenne to your liking.

1 large clove garlic
⅔ cup olive or vegetable oil
⅓ cup sour cream
¼ cup fresh lime juice
2 teaspoons Dijon mustard
¾ teaspoon chili powder
½ to ¾ teaspoon cayenne
½ teaspoon salt

1. With the machine running, drop the garlic into a food-processor workbowl fitted with the metal blade; process until garlic is chopped and clinging to sides of bowl. Scrape down sides of food processor bowl. Or mince garlic and turn into a blender jar.

2. Add the remaining ingredients; process 20 seconds, or until creamy. Cover and refrigerate until ready to use. Whisk before dressing salads.

. . . .

CREAMY GARLIC DRESSING

Makes about 1 cup

Though fresh garlic can be used for this dressing, I much prefer the milder, sweeter flavor of Roasted Garlic (page 309).

⅓ **cup heavy whipping cream**
¼ **cup vegetable oil**
2 **tablespoons fresh lemon juice**
10 **to 15 medium cloves Roasted Garlic, pulp squeezed from skins, or 2 medium fresh cloves garlic, peeled and crushed**
½ **teaspoon salt**
¼ **teaspoon freshly ground pepper**

1. In a blender jar or food-processor workbowl fitted with the metal blade, combine all the ingredients. Or combine the ingredients in a 12- to 16-ounce jar and use an immersion blender. Process until smooth.

2. Cover and store in the refrigerator up to 1 week. Let stand at room temperature for 30 minutes before using. If you forget to take dressing out of the refrigerator, microwave on HIGH 10 seconds to thin.

. . . .

CHUTNEY CREAM DRESSING

Makes about 1 cup

This dressing is great with all manner of meat salads—chicken, duck, turkey, beef. Try it with chicken, nectarines, and walnuts—it's wonderful! If you use walnuts, substitute one or two tablespoons walnut oil for an equal amount of the vegetable oil.

One of this recipe's special features is that it can be tailored to the dish simply by varying the chutney. Cranberry chutney, for example, is an ideal choice for a post-holiday turkey salad. Today's gourmet-market shelves carry an array of chutneys made with ingredients ranging from tomatoes to papayas to spinach—something for everyone!

½ cup heavy whipping cream
¼ cup vegetable oil
⅓ cup Major Grey or other chutney
¼ teaspoon curry powder
⅛ teaspoon cayenne
salt (optional)

In a blender jar or food-processor workbowl fitted with the metal blade, combine all the ingredients. Or combine the ingredients in a 12- to 16-ounce jar and use an immersion blender. Process until smooth. Cover and refrigerate at least 1 hour to allow flavors to meld. May be refrigerated up to 1 week. Taste just before using and add salt to taste, if necessary. Shake dressing well before tossing with salad ingredients.

. . . .

ROASTED GARLIC VINAIGRETTE

Makes about 1 cup

Don't be afraid of the garlic in this dressing. Roasting takes away the bite and gives it a nutty, slightly sweet flavor.

⅔ cup olive or vegetable oil
2 tablespoons fresh lemon juice
1 tablespoon balsamic or red wine vinegar
8 to 12 medium cloves Roasted Garlic (page 309), pulp squeezed from skins
½ teaspoon salt
¼ teaspoon freshly ground pepper

In a blender or food-processor workbowl fitted with the metal blade, combine all the ingredients. Or combine the ingredients in a 12- to 16-ounce jar and use an immersion blender. Process until smooth. Refrigerate until 30 minutes before using. If you forget to take the dressing out of the refrigerator on time, microwave it on HIGH for 10 seconds to thin.

. . . .

ORANGE–CURRY VINAIGRETTE

Makes about 1 cup

Though I created this dressing for the Sweet Potato and Smoked Turkey Salad (page 97), I find it equally delicious on other salads including spinach, citrus, and slaws.

⅔ cup canola or other vegetable oil
¼ cup red wine vinegar
3 tablespoons orange juice
  about 3 tablespoons finely grated zest from 1 medium orange
2 teaspoons minced fresh gingerroot
½ teaspoon curry powder
½ teaspoon salt

Combine all the ingredients in a blender jar or food-processor workbowl fitted with the metal blade. Or combine the ingredients in a 12- to 16-ounce jar and use an immersion blender. Process for 30 seconds.

. . . .

HONEYED MUSTARD VINAIGRETTE

Makes about 1 cup

This dressing is wonderful on an orange and avocado salad or a simple composition of greens as well as the Hoppin' John Salad (page 88) for which it was created. The type of honey you use can make a huge difference in the dressing's flavor. A strong sage honey, for example, can overpower the flavor of the other ingredients, while a fruity honey—such as blackberry—complements it.

½ cup canola or other vegetable oil
3 tablespoons red wine vinegar
1½ tablespoons honey
1½ tablespoons Dijon mustard
2 teaspoons Worcestershire sauce
¾ teaspoon salt

Combine all ingredients in a blender jar or in food-processor workbowl fitted with the metal blade. Or combine in a 12- to 16-ounce, wide-mouthed jar and use an immersion blender. Blend 30 seconds at high speed.

♦ ♦ ♦

♦ ♦ ♦

I have a singular passion for pasta. The proliferation of fresh and dried pasta now available means demand is high, so I'm obviously not alone in my ardor. That's probably because few foods can rival pasta's ability to give both body and spirit a lift. Pasta's the perfect foil for vegetables, meats, seafood, and cheese. Could it be (for some of us, at least) that pasta's the perfect food? It's extremely versatile, easy to cook, economical, and nutritious (about 1½ percent fat; 15 percent protein). What more can one ask?

The secret of pasta's success is undoubtedly that it's a food of a thousand faces. Manufacturers of pasta have become extraordinarily creative, generating a multitude of shapes, sizes, colors, and flavors. Sizes range from the tiny, rice-shaped orzo, to the jumbo conchiglie (shells). Colors span the spectrum from orange (tinted with carrot and/or paprika), to red (tomato or red bell pepper), to green (spinach), to black (squid ink or olives), and many hues in-between. You'll also find tricolor pastas—both fresh and dried—which combine red-, green-, and natural-colored noodles.

> Put a generous lump of sweet butter on top of a pile of spaghetti; shake and twist on the salt and pepper, also generously; pile Parmesan on top, and with your fork mix the whole into an odorous, steamy, rich, Medusa-like tangle. All that is left is to eat it.
>
> —M. F. K. Fisher

Flavors run the gamut from the traditional whole-wheat, tomato, and spinach, to the newer pastas seasoned with flavorings including chili peppers, spices, herbs, garlic, and even smoked salmon. Pasta shapes are inventive, as well. There are bows, spirals (long, short, fat, and thin), stuffed pastas, little wheels, thin round noodles, narrow to wide flat noodles, ruffled noodles, tubes, and radiator-shapes—just to name a few. Pasta shapes can get confusing because manufacturers sometimes use different names for the same shape pasta. See Pasta Shapes (page 112) for more detail.

Basically, there are two types of European-style pasta: The flour-and-water variety, which is made of semolina, milled from hard durum wheat, such as macaroni and spaghetti, and the egg-enriched variety, such as noodles. Almost every country has its own form of pasta. The Germans have *Spätzle* (little dumplings), the Poles *pierogi* (filled noodle squares), and the Chinese won ton skins, which they use in dozens of ways. Throughout the Orient, noodles are made with rice and mung beans, as well as wheat.

There's a plentitude of good fresh and dried commercial pasta available today. Their variety and ease of preparation certainly compete with homemade pasta, which few of us have time to do. Whether you buy fresh or dried pasta, the secret to success is to read the ingredients on the label. Only buy brands made with durum wheat, also called semolina. This is the pasta of preference because it absorbs less water, has a mellow flavor, and retains a pleasant bite when cooked. Fresh pasta can be wrapped airtight in a plastic bag and refrigerated for up to five days, double-wrapped and frozen for up to three months. Dried pasta will last almost indefinitely if tightly sealed and stored in a cool, dry place.

The key to preparing pasta is not to overcook it. Overdone pasta can be either rubbery or on the mushy side. Use plenty of water (about four quarts to one pound of pasta) and don't add the pasta until the water reaches a full rolling boil. Most commercial dried pasta needs far less time to cook than the package recommends; some fresh pasta takes as little as five or ten seconds and should be tested almost as soon as it hits the water. The best way to test pasta for doneness is to fish out a strand and bite into it. Ideally, the finished pasta should be *al dente*—tender but still firm to the bite. Immediately drain the cooked pasta, either in a colander or in the perforated section of a spaghetti pot. Shake the draining container well to drain as much moisture as possible from the pasta. You can also cook the pasta a day or so ahead of time to be sauced just before serving (page 111).

Common sense should prevail when saucing pasta. Thin, delicate styles like capelli d'angelo or capellini (angel hair) require a light sauce that won't overpower and weigh down the noodles. On the other hand, sturdy pasta shapes such as rotini (spirals) and farfalle (bows or butterflies) have wonderful nooks and crannies for catching chunkier sauces. Sauces can be creamy-rich, as for Creamy Confetti Corn Pasta, or fresh, light, and low in calories, like the Summertime Fettuccine. None of the sauces in this chapter takes long to cook, and all are suited to the noodles suggested. Don't think, however, that pasta has to have a composed sauce to be good. One of the best pasta dishes I ever tasted was steaming-hot fettuccine tossed with fresh basil and chunks of creamy Boursin cheese. The cheese melted seductively over the pasta and the result was sheer gastronomic ecstasy!

It's not even necessary to dirty a bowl to combine the pasta with its sauce.

It can be tossed either in the pan in which the sauce was cooked, or in the pasta cooking pot, after the water is drained. Because pasta cools quickly, always heat the pasta serving bowl or plates.

With the hundreds of different pasta sizes and shapes—and even more potential sauce variations—the possibilities for combinations are endless. Pasta can be served as a first course, side dish, salad, or entree. The temperature can be hot, cold, or room temperature. Just remember one thing: no matter how you cook or sauce pasta, there's only one way to eat it—with undaunted enthusiasm and a great deal of gusto!

✦✦✦✦✦✦✦✦✦✦✦✦✦✦✦ MAKING PASTA AHEAD ✦✦✦✦✦✦✦✦✦✦✦✦✦✦✦✦✦

One thing I often do—particularly when entertaining—is cook pasta a day in advance and sauce it just before serving. That way, I don't have to bother with last-minute hassle or steaming up the kitchen with a huge pot of boiling water. Instead, I can give my attention to finishing the rest of the meal.

Simply cook the pasta as usual, being particularly careful to cook it only until *al dente*—tender, but still firm to the bite. Drain, rinse under cold running water to stop the cooking, and again drain thoroughly. Let the pasta cool completely, then toss with a couple of teaspoons of oil so it won't stick together. Store the pasta in a plastic bag or a covered bowl in the refrigerator for up to three days.

The pasta can be reheated in one of several ways. I prefer to microwave it right in the storage container on HIGH for one to three minutes, tossing the pasta halfway through. The length of time in the microwave depends on how much pasta you have.

You can also reheat the pasta in the pan of hot sauce or put it in a colander and run very hot tap water over it. If using the hot-water method, be sure to drain the pasta well before saucing it.

You can also reheat pasta that's already been sauced. Do so either in the microwave (as suggested above), or in a covered pan over low heat. If making pasta ahead specifically to reheat it be sure to undercook it slightly. It will continue to cook when reheated in the sauce.

PASTA SHAPES

There are hundreds of pasta shapes and sizes—no one really knows exactly how many. The confusion is increased by the fact that manufacturers often use different names for the same shape (fusilli and rotini, for example). The following glossary describes those pastas shapes most commonly available either in supermarkets or in Italian markets.

ACINI DI PEPE Tiny peppercorn-shape pasta.

AGNOLOTTI Small, crescent-shape stuffed pasta.

ANELLINI Tiny pasta rings.

BAVETTINE Narrow linguine.

BUCATINI Hollow, spaghettilike strands.

CANNARONI Wide tubes; also called zitoni.

CANNELLONI Large, round tubes, used for stuffing.

CAPELLI D'ANGELO, CAPELLINI Long, extremely fine strands.

CAPELVENERI Very thin noodles.

CAPPELLETTI Hat-shape stuffed pasta.

CAVATAPPI Short, thin, spiral macaroni.

CAVATELLI Short, narrow, ripple-edged shells.

CONCHIGLIE Shell-shape pasta, sometimes called maruzze.

CORALLI Tiny tubes, generally used in soup.

DITALI Small macaroni about ½ inch long.

DITALINI Smaller ditali.

ELBOW MACARONI From small to medium tubes.

FARFALLE Bow- or butterfly-shape pasta.

FARFALLINE Small farfalle.

FARFALLONE Large farfalle.

FEDELINI Very fine spaghetti.

FETTUCCE Flat egg noodles (about ½ inch wide); the widest of the fettuccines.

FETTUCCELLE Narrow (about ⅛ inch wide), flat egg noodles; the thinnest of the fettuccine family.

FETTUCCINE Thin, flat egg noodles about ¼ inch wide.

FIDEO Thin, coiled strands of pasta that, when cooked, resemble vermicelli.

FUSILLI Traditional fusilli comes in spaghetti-length spiral-shape noodles. Cut fusilli is about 1½ inches long.

GEMELLI Short (1½-inch) twists that resemble 2 strands of spaghetti twisted together.

GNOCCHI Small, ripple-edged shells.

LASAGNE Long, very broad noodles (2 to 3 inches wide); straight or ripple-edged.

LINGUINE Very narrow (⅛ inch wide or less) ribbons.

LUMACHE   Large shells, used for stuffing.

MACARONI   Tube-shape pasta of various lengths.

MACCHERONI   The Italian word for all types of macaroni, from hollow tubes, to shells, to twists.

MAFALDE   Broad, flat, ripple-edged noodles.

MAGLIETTE   Short, curved tubes of pasta.

MANICOTTI   Very large tubes, used for stuffing.

MARGHERITE   Narrow flat noodles, with one rippled side.

MARUZZE   Shell-shape pasta; several sizes, from tiny to jumbo.

MEZZANI   Very short, curved tubes.

MOSTACCIOLI   Pasta tubes about 2 inches long.

ORECCHIETTE   Tiny disk shapes.

ORZO   Rice-shape pasta.

PAPPARDELLE   Wide noodles (about 5/8 inch) with rippled sides.

PASTINA   Tiny pasta (such as acini de pepe), generally used in soups.

PENNE   Diagonally-cut tubes with either smooth or ridged sides.

PERCIATELLI   Thin, hollow pasta about twice as thick as spaghetti; similar to bucatini.

PEZZOCCHERI   Thick buckwheat noodles.

QUADRETTINI   Small, flat pasta squares.

RADIATORI   Short, chunky shapes that resemble tiny radiators with rippled edges.

RAVIOLI   Square-shape stuffed pasta.

RIGATONI   Large (about 1½ inches wide) grooved macaroni.

ROTELLE   Small spoked-wheel shapes.

ROTINI   Short (1 to 2 inches long) spirals.

RUOTE, RUOTE DI CARRO   Small spoked-wheel shapes.

SEMI DI MELONE   Tiny, flat melon-seed shapes.

SPAGHETTI   Long, thin, round strands.

SPAGHETTINI   Very thin spaghetti.

TAGLIATELLE   Long, thin (about ¼ inch wide) flat egg noodles.

TAGLIARINI   Long, paper-thin (less than ⅛ inch wide) ribbons.

TAGLIOLINI   Another name for tagliarini.

TORTELLINI   Small stuffed pasta; similar to cappelletti.

TORTELLONI   Large tortellini.

TRENETTE   A narrower, thicker version of tagliatelle.

TRIPOLINI   Small bow-ties with rounded edges.

TUBETTI   Tiny, hollow pasta tubes.

VERMICELLI   Very thin strands of spaghetti.

ZITI   Slightly curved tubes, ranging in length from 2 to 12 inches.

SCOTCHED SALMON PENNE

*Makes 4 main course or
6 first course or
side dish servings*

James Beard and Barbara Kafka used to give week-long cooking classes at San Francisco's Stanford Court Hotel. It was always a week of intensive learning and inspiration. I particularly remember one special afternoon when a few of us were sitting around talking after class. Outside, the winter day was cold and rainy, making the warmth of the kitchen and our camaraderie all the more cozy. In his quiet, thoughtful manner, Beard began to expound on pasta. One of his favorite ways of saucing it, he said, was to toss it with reduced heavy cream, a goodly amount of Scotch whiskey, and lots of smoked salmon.

Those remembrances inspired this recipe but, unlike James Beard, I use half-and-half instead of heavy cream, which enrobes the pasta in a lighter (less caloric) fashion. I also add leeks and long, thin strands of lemon zest, and use smoked salmon ends and trimmings for a more economical dish. This has become one of my very favorite ways with pasta. It's quick and delicious and even tastes wonderful cold the next day.

> ◆ TIP ◆
> Use a citrus zester (available in gourmet specialty shops) to obtain long thin strands of citrus zest. Press firmly as you draw the zester down along the skin of the fruit. For continuous strips of zest, begin at one end of the fruit, and cut in a spiral around and down.

 3 tablespoons extra virgin olive oil
 ½ cup finely chopped leeks (white part only) or 2 small scallions, finely chopped
 1½ cups half-and-half
 ⅔ cup Scotch whisky
   about 1½ tablespoons grated lemon zest (1 large lemon)
 ½ pound smoked salmon, coarsely chopped
   salt and white pepper
 1 pound dried penne

1. Heat oil in a medium saucepan over medium heat. Add the leeks; sauté 1 minute. Stir in the half-and-half and Scotch; bring to a boil. Reduce heat to medium-low. Cook, stirring occasionally, for 10 minutes. Add the lemon zest; cook additional 5 minutes. Stir in the salmon; heat for 1 minute. Remove from heat; salt and pepper to taste.

2. Meanwhile, in a large pot of boiling salted water, cook the penne until al dente. Drain well; turn into large, heated bowl. Pour sauce over pasta; toss to coat. Serve warm or at room temperature.

FUSILLI NIÇOISE

Makes 6 servings

Fusilli Niçoise is patterned after the classic salade niçoise, noted for its felicitous combination of tuna, green beans, potatoes, onions, black olives, and anchovies. The potatoes, green beans, and pasta can be cooked a few hours or a day ahead and refrigerated. Toss the pasta with a tablespoon of oil to make sure it doesn't stick together. Bring refrigerated ingredients to room temperature before assembling the dish.

- 1 **pound small red potatoes, scrubbed**
- ¾ **pound fresh tender green beans**
- 1 **pound dried fusilli**
- ⅓ **cup olive oil**
- 1 **small red onion, finely chopped**
- 1 **large clove garlic, minced**
- 2 **tablespoons butter, softened**
- 2 **teaspoons anchovy paste**
- 1 **tablespoon fresh lemon juice**
- ⅓ **cup niçoise olives**
- 2 **large tomatoes, seeded and chopped**
- 1½ **cups water-packed albacore tuna, drained and coarsely flaked (12½-ounce can)**
   salt and freshly ground pepper
- 2 **tablespoons capers, rinsed and drained**
- 2 **tablespoons finely chopped chervil or parsley**

> No man is alone while eating spaghetti—it requires so much attention.
> —CHRISTOPHER MORLEY

1. Place the potatoes in a large saucepan, add enough water to cover by 1 inch, and bring to a boil. Boil gently for 15 to 20 minutes, or until potatoes test done when pierced by a fork. Drain potatoes, then rinse with cold running water. Set aside to drain thoroughly. When cool, cut into bite-size pieces.

2. In a large saucepan, bring 4 quarts water to a boil. Wash, trim, and remove strings, if any, from beans; cut into 1½-inch lengths. Cook beans until crisp-tender, about 5 minutes. Drain, then plunge into a bowl of ice water to stop further cooking. Drain again and blot dry.

3. In a large pot of boiling water, cook pasta until al dente. Drain and set aside.

4. Use a paper towel to dry the pot the pasta was cooked in. Add the oil; heat over medium-high heat. Add onion and sauté, stirring often, until soft, about 5 minutes. Add garlic; cook for additional 2 minutes.

5. While onion and garlic are cooking, combine butter and anchovy paste in a small bowl. Add to onion mixture, along with the lemon juice.

6. Reduce heat to medium. Add pasta, potatoes, beans, and olives; toss to combine. Heat until warmed through. Add the tomatoes and tuna; toss to combine. The heat of the other ingredients will warm the tomatoes and tuna. Salt and pepper to taste. Serve immediately, garnished with capers and chervil.

. . . .

MARINATED SHRIMP PASTA

Makes 6 main course or 8 to 10 first course or side dish servings

Created for an appearance on ''Hour Magazine,'' this make-ahead, one-dish meal requires only tossed greens, crusty French bread, and maybe a chilled white wine to complete the picture. You can also serve it in smaller portions as a first course. But don't serve this dish cold: Remove it from the refrigerator at least an hour before serving; the flavors will be more intense. Grilling the shrimp adds wonderful flavor. Use long fusilli, if available, for a showier dish.

MARINADE:

 2 **small cloves garlic**
½ **cup olive oil**
¼ **cup canola or other vegetable oil**
¼ **cup red wine vinegar**
 2 **tablespoons Worcestershire sauce**
¾ **teaspoon salt**
¼ **teaspoon freshly ground black pepper**
⅛ **teaspoon cayenne**

  1 **pound medium shrimp, peeled and grilled or boiled**
½ **to ⅔ cup chopped fresh dill**
  1 **pound dried fusilli**
  2 **medium tomatoes, seeded and chopped**
  1 **medium red bell pepper, thinly sliced**
  1 **medium green bell pepper, thinly sliced**
  1 **cup chopped chives or scallions, green parts only**

1. With the machine running, drop the garlic into a food-processor workbowl fitted with the metal blade; process until garlic is chopped and clinging to sides of bowl. Scrape down sides of workbowl. Or mince garlic and turn into a blender jar. Add remaining marinade ingredients; process until well blended.

2. Pour marinade into a large bowl. Add shrimp and dill; toss to combine. Cover tightly and refrigerate at least 3 hours, preferably overnight. Stir once or twice during marinating time.

3. Cook the pasta in a large pot of boiling salted water until al dente. Rinse with cold running water; drain well.

4. Drain off ⅓ cup marinade; reserve. Add pasta to marinated shrimp; toss to coat pasta. Cover and refrigerate until 1 hour before serving.

5. Divide pasta evenly among plates. Top each serving with tomatoes and bell peppers. Sprinkle with chives; drizzle each serving with a small amount of the reserved marinade.

. . . .

POPEYE PASTA

*Makes 4 main dish or
6 first course or
side dish servings*

This spinach-clad pasta packs a delicious power punch to the tastebuds! The contrast of the pale green spinach pasta and the dark greens is as much of a treat for the eye as the feta, sundried tomatoes, and pine nuts are for the palate. Popeye never had it so good!

¼ to ⅓ **cup pine nuts (about 2 ounces)**
  1 **pound dried fettuccine**
  4 **tablespoons olive oil**
  2 **large cloves garlic, each cut into 4 slices**
 ⅓ **cup finely chopped sundried tomatoes, commercial
    or homemade (page 289)**
1½ **pounds spinach, washed, dried, stemmed, and shredded**
  1 **teaspoon balsamic or red wine vinegar**
 ¾ **cup crumbled feta (4 ounces)**
    freshly grated nutmeg
    salt and freshly ground pepper

1. In a large ungreased skillet, toast pine nuts over medium-high heat until golden brown. Turn out onto a plate; set aside to cool.

2. Cook the pasta in a large pot of boiling salted water until al dente.

3. While pasta is cooking, combine 2 tablespoons of the oil and 1 of the sliced cloves garlic in each of 2 large skillets. Cook over medium-high heat until garlic turns golden, 2 to 3 minutes. Use a slotted spoon to remove and discard garlic. Add half the sundried tomatoes to each skillet; sauté 2 minutes. Add half the spinach to each skillet. Cook over medium-high heat until spinach is slightly wilted, turning carefully so that spinach doesn't spill from pan. Sprinkle ½ teaspoon vinegar over each pan of spinach; toss to combine.

4. Drain pasta. Add spinach mixture (including any excess oil in skillets) and feta; toss to combine. Season to taste with nutmeg, salt, and pepper.

Microwave Method: Spread pine nuts in a single layer on a paper plate. Cook on HIGH for 1½ to 2 minutes, or until nuts begin to brown, rotating plate halfway through. Set aside to cool. Cook pasta as in Step 2. While pasta is cook-

> ♦ TIP ♦
>
> Feta is a Greek cheese traditionally made of sheep's or goat's milk, though today most is made with cow's milk. It is cured and stored in a salty whey brine. Feta's crumbly texture makes it perfect for combining with pastas, sprinkling over salads, or tossing with hot vegetables.

ing, combine oil and garlic in a very large bowl. Cook, uncovered, on HIGH for 1 minute. Add sundried tomatoes; cook, uncovered, on HIGH for 1 minute. Add spinach and vinegar; cook, uncovered, on HIGH for 1 minute, tossing after 30 seconds. Add drained pasta, tossing to combine. Cook, uncovered, on HIGH for 1 to 1½ minutes, or until hot throughout, tossing halfway through. Add feta; season to taste with nutmeg, salt, and pepper. Toss to combine.

5. Serve immediately, garnished with toasted pine nuts.

. . . .

CREAMY CONFETTI CORN PASTA

*Makes 4 to 6 main course or
6 to 8 first course or
side dish servings*

This multihued dish is quick and colorful. Tricolor pasta comes in both dried and fresh forms. Among those available are fettuccine, radiatori, spaghetti, and rotini.

  1 **pound dried tricolor pasta**
1½ **cups heavy whipping cream**
  2 **medium cloves garlic, quartered**
  ½ **cup finely chopped sundried tomatoes, commercial
       or homemade (page 289)**
  ⅛ **teaspoon freshly grated nutmeg**
  2 **cups fresh or thawed frozen corn kernels (about
       2 large ears of corn)**
  3 **to 4 tablespoons capers, rinsed and well drained**
  1 **cup grated aged Asiago, Parmesan, or Monterey Jack
       (about 4 ounces)**
  ¼ **cup finely chopped watercress
       salt and freshly ground pepper**

1. Cook the pasta in a large pot of boiling salted water until al dente.

2. Meanwhile, combine the cream and garlic in a large

saucepan. Bring to a boil over medium-high heat. Cook for 2 minutes. Use a slotted spoon to remove garlic.

3. Stir in sundried tomatoes and nutmeg. Reduce heat to medium; cook, uncovered, for 5 minutes. Add corn and capers; continue to cook for 2 minutes. Remove from heat.

Microwave Method: Combine cream and garlic in a large microwavesafe bowl. Cook on HIGH, uncovered, until mixture comes to a boil, about 3 minutes. Use a slotted spoon to remove garlic. Stir in sundried tomatoes and nutmeg. Cook on MEDIUM-HIGH (70% power) for 4 minutes. Add corn and capers; cook on HIGH for 1 minute.

4. Drain pasta; add to cream mixture in pan or bowl. Add cheese and watercress; toss to combine. Salt and pepper to taste. Serve hot.

> The discovery of a new dish does more for the happiness of mankind than the discovery of a star.
> —ANTHELME BRILLAT-SAVARIN

SUMMERTIME FETTUCCINE

Makes 4 main course or 6 to 8 first course or side dish servings

This dish takes its name from the summer-fresh combination of mint leaves, lemon, and juicy, ripe tomatoes. This is one of those dishes that's just as good cold or at room temperature as it is hot.

1 **pound dried or 1¼ pounds fresh fettuccine**
¼ **cup olive oil**
1 **medium clove garlic, minced**
2½ **pounds tomatoes, peeled, seeded and coarsely chopped, or about 3 cups chopped canned Italian tomatoes (28-ounce can)**
  about 2½ teaspoons finely grated lemon zest (1 medium lemon)
½ **cup, packed, fresh mint leaves, chopped**
  salt and freshly ground pepper
  sprigs mint for garnish

1. Cook the pasta in a large pot of boiling salted water until al dente.

2. Meanwhile, heat the oil in a medium saucepan over

medium-high heat. Cook garlic for 1 minute. Reduce heat to medium; add tomatoes and lemon zest. Cook, stirring often, for 2 minutes. Stir in the mint and cook 1 more minute. Salt and pepper to taste. Keep warm over low heat just until pasta is done. Do not overcook, or sauce will lose its fresh flavor.

3. Drain pasta and toss with sauce. Garnish with mint sprigs.

. . . .

PASTA-GORGONZOLA GRATIN

Makes 6 servings

Roasted eggplant adds smoky nuance to this dish, made with two popular Italian cheeses—Gorgonzola and fontina. I use radiatori—radiator-shape pasta that catches and holds sauce in every bite. If you can find it, use tricolor (red, green, and white) radiatori to add visual interest. Almost any pasta can be used for this gratin, though, just as long as it's not too fine. If you can't find radiatori, try mostaccioli, rotini, farfalle, or little shells.

Pasta-Gorgonzola Gratin is a great dish for guests because it can be made and refrigerated the day before and baked a half hour before serving.

2 pounds eggplant
6 to 7 tablespoons olive oil
12 ounces dried radiatori
1 pound tomatoes, peeled, seeded, and coarsely chopped
1½ cups finely crumbled Gorgonzola (6 ounces)
2 cups grated fontina (8 ounces)
3 tablespoons all-purpose flour
1 large clove garlic, crushed
½ teaspoon salt
3 cups half-and-half
   about 2½ teaspoons finely grated lemon zest (1 medium lemon)
⅛ teaspoon cayenne
½ cup chopped chives or scallion, green parts only

1. Preheat oven to 400°F.

2. Cut stems from eggplants. Cut each eggplant in half lengthwise; slice each half lengthwise into 3 segments. Place eggplant pieces, skin side down, on a large baking sheet. Lightly brush exposed flesh with olive oil. Roast 45 to 55 minutes, or until well browned. Cool to room temperature.

3. Meanwhile, cook the pasta in a large pot of boiling salted water until *al dente.* Turn cooked pasta into a large colander. Drain and set side.

4. Place tomatoes in a colander; set aside to drain excess juice. In a medium bowl, combine cheeses; set aside. Remove skin from eggplant. Cut flesh into large chunks; set aside.

5. In a medium saucepan, heat 3 tablespoons of the remaining oil. Stir in the flour and garlic. Cook over medium-high heat, stirring constantly, for 2 minutes. Gradually stir in the half-and-half. Add lemon zest and cayenne. Stirring often, bring mixture to a boil. Reduce heat to medium; cook 5 minutes, stirring often. Remove from heat. Add half the cheese; stir to combine.

6. Lightly oil a large gratin dish. Turn pasta and sauce into dish; toss until pasta is well coated. Sprinkle surface with tomatoes, eggplant, and chives; top with remaining cheese. Dish may be covered and refrigerated for up to 24 hours at this point. If made in advance, remove dish from refrigerator 1 hour before baking.

7. Preheat oven to 350°F. Bake 30 minutes, or until slightly bubbly around edges. Place on a rack 6 inches from broiling unit. Broil 3 to 5 minutes, or until lightly browned.

. . . .

> Cheese is milk's leap toward immortality.
> —CLIFTON FADIMAN

TOASTED ORZO PILAF

Makes 6 servings

Orzo, a rice-shape pasta, is a delicious substitute for rice.

2 cups orzo
3 tablespoons olive or vegetable oil
¼ cup minced peeled fresh gingerroot
¼ cup chopped shallots
1 medium clove garlic, minced
½ teaspoon freshly grated nutmeg
3½ cups homemade chicken stock or canned chicken broth
½ cup dry sherry or additional chicken broth
⅓ cup dark raisins (optional)
2 tablespoons butter
   salt

1. In a large dry skillet over medium-high heat, toast the orzo, stirring constantly, until lightly browned. Remove from heat; set aside.

2. In a large saucepan over medium heat, combine the oil, ginger, shallots, garlic, and nutmeg. Sauté, stirring constantly, 1 minute. Add orzo; sauté additional 3 minutes.

3. Add broth, sherry, and raisins, if desired; bring to a boil. Cover and cook over low heat 12 to 15 minutes, or until barely tender; add butter. Use a fork to fluff orzo and incorporate butter. Season to taste with salt.

SAFFRON-
BUTTERED
SPÄTZLE

*Makes 6 side dish or
first course servings*

This nontraditional spätzle (SHPEHT-sluh or SHPEHT-sehl) is fragrant with saffron and sauced with saffron butter. Spätzle is a German dish of small free-form noodles made from a dough that's firm enough to cut into slivers or soft enough to be forced through a spätzle-maker (available in cookware shops) or any other utensil with small holes (such as a flat grater, a slotted spoon, or a colander). The dough falls into boiling water and two minutes later —spätzle!

¼ cup very hot water
½ teaspoon saffron threads (about 2 0.2-gram vials)
 2 cups all-purpose flour
 3 large eggs, lightly beaten
½ cup milk
½ teaspoon salt
 6 tablespoons butter
    salt and freshly ground pepper

   1. In a small bowl, combine the hot water with ¼ teaspoon (1 vial) saffron threads. Set aside 5 minutes to steep.
   2. In a medium bowl, stir together the flour, eggs, milk, salt, and saffron water. Set batter aside for 15 minutes.
   3. Meanwhile, fill a large saucepan two-thirds full with water; bring to a boil.
   4. Reduce heat so water is barely boiling. Choose a utensil with ¼-inch holes, such as a slotted spoon, flat grater, or colander. Hold or set utensil on pan over water. Use a rubber spatula to press several tablespoons of the batter at a time through the utensil, so that small bits of the batter fall into the water. Cook about ¼ of the batter at a time. After spätzle float to the water's surface, cook about 2 minutes, or until noodles are cooked through. Use a slotted spoon to transfer cooked spätzle to a colander. Continue with remaining batter in batches.
   5. Rinse spätzle with cold running water; set aside to drain.

6. In a large skillet over medium-high heat, combine butter and remaining ¼ teaspoon (1 vial) saffron. Heat, stirring, until butter is melted. Cook 2 minutes more. Add drained spätzle. Either cook, stirring occasionally, until noodles are golden brown, about 8 minutes, or toss noodles with saffron-butter. Salt and pepper to taste. Serve hot.

✦✦✦✦✦✦✦✦✦✦✦✦ **THE WORLD'S MOST EXPENSIVE SPICE** ✦✦✦✦✦✦✦✦✦✦✦✦

Saffron—the yellow-orange stigmas from a small purple crocus—is the world's most expensive spice. That's because each flower provides only three stigmas (which must be painstakingly hand-picked and dried), and it takes fourteen thousand of these tiny threads for each ounce of saffron! This pricey, pungently aromatic spice comes either powdered or in threads (the whole stigmas). Powdered saffron loses its flavor more rapidly and can easily be adulterated with less expensive powders like turmeric. Buying cheaper saffron won't save money in the long run, since more will be needed for the same flavor impact. Since heat releases saffron's flavor essence, it's usually steeped in hot water before being added to foods.

ORANGE-POPPY SEED NOODLES

*Makes 4 main course or
6 to 8 first course or
side dish servings*

Toasted sesame seeds make a delicious substitute for the poppy seeds. If you do so, use half Oriental sesame oil and half butter for the sauce.

1 **pound dried linguine**
1 **large orange**
1 **teaspoon cider vinegar**
8 **tablespoons (1 stick) butter, cut into 6 pieces, at room temperature**
¼ **teaspoon freshly grated nutmeg**
2 **tablespoons poppy seeds**
  salt and freshly ground pepper
1 **tablespoon additional grated orange zest (optional)**

1. Cook the pasta in a large pot of boiling salted water until al dente.

2. Meanwhile, remove zest from orange with a swivel-bladed vegetable peeler. Chop fine; set aside. Squeeze juice from orange.

3. In a small saucepan over medium-high heat, cook the juice and vinegar until reduced to 2 tablespoons. Add butter and nutmeg; whisk until butter is melted.

4. Drain pasta. Toss with butter mixture and poppy seeds. Salt and pepper to taste. If desired, garnish with additional orange zest.

◆ TIP ◆

A bit of freshly grated orange, lemon, or lime zest will give a dish much more pizzazz than dried peel.

FENNELED FARFALLE WITH TOASTED PINE NUTS

*Makes 6 to 8 main course or
8 to 10 first course or
side dish servings*

Rotini and radiatori are two pastas that can be substituted for farfalle. Just choose a shape that has lots of nooks and crannies for the fennel seed.

The food processor will make quick work of grating the romano. You can also use it to chop the parsley, though using a knife and cutting board takes only a few additional seconds and will retain more of the herb's natural moisture.

1½ **pounds dried farfalle or other pasta**
 4 **tablespoons butter, softened**
 ½ **cup olive oil**
 2 **to 2½ tablespoons fennel seed, crushed**
 2 **teaspoons grated or minced fresh gingerroot**
 1 **large clove garlic, minced**
 ⅔ **cup grated romano**
 ½ **cup finely chopped parsley**
   salt and pepper
 ⅓ **cup toasted pine nuts (2 ounces)**

1. In a large pot of boiling salted water, cook the pasta until al dente. Drain; turn into a serving bowl. Add butter; toss to coat pasta.

2. Meanwhile, heat the olive oil in a large skillet over medium heat. Add the fennel seeds and ginger; cook 5 minutes. Add the garlic; cook additional 2 minutes. Pour over pasta; toss to coat. Add cheese and parsley; toss. Salt and pepper to taste. Sprinkle with pine nuts. Serve hot or at room temperature.

♦ ♦ ♦

♦ ♦ ♦

Gratifying Grains and Beans

....

With Americans eating less meat, there's been a renewed interest in grains and dried beans. Both are low in fat, high in protein, and rich with vitamins; both offer a wide variety of palate- pleasing tastes and tex- tures. Don't think of beans and grains only as side dishes. More and more, Americans are choosing these nu- tritious, protein-packed foods as the meal's main event. Join the complex-carbohydrate fan club—you'll be glad you did!

> The gentle art of gastronomy is a friendly one. It hurdles the language barrier, makes friends among civilized people, and warms the heart.
> —Samuel Chamberlain

....

GRAINS

Among the more popular grains today are wheat, corn, oats, rice (and wild rice), barley, buckwheat, and the high-protein quinoa.

What exactly are grains? They're the edible seed-bearing fruits of cereal grasses. At the heart of each kernel is the embryo (or germ), surrounded by the endosperm (the part most commonly consumed), a bran layer, and—in most grains—an inedible hull. Whole grains are more nutritious than pro- cessed grains because 25 percent of the protein and most of the fiber, B vitamins, and fat are in the germ and bran, which are removed during pro- cessing. The only downside for whole grains is that their nutritious germ and bran causes them to have a shorter shelf life and to take longer to cook.

◆◆◆◆◆ Barley ◆◆◆

A grain that dates back to the Stone Age, barley is marketed in several forms today. *Pearl barley*, easily found in most supermarkets, has had the husk and bran removed before the grain is steamed and polished. The brownish gray *whole hulled barley* has been husked but retains its bran, which gives it a higher nutritional content. It is, however, almost twice the price of pearl barley, too fibrous for all but the most ardent grain enthusiasts, and usually only available in health-food stores. When whole hulled barley is coarsely ground, it is called *Scotch barley*. Store barley airtight in a cool, dry place for up to one year.

✦✦✦✦✦ Bulgur ✦✦✦

Also called burghul, bulgur is steamed, dried, and crushed wheat kernels. It's often confused with cracked wheat, which is uncooked wheat that has been dried before being cracked. Bulgur comes in coarse, medium, and fine grinds. It has a tender, chewy texture. Store bulgur in a cool (below 60°F.) dark place—the refrigerator is perfect. Be sure it's wrapped airtight in a plastic bag, or store it in a screwtop glass jar.

✦✦✦✦✦ Corn ✦✦✦

When it's fresh, corn is treated as a vegetable, though it is, in truth, a grain. This section deals only with ground corn (see the Versatile Vegetables chapter for information on fresh corn). Cornmeal is either yellow, white, or blue, depending on the type of corn. Yellow cornmeal has slightly more vitamin A than the other two. The type found in most supermarkets is *steel-ground cornmeal* (ground by huge, high-speed steel rollers). This process removes almost all of the husk and germ. *Stone-ground cornmeal* (ground by stone wheels that move at a slower rate), is more nutritious because it retains some of the hull and germ. Stone-ground cornmeal will always be labeled as such. It is found in health-food stores and many supermarkets. Cornmeal comes in three textures—coarse, medium, and fine. Coarse cornmeal—also labeled polenta—can be found in many supermarkets and all Italian markets. Medium- and fine-ground cornmeal are readily available in supermarkets. Because of the fat in the germ, you should store stone-ground meal airtight, in the refrigerator, for no more than four months. Store steel-ground cornmeal in an airtight container in a cool, dry place.

✦✦✦✦✦ Kasha ✦✦

Hulled and roasted buckwheat groats are referred to in the United States as kasha. It's the roasting process that gives kasha its characteristic nutlike flavor. Though it's treated as a grain, buckwheat is technically a fruit of the genus *Fagopyrum*. Not only is this grain gluten free, but it's rich in protein and contains all eight amino acids—making kasha a nutritional powerhouse.

Though once only available in health-food stores or ethnic markets, today kasha can often be found in large supermarkets. It comes in several grinds—

fine, medium, coarse, and whole—the last two being easier to find. The grind should be clearly indicated on the package label. Store kasha airtight in a cool, dry place for up to a year.

✦✦✦✦ Quinoa ✦✦✦

Although relatively new to the United States, quinoa (KEEN-wah) was known to the ancient Incas as "the mother grain." This supergrain contains a rich source of vital nutrients and more protein than any other grain. The protein in quinoa is considered a *complete protein* because it contains all eight essential amino acids. Quinoa provides a rich and balanced source of vital nutrients. It is higher in unsaturated fats and lower in carbohydrates than most other grains. Tiny and bead-shaped, the ivory-colored quinoa has a delicate, light flavor. It cooks like rice, but takes half the time. When cooked, it expands to four times its original volume. It can be stored in the refrigerator for up to four months, but should be brought to room temperature before cooking. Quinoa can be found in many supermarkets, gourmet markets, and health-food stores. Store quinoa airtight in a cool, dry place for no more than a month (its higher fat content makes it more perishable than other grains).

✦✦✦✦ Rice ✦✦✦

This grain is a staple for almost half the world's population, and there are more than seven thousand varieties of rice grown around the globe. Rice is commercially classified by size—long-, medium- or short-grain. The length of *long-grain rice* is four to five times its width. There are both white and brown varieties of long-grain rice which, when cooked, produce light, dry grains that separate easily. One of the more exotic varieties in the long-grain category is the expensive aromatic *basmati*. See Aromatic Rices (page 137) for details about fragrant rice varieties.

Short-grain rice has fat, almost round grains that have a higher starch content than either of the other two rice types. There are three main types of short-grain rice: pearl rice, Italian Arborio, and the Oriental glutinous rice. Pearl short-grain rice, prized for its adhesive quality, is the rice that's used for sushi. Arborio, which has the ability to absorb a high proportion of liquid, is the basis of the wonderfully creamy rice dish known as risotto. Oriental glutinous rice, also called "sweet rice," is what the Japanese use for rice cakes and many desserts, the most well-known being *mochi*.

Medium-grain rice is shorter and moister than long-grain rice and generally not as starchy as the short-grain varieties. Though fairly fluffy right after being cooked, medium-grain rice begins to clump once it starts to cool.

Rice can be further divided into brown and white rice. *Brown rice* is the entire grain with only the inedible outer husk removed. The nutritious, high-fiber bran coating gives it a light tan color and nutlike flavor. Regular brown rice takes longer to cook than white long-grain rice—about 50 minutes. There is, however, a quick brown rice that cooks in about 15 minutes. Because of its high fat content, brown rice has a tendency to go rancid and should only be stored for up to six months. Store it in an airtight container in a cool, dark, dry place.

   White rice has had the husk, bran, and germ removed. Regular white rice is sometimes referred to as polished rice. Converted or parboiled white rice is the unhulled grain that has been soaked, pressure-steamed and dried before milling. Converted rice has a pale beige cast and takes slightly longer to cook than regular white rice. Instant white rice has been fully or partially cooked before being dehydrated and packaged. It takes only a few minutes to prepare but delivers lackluster results in both flavor and texture. Store white rice in an airtight container in a cool, dark, dry place.

♦♦♦♦♦ Wild Rice

Known for its luxuriously nutty flavor, wild rice isn't really rice at all. Rather, it's a long-grain marsh grass native to the northern Great Lakes area. There is also commercial wild rice production in California as well as several Midwest states. Because of its labor-intensive harvesting process, wild rice is quite expensive. Both pleasure and budget can be extended by combining it with brown rice or bulgur. Wild rice can be stored indefinitely if kept airtight in a cool, dark, dry place.

Cleaning wild rice: It's important to clean wild rice thoroughly before cooking it. The best method is to place the rice in a strainer and rinse well with cold running water.

DRIED BEANS

All members of the dried-bean family are rich in protein, calcium, phosphorous, and iron. Their high protein content, along with the fact that they're easily grown and stored, has made them a staple throughout many parts of the world where animal protein is scarce, expensive, or both. Dried beans are available to us prepackaged or in bulk. With the exception of lentils and split peas, dried beans must be soaked in water for several hours (or quick-soaked) to rehydrate them before cooking. Beans labeled quick-cooking have been presoaked and redried before being packaged. They take considerably less time to prepare, but their texture is not as firm to the bite as regular dried beans. Store dried beans in an airtight container for up to a year.

Quick-soak Method: Cover dried beans with hot water, bring them to a boil, and boil for 1 minute. Cover the beans and set aside for 1 hour. Drain and cook as usual.

. . . .

RISOTTO À LA GRECQUE

Makes 4 to 6 first course or side dish servings

French for "in the Greek style," *à la grecque* in the recipe title refers to the Greek olives, feta cheese, and lemon used to flavor this creamy concoction. Like all rice dishes, risotto is perfect for culinary improvisation.

2 tablespoons olive oil
2 large shallots, minced
1 large clove garlic, minced
1 cup Arborio rice
¼ teaspoon freshly grated nutmeg
1 tablespoon fresh lemon juice
3 cups homemade chicken stock or canned chicken broth, at room temperature if using microwave, simmering if using stovetop
2 teaspoons finely grated lemon zest
3 tablespoons finely chopped, pitted kalamata olives
2 tablespoons finely chopped sundried tomatoes, commercial or homemade (page 289)
¼ cup chopped fresh parsley
1 cup crumbled feta (4 ounces)
salt and freshly ground pepper
¼ cup whole kalamata olives (optional)

1. *Microwave Method* (HIGH—100% power—is used and dish is uncovered throughout all steps): Heat the oil in a shallow, 2½- to 3-quart, microwavesafe casserole for 2 minutes. Add the shallots, stirring to coat with oil; cook for 2 minutes. Stir in the garlic, rice, and nutmeg; cook for 1 minute, or until rice is opaque.

2. Stir in lemon juice and 2 cups of the chicken stock. Cook for 12 minutes, stirring halfway through.

3. Add the lemon zest, chopped olives, tomatoes, and remaining stock. Cook for 6 minutes. Test for doneness;

the rice should be tender but still firm to the bite. Remove from oven. Stir, then let stand, uncovered, for 5 minutes.

4. Add parsley and feta; toss to combine. Salt and pepper to taste. Serve immediately, garnished with whole kalamata olives, if desired.

5. *Stovetop Method:* In a large heavy saucepan, heat the oil over medium heat. Add the shallots; cook until golden, about 5 minutes. Stir in the garlic, rice, and nutmeg; cook for 2 minutes, or until rice is opaque.

6. Reduce heat to medium-low. Slowly add lemon juice and 1 cup of simmering broth. Cook, stirring constantly, until liquid is absorbed, about 10 minutes.

7. Add remaining simmering broth, ½ cup at a time, stirring constantly until liquid is absorbed after each addition. Add lemon zest, olives, and tomatoes with the last ½ cup of broth. Altogether, the cooking time should be 25 to 30 minutes. Test for doneness; the rice should be tender but still firm to the bite.

8. Add parsley and feta; toss to combine. Salt and pepper to taste. Serve immediately, garnished with whole kalamata olives, if desired.

ABOUT RISOTTO

Risotto is a classic northern Italian dish made with short-grain, high-starch rice. Arborio rice is what we commonly use in the United States, and it can now be found in most supermarkets and all Italian markets. The rice's higher starch content gives risotto its creamy texture. Adding hot liquid a little at a time—and constantly stirring until the rice absorbs it—are the other elements of a successful risotto. All of which means that the classic method of preparing risotto is very labor intensive indeed.

The magic of microwaving, however, changed all that. Even though it takes about the same amount of time to cook risotto in the microwave, it doesn't require constant stirring. And that means that the cook can be preparing the rest of the meal while the risotto bubbles away in the microwave oven. Microwave risotto is slightly less creamy than stovetop risotto, but still delicious. This simple cooking method has moved risottos from a special-occasion treat to a whenever-you-feel-like-it dish.

Other types of rice—such as medium- and long-grain—can be used to make risotto, but the texture of the final dish will be entirely different.

THAI RISOTTO

Makes 4 first course or side dish servings

Thai ingredients transport risotto into exotic regions miles away from its Italian homeland. This is a fragrant, spicy version of risotto that will warm your palate with pure pleasure. Coconut Milk (page 299) lends subtle flavor and silky texture to this dish, and the basil and mint added shortly before serving give it a fresh taste.

1½ teaspoons hot pepper oil
1½ teaspoons Oriental sesame oil
  1 tablespoon minced fresh gingerroot
  2 medium cloves garlic, minced
  1 cup Arborio rice
1½ cups unsweetened coconut milk, canned or homemade at room temperature if using microwave, simmering if using stovetop
  5 tablespoons finely chopped scallions
  1 tablespoon fresh lime juice
  ¼ teaspoon crushed red pepper (optional)
1½ cups homemade chicken stock or canned chicken broth, at room temperature if using microwave, simmering if using stovetop
  2 tablespoons finely chopped fresh basil
  2 tablespoons finely chopped fresh mint
  3 tablespoons finely chopped roasted peanuts
    salt and freshly ground pepper
  5 or 6 sprigs basil or mint for garnish (optional)

Tell me what you eat, and I will tell you what you are.
—ANTHELME BRILLAT-SAVARIN

  1. *Microwave Method* (HIGH—100% power—is used and dish is uncovered throughout all steps): Heat the oils in a shallow, 2½- to 3-quart, microwavesafe casserole for 1 minute. Add the ginger, garlic, and rice, stirring to coat with oil. Cook for 1 minute, or until rice is opaque.

  2. Stir the coconut milk well, then stir in with 3 tablespoons of the scallions, the lime juice, and crushed red pepper, if using. Cook for 12 minutes, stirring halfway through.

  3. Add the chicken stock. Cook for 6 minutes. Test for doneness; the rice should be tender but still firm to the bite. Remove from the microwave oven and continue in Step 7.

  4. *Stovetop Method:* In a large heavy saucepan, heat the oils over medium heat. Add the ginger, garlic, and rice. Cook for 2 minutes, or until rice is opaque.

5. Reduce heat to medium-low. Slowly add 1 cup of simmering coconut milk, 3 tablespoons of the scallions, the lime juice, and crushed red pepper, if using. Cook, stirring constantly, until liquid is absorbed, about 10 minutes.

6. Add remaining ½ cup simmering coconut milk, stirring constantly until liquid is absorbed. Add 1½ cups simmering chicken broth, ½ cup at a time, stirring constantly until liquid is absorbed after each addition. Altogether, the cooking time should be about 30 minutes. Test for doneness; the rice should be tender but still firm to the bite.

7. Stir in the basil, mint, 2 tablespoons of the peanuts, and remaining scallions. Salt and pepper to taste. Sprinkle top of risotto with remaining peanuts. Serve immediately, garnished with sprigs of basil or mint, if desired.

. . . .

CINNAMON RICE

Makes 4 to 6 side dish servings

This fragrant rice goes with fish, meat, or chicken, and it lends itself to both spicy-hot and creamy-mild accompaniments. It's a natural with the Spiced Tomato–Orange Scallops (page 199), and the Crispy Duck with Onion–Orange Marmalade (page 231). For a vegetarian dish, toss the rice with a little sesame oil and lightly sautéed, finely chopped vegetables such as onions, eggplant, green bell peppers, and zucchini. Make a double batch of vegetarian cinnamon rice and serve it chilled, tossed with your favorite salad dressing, the next day.

3 cups homemade chicken stock or canned chicken broth
1 teaspoon ground cinnamon
¼ teaspoon ground ginger
1½ cups medium- or long-grain brown rice or long-grain white rice
salt and freshly ground pepper

♦ TIP ♦

Brown rice takes about 50 minutes to cook, compared to 15 to 20 minutes for long-grain white rice. If time is a concern, use quick brown rice; it takes only 15 to 20 minutes. Or soak regular brown rice in the cooking liquid overnight and reduce the cooking time to about 20 minutes.

1. In a medium saucepan, combine the chicken stock, ginger, and nutmeg; bring to a rolling boil.

2. Stir in the rice and return to a boil. Reduce heat; cover and simmer until tender, 15 to 20 minutes for quick brown rice, about 50 minutes for regular brown rice, 15 to 20 minutes for long-grain white rice. If the brown rice is not tender enough after the liquid has been absorbed, add an additional ¼ to ½ cup stock, cover and continue to cook an additional 10 minutes.

3. Remove rice from heat. Salt and pepper to taste, and fluff with a fork. Cover with a cloth to absorb moisture; let stand 10 minutes, or longer in a warm low oven.

AROMATIC RICES

Aromatic rices have a perfumy, nutlike flavor and aroma. Probably the best-known of these fragrant rices is the long-grain basmati (bahs-MAH-tee). Literally "queen of fragrance," basmati has been grown in the foothills of the Himalayas for thousands of years. The grain is aged to decrease its moisture content. Basmati is available in Indian markets, some health-food stores, and the gourmet section of many supermarkets.

Another aromatic rice gaining popularity in the United States is jasmine (jasmin) rice from Thailand. It's extremely close to the flavor and fragrance of basmati, yet a fraction of the cost. A domestic version was recently developed (using Thai grains) at the International Rice Research Institute in the Philippines. It is now being grown in Texas and will soon be readily available throughout the United States. Even now, you can find it at some large supermarkets, and it's almost always available in Asian markets.

In addition to basmati and jasmine are American-bred aromatics, including California's Wehani and Calmati, Louisiana's wild pecan, and Texas's Texmati. Though quite good in their own right, none of these varieties come close to the fragrance and flavor of basmati and jasmine. Domestic aromatics are available in most supermarkets.

GINGERROOT RICE

Makes 4 to 6 servings

This dish comes from Kitti Suthipipat, a native Thai and one of the chefs at one of my favorite Marin County restaurants, Comforts. It's made with jasmine rice, an aromatic long-grain white rice from Kitti's homeland, Thailand. Kitti bakes the rice, giving it a mellow, nutty flavor. I've also given the more traditional stovetop method for those who prefer that. Cooking rice in the microwave has no flavor or time advantage.

Gingerroot Rice is very special in cold rice salads, stir-fried with vegetables and meat or shellfish, particularly shrimp, and in rice pudding. Try the Mango–Macadamia Rice variation, which adds excitement to almost any pork and poultry dish.

1 **piece peeled fresh gingerroot, 1 x 3 inches**
2¾ **cups homemade chicken stock or canned chicken broth**
2 **tablespoons light soy sauce**
2 **tablespoons vegetable oil**
1½ **cups jasmine rice or long-grain white rice**
2 **large cloves garlic, minced**
    salt

1. Preheat oven to 400°F.

2. Cut the gingerroot in half lengthwise. Place on a cutting board, cut side down. Lay the flat side of a chef's knife on top of each piece and give the knife a sharp, powerful rap with your fist or heel of your hand.

3. Put the smashed gingerroot in a medium saucepan; add the chicken stock and soy sauce. Bring to a boil.

4. Meanwhile, in a heavy ovenproof skillet or sauté pan with a lid or in a shallow flameproof casserole with lid, heat the oil over medium-high heat. Add the rice. Sauté, stirring often, just until rice begins to brown, about 5 minutes. Stir in the garlic; cook for 1 more minute. Remove from heat.

5. Pour the boiling chicken stock, with the ginger, into the rice, stirring to combine. Immediately cover tightly. Bake until rice is tender and all liquid is absorbed, about 20 minutes. Remove chunks of gingerroot. Salt to taste; stir rice to fluff. Serve hot.

Stovetop Method: Follow Steps 2–5, sautéing rice in any large skillet. Stir rice into boiling stock. Reduce heat; cover tightly and simmer for 15 to 20 minutes, or until rice is tender and liquid is absorbed. Remove gingerroot. Salt to taste.

♦ **VARIATION: Mango–Macadamia Rice:** Substitute 2 tablespoons fresh lime juice plus 2 teaspoons sugar for the soy sauce; add ⅛ teaspoon cayenne to the chicken stock. After rice is cooked, stir in 1 large mango, peeled, seeded, and chopped, 2 tablespoons finely chopped chives, and ½ cup finely chopped toasted macadamias.

♦♦♦♦♦♦♦♦♦♦♦♦♦♦♦♦♦ FRESH GINGER ♦♦♦♦♦♦♦♦♦♦♦♦♦♦♦♦♦♦♦

Fresh gingerroot has a peppery, slightly sweet flavor and a pungent, spicy aroma. Its flavor is fresher and entirely different from ground ginger, which is more commonly used in baked goods. This knobby root can be found in most supermarkets today. Look for firm roots with smooth skin; wrinkled skin indicates the root is past its prime. The root should smell fresh.

When peeling ginger, use a sharp knife to carefully remove the thin skin, leaving as much as possible of the flesh just under its surface. In the springtime, you can often find young or spring ginger in Oriental markets. The skin of this tender root doesn't require peeling.

Store fresh unpeeled ginger, tightly wrapped, in the refrigerator for up to a week or in the freezer for up to two months. Or place peeled ginger in a screwtop jar, cover with dry sherry or Madeira, and refrigerate for up to a month. The wine will impart some of its flavor to the ginger, but that's a minor disadvantage when weighed against having peeled ginger ready and waiting. The ginger-flavored liquid can be used for cooking or in salad dressings.

CHUTNEY WILD RICE WITH APPLES AND NUTS

Makes 6 servings

Elegant yet earthy, this baked rice dish is really quite easy —just pop it in the oven and walk away. Almost any type of chutney can be used. Cranapple–Apricot Chutney (page 295) is a natural for this dish, but I've also used a commercially prepared sundried tomato chutney and it was wonderful. Finely chop any large pieces of fruit before measuring the chutney.

Add chicken broth, cream, and a few vegetables to leftovers for a quick wild-rice soup.

> 1 **cup wild rice (about 6 ounces)**
> 3 **cups homemade chicken stock or canned chicken broth**
> ⅔ **cup chopped walnuts or pecans**
> 2 **tablespoons olive oil**
> ½ **cup chopped onion**
> ¼ **teaspoon ground cinnamon**
> ¼ **teaspoon ground ginger**
> ¼ **to ⅓ cup chutney, large pieces of fruit finely chopped**
> ⅔ **cup heavy whipping cream, half-and-half, or additional chicken broth**
> 2½ **cups coarsely chopped, tart apples, peeled or unpeeled (about 2 large apples)**
> **salt and freshly ground pepper**

1. Place wild rice in a strainer and rinse well with cold running water. Turn wild rice out onto several layers of paper towel; blot dry with additional paper towels.

2. Preheat oven to 350°F.

3. Bring the chicken stock to a boil. While stock is heating, toast the nuts in a large, ungreased sauté pan or skillet with an oven-proof handle over medium-high heat until golden-brown. Turn out onto a plate; set aside to cool.

4. In same pan, heat the oil over medium-high heat. Add the rice and onion; cook until the onion begins to brown. Stir in the cinnamon and ginger; cook 3 minutes. Stir in the chutney and chicken stock. Cover and bake for 1½ hours.

5. In a small saucepan, heat the cream just to the boil. Or pour the cream into a 1-cup glass measure; microwave on HIGH just until it comes to a boil, about 90 seconds.

6. Remove rice from oven; stir in hot cream. Cover and return to oven for 25 minutes.

7. Remove rice from oven. Taste for doneness; rice should be al dente, even on the chewy side. If rice isn't quite done, add ¼ cup hot water or chicken broth and return, covered, to oven for 10 minutes. If rice is done, stir in apples. Cover and continue to bake 5 to 10 minutes, or until apples are crisp-tender.

8. Salt and pepper to taste. Add nuts; toss to combine. Serve immediately.

. . . .

PUFFED WILD RICE

Makes about 1 cup

This crunchy and nutty-tasting treat can be used as a garnish for soups (see Creamy Wild Rice Soup, page 74), salads, and vegetables. It's also a component in the Wild Rice Breadsticks (page 247), and it is absolutely addictive —though rather extravagant—as a snack.

⅔ **cup wild rice (about 4 ounces)**
 1 **tablespoon olive oil**
    salt and freshly ground pepper

1. Place wild rice in a strainer and rinse well with cold running water. Turn wild rice out onto several layers of paper towel; blot with additional paper towels. It should be as dry as possible before sautéing.

2. In a large skillet, heat oil for 1 minute. Add wild rice and, stirring often, sauté over medium heat until most of the grains have cracked open and puffed slightly. Turn out onto paper towels; salt and pepper to taste. Serve warm or at room temperature.

. . . .

SICILIAN KASHA

Makes 6 to 8 servings

The flavors of southern Italy combine here in this full-bodied dish. The classic method for preventing kasha from turning mushy is to coat it with egg. Then it's sautéed until the egg dries, giving the kernels a protective seal that will keep them separate during cooking. See page 130 for general information on kasha.

  1 medium eggplant, peeled and cut into ½-inch cubes (about ¾ pound)
     salt
  1 large egg
1½ cups whole ground kasha
1½ pounds Italian sausage, half sweet and half hot
     about 4 tablespoons olive oil
  1 large onion, chopped
  ½ pound mushrooms, chopped (2½ to 3 cups)
  1 large green bell pepper, stemmed, seeded, and chopped
  1 large red bell pepper, stemmed, seeded, and chopped
  2 large cloves garlic, minced
  1 tablespoon minced fresh oregano or 1 teaspoon dried oregano
2½ cups simmering homemade chicken stock or canned chicken broth
  2 cups grated fontina (8 ounces)

1. Sprinkle eggplant with salt. Place it in a colander; set aside for 1 hour to drain.

2. Meanwhile, lightly beat the egg in a medium bowl. Add the kasha; stir to coat thoroughly. Turn into a large dry skillet over medium heat. Cook, stirring constantly, until kasha is dry and grains are separated, about 5 minutes. Turn into a large bowl; set aside.

3. Heat the same skillet over medium-high heat. Squeeze the sausage out of its casings into the skillet. Cook until nicely browned, coarsely crumbling as it cooks. Use a slotted spoon to transfer sausage to the bowl containing the kasha.

4. Blot eggplant with paper towels. If necessary, add up to 2 tablespoons olive oil to sausage drippings in skillet. Over medium-high heat, sauté eggplant cubes until nicely browned, about 8 minutes. Use a slotted spoon to transfer eggplant to a plate; set aside.

5. Add 2 tablespoons olive oil to skillet. Heat over medium-high heat. Sauté onion for 5 minutes. Add mushrooms, green and red peppers, and garlic; sauté an additional 3 minutes.

6. Add the oregano and reserved kasha and sausage; stir to combine. Slowly stir in simmering broth, being careful of spattering liquid. Stirring often, bring mixture to a boil.

7. Reduce heat to low. Cover and simmer for 18 to 20 minutes, or until kasha is tender and liquid is absorbed. If not, cover and simmer an additional 3 to 5 minutes.

8. Add reserved eggplant and 1 cup of the fontina; toss to combine. Sprinkle remaining cheese over top of dish. Serve hot.

. . . .

RED-LETTER QUINOA

Makes 6 servings

♦ TIP ♦

Add chicken or beef broth to leftover rice, risotto, or beans, stir in some sautéed vegetables, and you have soup in minutes.

The tiny quinoa grain is lighter and more delicately flavored than rice and easily takes on flavorings, such as the tomato in this dish. For more information on quinoa, see page 131.

1½ **cups quinoa**
  2 **tablespoons olive or vegetable oil**
 ½ **cup finely chopped shallots**
 ½ **pound mushrooms, finely chopped (2½ to 3 cups)**
  1 **medium clove garlic, minced**
  2 **cups homemade chicken stock or canned chicken broth**
 ¾ **cup tomato juice**
  2 **tablespoons balsamic or red wine vinegar**
    salt and freshly ground pepper
  2 **medium tomatoes, seeded and finely chopped**

1. Place quinoa in a fine strainer; rinse under cold, running water. Drain thoroughly; blot dry on paper towels. Set aside.

2. In a large saucepan or a large 3-inch-deep skillet, heat oil over medium-high heat. Add the quinoa; cook, stirring often, 2 minutes. Stir in the shallots, mushrooms, and garlic; cook 3 minutes.

3. Add the stock, tomato juice, and vinegar; bring to a boil. Reduce heat; cover and simmer until quinoa is tender, 12 to 15 minutes. Salt and pepper to taste. Add tomatoes; stir to combine. Cover and set aside 1 minute. Heat from quinoa will cook the tomatoes. Serve hot.

. . . .

BLACK-BEAN POLENTA CAKES

Makes 8 to 12 side dish or 4 luncheon servings

Don't think of these little polenta cakes only as a side dish for dinner—they're sensational served with eggs for breakfast. Or arrange three polenta cakes on a plate with a tossed green salad for a satisfying lunch.

    about 2 tablespoons vegetable oil
3 cups homemade chicken stock or canned chicken broth, at room temperature
1 medium clove garlic, minced
⅛ teaspoon cayenne
2 teaspoons balsamic vinegar (optional)
1½ cups polenta or coarse yellow cornmeal
⅓ cup finely chopped smoked ham
1 cup cooked black turtle beans (about ⅓ cup uncooked)
¼ cup chopped chives or scallions, green parts only
2 tablespoons finely chopped cilantro
1 cup grated cheddar (about 4 ounces)
    salt
    about 1½ tablespoons olive oil
1½ cups Black Bean Relish (page 287; optional)

1. Generously oil 12 standard muffin cups; set aside.

2. In a large saucepan over high heat, bring the stock, garlic, cayenne, and vinegar, if using, to a full rolling boil. Whisking rapidly, gradually add polenta. When polenta is incorporated, reduce heat to low; stir in ham. Cook, stirring occasionally, about 5 minutes, or until mixture is very thick and pulls away from side of pan. This is extremely important because if the polenta doesn't cook long enough, it won't set firmly enough for broiling.

Microwave Method: In a 2-quart casserole, combine the

stock, garlic, cayenne, vinegar, if using, and polenta. Microwave on HIGH for 3 minutes. Stir mixture, making sure no cornmeal is clinging to the bottom or sides of dish. Cover and continue to cook on HIGH another 3 minutes. Stir in ham; cook 3 more minutes, or until polenta is very thick and pulls away from side of dish.

3. Remove polenta from stovetop or microwave oven; stir in black beans, scallions, cilantro, and cheddar. Salt to taste.

4. Immediately spoon mixture into prepared muffin cups. Don't smooth tops; they should look a little uneven. If muffin cups are only 1½ inches deep, the polenta will mound slightly above edge of cups. Generously brush top of polenta with olive oil. Refrigerate, uncovered, 3 hours or until very firm. Polenta may then be covered and refrigerated overnight.

5. Preheat broiler. Position rack 6 inches from broiling unit. Lightly oil a large baking sheet; set aside.

6. Use a dinner knife to loosen polenta cakes from pan. Place cakes, bottom side up, 2 inches apart, on prepared baking sheet. Broil 6 minutes, or until pale golden-brown. Don't broil too long, or polenta will soften too much to flip easily. Remove from oven; use a spatula to gently turn polenta cakes right side up. Broil about 6 minutes, or until golden brown. Serve hot, accompanied by Black Bean Relish, if desired.

. . . .

CREAMED CORN POLENTA

Makes 4 to 6 servings

2½ cups homemade chicken stock or canned chicken broth

1½ cups heavy whipping cream

1 small clove garlic, minced

2 teaspoons sugar

⅛ teaspoon cayenne

1 cup polenta or coarse yellow cornmeal

¼ cup finely chopped sundried tomatoes, commercial or homemade (page 289)

2 cups fresh or thawed frozen corn kernels (about 2 large ears of corn)

salt and freshly ground pepper

1 cup grated Jarlsberg (about 4 ounces), optional

1. In a large saucepan over high heat, bring the stock, cream, garlic, sugar, and cayenne to a full rolling boil. Whisking rapidly, gradually add the polenta, making sure no lumps form. Reduce heat to medium; cook, whisking often, for 5 minutes. Add the tomatoes; cook an additional 2 minutes, or until soft and thick. Remove from heat; stir in the corn. Salt and pepper to taste. Add the jarlsberg; blend quickly. It's not necessary for cheese to melt completely.

Microwave Method: In a 2-quart glass measuring cup or casserole, combine the stock, cream, garlic, sugar, cayenne, and polenta. Microwave, uncovered, on HIGH for 4 minutes; whisk to combine. Cook on HIGH for 5 more minutes; whisk briskly after 3 minutes. Stir polenta well, making sure there are no lumps. Add tomatoes; cook on HIGH for 1 minute, or until thick. Stir in the corn; salt and pepper to taste. Add the Jarlsberg, if desired; blend quickly. It's not necessary for cheese to melt completely.

. . . .

FRUITED BARLEY– SAUSAGE BAKE

Makes 4 to 6 servings

This is one of the most satisfying dishes I know, just perfect for winter evenings. Complete the meal with a salad of tossed greens, mushrooms, and walnuts, and a loaf of warm bread.

¾ pound bulk sausage
2 tablespoons vegetable oil (optional)
1 medium onion, chopped
1 medium red or green bell pepper, seeded, and chopped, or half of *each*
2 medium cloves garlic, minced
½ teaspoon freshly grated nutmeg
1 cup pearl barley
1 cup chopped mixed, dried fruit, such as apples, pears, peaches, apricots, or prunes
4½ cups homemade chicken stock or canned chicken broth
1 tablespoon balsamic or red wine vinegar
  salt and freshly ground pepper
1 cup grated fontina (4 ounces)

♦ TIP ♦

To make easy work of cutting dried fruit into bite-size pieces, snip it with scissors, dipping them in hot water as necessary to prevent sticking.

1. In a large ovenproof sauté pan or skillet, or a large saucepan, sauté the sausage over medium-high heat until well browned. Use a wooden spoon to crumble sausage into bite-size chunks as it cooks. Use a slotted spoon to remove sausage to a double thickness of paper towels to drain.

2. Pour off all but 2 tablespoons of the sausage grease. Or pour off all grease and add 2 tablespoons of oil to pan. Add the onion, pepper, garlic, and nutmeg. Sauté over medium-high heat, stirring often, until onion begins to soften, about 5 minutes.

3. Add the barley, fruit, stock, and vinegar; bring to a boil. Reduce heat, cover pan, and simmer for 25 minutes.

4. Preheat oven to 350°F.

5. If barley has been cooked in an ovenproof sauté pan, add sausage directly to pan; stir to combine. If not, turn barley mixture and accompanying liquid into a shallow, 3-quart covered casserole, then add the sausage. Cover and bake for 30 minutes, or until liquid is completely absorbed.

6. Preheat broiler. Stir barley; salt and pepper to taste. Sprinkle top with fontina. Broil 6 inches from heat until cheese is melted and bubbly. Serve hot.

♦ TIP ♦

Leathery dried fruit can be rehydrated by covering it with boiling water and setting aside for fifteen minutes. Drain off water, then blot fruit well on paper towel before chopping.

. . . .

BLACK AND WHITE CHILI

Makes 8 to 10 servings

Black beans and pearl barley are the black and white of this delicious mélange. I like to make the chili the day before so the flavors have plenty of time to mingle and bring out the best in each other.

This recipe makes a huge batch of chili. I've been known to serve leftovers a couple of days in a row, or I

♦ TIP ♦

If using dried herbs instead of fresh, substitute 1 teaspoon dried herbs for every tablespoon of fresh herbs. Intensify the flavor of dried herbs by crushing them between your fingers.

freeze the chili in individual servings and reheat it in the microwave. The nice thing about chili—particularly this one—is that it just keeps getting better.

If you prefer, substitute an equal amount of crumbled, well-browned sausage for the ham. Or omit the meat entirely for a vegetarian chili.

Pass bowls of Avocado Salsa (page 286), sour cream, chopped cilantro, grated cheddar or Monterey Jack cheese, and lime wedges as accompaniments to this chili. The only other partner it needs is some wonderful bread or soft tortillas and, if you're so inclined, an ice-cold brew.

      2 cups dried black turtle beans
      5 tablespoons vegetable oil
   1½ cups pearl barley (about 11 ounces)
      2 large onions, finely chopped
      1 large green bell pepper, cored, seeded and finely chopped
      1 pound smoked ham, finely chopped (about 2¾ cups)
      4 large cloves garlic, minced
      2 tablespoons chili powder
      1 tablespoon unsweetened cocoa powder
      2 teaspoons dried oregano
      2 teaspoons dried basil
      2 teaspoons ground cumin
      1 teaspoon crushed red pepper
      6 to 8 cups homemade beef stock or canned beef broth
      3 cups canned ready-cut tomatoes with juice (2 14½-ounce cans)
      1 cup canned diced green chilies (2 4-ounce cans) salt and cayenne

1. In a large pot, place beans in hot water to cover. Bring to a boil; boil 1 minute. Remove from heat; cover and let stand 1 hour.

2. Drain beans (rinsing optional); cover with 6 cups fresh cold water. Bring to a boil. Reduce heat and simmer, covered, until *barely* tender, 30 to 40 minutes.

3. About 15 minutes before beans are ready, heat 2 tablespoons of the oil in a large skillet over medium-high

♦ TIP ♦

Epazote is a pungent herb that's long been popular in Mexico as a flavoring for beans. One of its main attributes is that it's a carminative, which means it reduces stomach gas. Epazote has a strong flavor. It has flat, pointed leaves and is available dried, and sometimes fresh, in Latin-American markets and some gourmet specialty stores.

heat. Add the barley. Cook, stirring often, until it begins to brown, about 5 minutes. Transfer barley to a medium bowl; set aside.

4. Add remaining oil to skillet over high heat. Cook onions, green pepper, and ham just until onions begin to soften, about 4 minutes. Add garlic, chili powder, cocoa, oregano, basil, cumin, and crushed red pepper; sauté for 2 minutes. Add ½ cup of the beef stock; stir to loosen all the flavor bits from bottom and sides of pan. Remove from heat.

5. Drain beans, reserving the cooking water. Return beans and 3 cups of the reserved cooking water to pot (if you don't have 3 cups, add beef broth or water to equal that amount). Add barley, sautéed vegetable mixture, tomatoes and their juice, chilies, and remaining beef stock. Bring to a boil. Reduce heat and simmer, covered, for about 45 minutes, or until barley is tender. Season to taste with salt and cayenne. The chili can be covered and refrigerated overnight at this point, if desired.

6. Reheat over medium heat, stirring often. If chili has thickened too much for your liking, add beef broth. Serve hot.

. . . .

PERSIAN STIR-FRY

Makes 6 servings

Lentils play a starring role in this full-flavored dish, fragrant with spices and dotted with carrots, raisins, and pistachios. Lentils, tiny, lens-shaped pulses (dried seeds), range in color from brown to green to orange (called red). Lentils vary widely in cooking time, taking anywhere from 20 to 50 minutes, and overcooked lentils can easily turn to mush. Check them often after 20 minutes cooking time to prevent overcooking.

Pistachios are available shelled and unshelled, raw or roasted, and salted or not. I always buy packages of shelled, chopped, and roasted pistachios. If you buy them whole, make sure they're the natural pistachios and not those that are dyed red. Cashews or almonds can be substituted for the pistachios.

Cook the lentils and rice up to three days ahead for a quick, last-minute stir-fry. The carrots and onions can be chopped a day ahead.

½ cup raisins
¼ cup fresh orange juice
1 cup red lentils
1 cup regular or quick brown rice
2 to 2½ cups homemade chicken stock or canned chicken broth
¼ to ⅓ cup olive oil
1 cup chopped onion
1 cup finely chopped carrots
2 tablespoons minced fresh gingerroot
2 medium cloves garlic, minced
¾ teaspoon ground allspice
½ teaspoon ground cinnamon
½ teaspoon ground coriander
¼ teaspoon ground cumin
¼ teaspoon cayenne
1½ tablespoons grated orange zest (½ medium orange)
    salt and additional cayenne
⅓ to ½ cup chopped toasted pistachios

1. In a 1-cup glass measuring cup, combine the raisins and orange juice. Cover with plastic wrap; microwave on

HIGH for 1 minute. Or combine the raisins and juice in a small saucepan; bring to a boil. Cover and remove from heat. Set raisins aside to plump for at least 30 minutes. Or cool to room temperature and refrigerate, covered, for up to 3 days.

2. Sort through lentils to remove any pebbles. Rinse lentils thoroughly. In a medium saucepan with a cover, combine lentils and 3 cups water. Bring to a boil over high heat. Reduce to low heat; cover and simmer for about 20 minutes, or until lentils are tender but still hold their shape.

3. In a medium saucepan, combine the rice and 2 cups of the chicken stock; bring to a rolling boil. Reduce heat; cover and simmer until tender, 15 to 20 minutes for quick brown rice, 50 minutes for regular brown rice. If the rice is not tender enough, add an additional ¼ to ½ cup stock; cover and continue to cook an additional 10 minutes. Remove from heat. Let stand, covered, for 10 minutes. Turn rice into colander; rinse well with cool water. Set aside to drain.

4. In a wok or very large skillet, heat oil over medium-high heat. Add the onion, carrots, and gingerroot; sauté 2 minutes. Add the garlic, allspice, cinnamon, coriander, cumin, cayenne, orange zest, lentils, rice, and raisins with their soaking liquid. Sauté, stirring constantly, until rice just begins to brown, about 10 minutes. Season to taste with salt and additional cayenne. Sprinkle with pistachios; serve hot.

. . . .

SPICY CHICKPEA SAUTÉ

Makes 4 to 6 servings

East Indian in flavor, this spicy sauté takes only minutes to prepare once everything is set to go. The amount of crushed red pepper you use depends on your palate. If you're unsure, remember: You can always add more at the table, but there's no way to take the heat out once it's in. If you're not a cilantro fan, substitute chopped basil or mint. Gingerroot Rice (page 138), Aztec Salad (page 94), and ice-cold beer will make this meal complete.

> 1 large eggplant, peeled and cut into ½-inch cubes
>   (about 1½ pounds)
>   salt
> 3 tablespoons olive or vegetable oil
> 1½ teaspoons cumin seed
> 2 teaspoons ground coriander
> 1 teaspoon ground turmeric
> ¼ teaspoon ground cloves
> ¼ teaspoon ground cinnamon
> 3½ cups canned chickpeas, drained, rinsed, and blotted dry
>   (2 15-ounce cans)
> 2 medium cloves garlic, minced
> ¼ to ½ teaspoon crushed red pepper
> 1 pound fresh spinach, trimmed, washed, dried, and
>   coarsely chopped, or 1 packed cup (10-ounce package)
>   frozen chopped spinach, thawed and squeezed as dry as
>   possible
> 1 pound tomatoes, peeled, seeded, and coarsely chopped,
>   or 1½ cups canned ready-cut tomatoes, well drained
>   (14½-ounce can)
> 2 tablespoons finely chopped cilantro
> 2 tablespoons toasted sesame seeds
>   freshly ground pepper

1. Sprinkle the eggplant with salt. Place it in a colander; set aside for 1 hour to drain. Blot eggplant with paper towels, wiping off excess salt; set aside.

2. In a large skillet or wok, combine 2 tablespoons of the oil, cumin, coriander, turmeric, cloves, cinnamon, and eggplant. Saute over medium-high heat, stirring constantly, for 5 minutes, or until eggplant begins to brown.

3. Stir in the chickpeas, garlic, and crushed red pepper. Cook over medium-high heat for 3 minutes. Add the oil and the spinach; cook just until spinach begins to wilt. If using frozen spinach, cook 2 minutes.

4. Stir in the tomatoes. Cook just until warmed

through, 1 to 2 minutes. Add cilantro and sesame seeds; toss to combine. Salt and pepper to taste. Serve immediately.

. . . .

LENTIL-BULGUR PILAF

Makes 4 main dish or 6 side dish servings

This hearty pilaf can be served either as a side dish or main dish.

1   **cup brown lentils**
2   **tablespoons vegetable oil**
¾   **cup finely chopped scallions, both white and green parts**
2   **medium cloves garlic, minced**
1   **teaspoon fennel seed, crushed**
¼   **to ½ teaspoon cayenne**
⅛   **teaspoon ground cloves**
¼   **pound smoked ham, finely chopped**
1   **cup medium-grind bulgur**
2   **cups homemade beef stock or canned beef broth**
2   **medium tomatoes, peeled, seeded, and finely chopped**
    salt and freshly ground pepper
3   **tablespoons finely chopped fresh basil**

1. Sort through the lentils to remove any pebbles. Rinse lentils thoroughly. In a medium saucepan with a cover, combine lentils and 3 cups water. Bring to a boil over high heat. Reduce to a simmer; cover and cook 20 to 30 minutes, or until lentils are tender but still hold their shape. Drain and set aside.

2. Meanwhile, in a large saucepan, heat the oil over medium-high heat. Add the scallions, garlic, fennel, cayenne, cloves, ham, and bulgur. Cook, stirring often, until bulgur colors slightly, about 5 minutes.

3. Stir in stock; bring to a boil. Reduce heat to low. Cook, covered, until bulgur is tender, 15 to 20 minutes.

4. Stir in lentils and tomatoes. Cook over low heat 1 minute, or just until tomatoes and lentils are heated through. Remove from heat. Salt and pepper to taste. Add basil; toss to combine and fluff pilaf. Serve immediately.

♦ ♦ ♦

♦ ♦ ♦

Versatile Vegetables

With the remarkable quantity and variety of farm-fresh vegetables available year-round, is it any wonder that Americans are enjoying more and more of this fresh bounty? Vegetables, which are naturally low in fat and high in fiber, certainly fit the bill for today's nutri-tion-conscious consum-ers, on the alert for new ways of reducing their meat intake and increas-ing fiber consumption. It's no longer uncom-mon—even among non-vegetarians—for vege-tables to take the central role in a meal.

> There are many ways to love a vegetable. The most sensible way is to love it well-treated. Then you can eat it with the comfortable knowledge that you will be a better man for it, in your spirit and your body too.
>
> —M. F. K. Fisher

Through the ages, vegetables have been used in many ways, and at all meals. The Japa-nese have crisp salads for breakfast, Ameri-cans their hash browns. At the sweet end of the spectrum are zucchini bread, carrot pudding, and tomato devil's food cake. In fact, it's hard to find many dishes for which some type of vegetable couldn't be used. They're found in appetizers, soups, salads, pastas, stir-frys, condiments, sauces, breads, desserts, and side dishes. Some aromatic vegetables, such as garlic, leeks, shallots, and onions, are more often used as flavorings.

Unless you have your own garden, you must rely on your market for fresh vegetables, even in season. But that is less and less of a problem. Thanks to advanced technology and modern transportation methods, markets receive fresh vegetables faster and in better condition than ever before. In addition to a wider selection of the more common vegetables, you can find a selection of unusual greens, fresh wild mushrooms, and baby vegetables.

For superior quality, always buy vegetables at the peak of their season. You can't miss—the price will be lower, the quality higher. The best place to buy vegetables is at a farmers' market, where they've usually been harvested the previous day. Next best is a specialty produce market or a market that has a particularly well-tended produce section where turnover's frequent.

With the bounty of fresh vegetables available today, there's little reason to use lackluster canned vegetables or, for that matter, most frozen vegetables. Of course, there are times when the convenience of frozen vegetables can outweigh the bother of fresh. Frozen petite peas, for example, are quite good, and using them right out of the bag takes a fraction of the time necessary to shell fresh peas. And, since tomatoes are less than wonderful in the winter, canned Italian-style tomatoes and sundried tomatoes make a good stand-in.

Vegetables add color, flavor, and nutrition to meals, and can be the foundation of many a creative combination. If you haven't done so already, start making vegetables a highlight of your meals. The late food authority Bert Greene said it best: "Things that are supposed to be good for you should keep the secret of their good intentions strictly to themselves." A statement he appended with a huge grin, adding, "Eat your vegetables!"

✦✦✦✦✦ Beets ✦✦

The most common color for beets (called beetroots in the British Isles) is a garnet red. However, they can range in color from deep red to white, the most intriguing being the Chioggia (also called candy cane), with concentric rings of red and white. The leafy green tops are also edible and highly nutritious.

AVAILABILITY AND SELECTION: Fresh beets are available year-round, with a peak season from June to late September. Choose firm, smooth-skinned beets without any soft spots or other blemishes. Small or medium beets are generally more tender than large ones. If the beet greens are attached they should be crisp and bright.

STORAGE AND PREPARATION: Because they leach moisture from the bulb, beet greens should be removed as soon as you get them home. Leave about 1 inch of the stem and the root attached to prevent loss of nutrients, color, and flavor during cooking. Store beets in a plastic bag in the refrigerator for three to four weeks. Greens should be stored in a sealed plastic bag for up to a week. Just before cooking, wash beets gently so as not to break the thin skin, which could cause nutrient and color loss. Peel beets after cooking.

NUTRIENTS: Beets are high in potassium, contain a moderate amount of sodium, and small amounts of protein, vitamins, and minerals.

✦✦✦✦✦ Broccoli ✦✦

The name broccoli comes from an Italian word meaning cabbage sprout, and indeed, broccoli is a relative of cabbage, Brussels sprouts, and cauliflower. A deep emerald green vegetable, sometimes with a purple tinge, broccoli has tight clusters of tiny buds atop stout, edible stems.

AVAILABILITY AND SELECTION: Broccoli is available year-round, with a peak season from October through April. Look for broccoli with a deep, strong color—green, or green tinged with purple. The buds should be tightly closed and the leaves crisp.

STORAGE AND PREPARATION: Refrigerate, unwashed, in a plastic bag, for up to four days. Wash broccoli and if the stalks are tough, peel them before cooking. If separating broccoli into florets, cut into uniform pieces for even cooking.

NUTRIENTS: Broccoli is an excellent source of vitamins C and A, as well as riboflavin, calcium, and iron.

✦✦✦✦✦ Brussels Sprouts   ✦✦✦

Said to have been cultivated in sixteenth-century Belgium, Brussels sprouts are a member of the cabbage family that look like tiny cabbage heads. Many rows of sprouts grow on a single long stalk. They range from ½ to 1½ inches in diameter; the smaller sprouts are more tender.

AVAILABILITY AND SELECTION: Brussels sprouts are available from late August through March. Buy small bright green sprouts with compact heads, and no sign of yellowing on the leaves.

STORAGE AND PREPARATION: Store unwashed sprouts in a plastic bag in the refrigerator for up to three days. Longer than that, the sprouts will develop a strong flavor. Before cooking, remove any loose leaves. Wash sprouts, then lightly trim the stem. Cut an x in the bottom of each stem for even cooking.

NUTRIENTS: Brussels sprouts are low in sodium, high in vitamins A and C, and are a fair source of iron.

✦✦✦✦✦ Corn   ✦✦✦

Before settlers came to the New World, Europeans had never seen this food, which was called Indian corn by colonists. Today, Europeans call corn maize, a derivative of the early American Indian word *mahiz*. Everything on the corn plant can be used: the husks for tamales, the silk for medicinal tea, the kernels for food, and the stalks for fodder. The two most popular varieties of corn today are white and yellow. Yellow corn has larger, fuller-flavored kernels; white corn kernels are smaller and sweeter. There are also varieties with both yellow and white kernels on one cob. The multicolored Indian corn—used today mainly for decoration—has red, blue, brown, and purple kernels.

AVAILABILITY AND SELECTION: The peak season for fresh corn is June through September. As soon as corn is picked, its sugar immediately begins its gradual conversion to starch, which reduces the corn's natural sweetness. For that reason, it's important to buy corn as soon after it's picked as possible. Look for ears with bright green, snug-fitting husks and fresh-looking silk. The kernels should be plump and milky, and come all the way to the ear's tip; the rows should be tightly spaced.

STORAGE AND PREPARATION: Fresh corn should be cooked and served the day it's purchased, but it can be wrapped in a plastic bag and refrigerated for up to a day. Strip off the husks and silk just before cooking.

NUTRIENTS: Corn is a good source of potassium, contains a moderate amount of phosphorus, and small amounts of vitamins A and B.

✦✦✦✦ Eggplant ✦✦✦

There are many varieties of eggplant, ranging in color from rich purple to white, in length from 2 to 12 inches, and in shape from oblong to round. In the United States, the most common eggplant is large and pear-shaped with a smooth, glossy, dark purple skin. Then there's the very narrow, straight *Japanese* or *Oriental eggplant*, which ranges in color from violet to striated shades and has a tender, slightly sweet flesh. The *Italian* or *baby eggplant* looks like a miniature version of the common large variety, but has a more delicate skin and flesh. The small, firm *white eggplant* has a tougher skin, but firmer, smoother flesh than the larger eggplants.

AVAILABILITY AND SELECTION: Eggplant is available year-round, with the peak season during August and September. Choose a firm, smooth-skinned eggplant that is heavy for its size; avoid those with soft or brown spots.

STORAGE AND PREPARATION: Eggplants are very perishable and become bitter with age. They should be stored in a cool, dry place and used within a day or two of purchase. If longer storage is necessary, wrap eggplant in a plastic bag and store in the refrigerator. When young, the skin of most eggplants is edible; older eggplants should be peeled. Since the flesh discolors rapidly, an eggplant should be cut just before using. Most eggplants benefit from the ancient method of salting and weighting for 20 to 30 minutes, then blotting away the excess moisture and salt. The smaller varieties rarely require salting, and usually need only a short cooking time. Eggplant has an incredible capacity for soaking up oil, so it should be well coated with a batter or crumb mixture if deep-fried.

NUTRIENTS: Eggplant is high in fiber, and a good source of potassium.

✦✦✦✦✦ Fennel ✦✦✦

There are two types of fennel, both with pale green, celerylike stems and bright green, feathery foliage. *Florence fennel,* also called *finocchio*, is cultivated throughout the Mediterranean and in the United States. It has a broad, bulbous base that's treated like a vegetable. Both the base and stems can be eaten raw in salads or cooked in a variety of ways, including braising, sautéing, or in soups. The fragrant, graceful greenery can be used as a garnish or snipped like dill and used for a last-minute flavor enhancer. The flavor of fennel is sweeter and more delicate than that of anise and when cooked, becomes even lighter and more elusive than when raw. *Common fennel* is the variety from which the oval, greenish-brown fennel seeds come. The seeds are available whole and ground and are used in both sweet and savory foods, as well as to flavor many liqueurs. Though common fennel is bulbless, its stems and greenery are used the same way as Florence fennel. Common fennel is not usually available in U.S. markets.

AVAILABILITY AND SELECTION: Florence fennel is available from fall through spring. Choose clean crisp bulbs with no sign of browning. Any attached greenery should be a fresh green color.

STORAGE AND PREPARATION: Refrigerate fennel, tightly wrapped in a plastic bag, for up to five days. Fennel should be washed, the base trimmed, and the stalks and greenery removed before using. It can be used raw in salads, cooked as a vegetable, or added to soups and stews.

NUTRIENTS: Fennel is rich in vitamin A and contains a fair amount of calcium, phosphorus, and potassium.

✦✦✦✦✦ Green Beans ✦✦

The green bean is a long, slender, green pod with small seeds inside. The entire pod is edible. It's also called *string bean* (because of the fibrous string—now bred out of commercial varieties—running down the pod's seam) and *snap bean* (for the sound the bean makes when broken in half). The *wax bean* is a pale yellow variety of green bean.

AVAILABILITY AND SELECTION: Green beans are available year-round, with a peak season of May to October. Choose slender beans that are crisp, bright-colored, and free of blemishes.

STORAGE AND PREPARATION: Store green beans in the refrigerator, tightly wrapped in a plastic bag, for up to five days. Before cooking, wash the beans and trim the stem end.

NUTRIENTS: Green beans have good amounts of calcium, potassium, and vitamin A, and small amounts of phosphorus and vitamin C.

✦✦✦✦✦ Green Peas

The English pea, which is also known simply as the *green* or *garden pea*, has a sweet, fresh flavor that's anything but common. The French are famous for their tiny, young green peas known as *petits pois.* The bright green peas are enclosed in crisp pods of the same color.

AVAILABILITY AND SELECTION: The peak months for peas are March, April, and May, and from August to November. Choose fresh peas that have plump, unblemished, bright green pods. The peas inside should be glossy, crunchy, and sweet. Because peas begin the sugar-to-starch conversion process the moment they're picked, it's important to buy them as fresh as possible.

STORAGE AND PREPARATION: Refrigerate peas in their pods in a plastic bag for no more than two to three days. Shell just before using.

NUTRIENTS: Peas are a fair source of vitamins A and C, as well as potassium, niacin, and iron.

✦✦✦✦✦ Mushrooms

Mushroom sizes and shapes vary tremendously and colors go from white to black with a full gamut of colors in-between. The cap's texture can be smooth, pitted, honeycombed, or ruffled; flavors range from bland to rich, nutty, and earthy.

The cultivated mushroom is what's commonly found in most U.S. supermarkets today. Among the more exotic wild mushrooms available are porcini (or cèpe), chanterelle, enoki, morel, puffball, shiitake, and wood ear (see page 165). Because so many wild mushrooms are poisonous, it's vitally important to know which are edible and which are not. Extreme caution should be taken when picking them yourself.

The readily available cultivated mushroom has a mild, earthy flavor. It ranges in size from ½ to 3 inches in diameter and in color from white to pale tan.

AVAILABILITY AND SELECTION: Cultivated mushrooms are available year-round but are at their peak in fall and winter. Look for those that are firm and evenly colored with tightly closed caps. If all the gills are showing, the mushrooms are past their prime. Avoid any that are broken or damaged or have soft spots or a dark-tinged surface. If the mushrooms are to be cooked whole, select those of equal size so they will cook evenly.

STORAGE AND PREPARATION: Fresh mushrooms should be stored with cool air circulating around them. Place them on a tray in a single layer, cover with a damp paper towel, and refrigerate. Before using, wipe with a damp paper towel or, if absolutely necessary, rinse with cold water and dry thoroughly. Mushrooms should never be soaked because they absorb water and will become mushy. The stem ends should be trimmed before cooking.

NUTRIENTS: Mushrooms have moderate amounts of potassium and phosphorous, and small amounts of the B vitamins.

♦♦♦♦♦ Wild (and not-so-wild) Mushrooms   ♦♦♦♦♦♦♦♦♦♦♦♦♦♦♦♦♦♦♦♦♦♦♦♦♦♦♦♦

Many of the so-called wild mushrooms—once available only to those willing to forage the woods for them—are now being cultivated. These tamed mushrooms may not be as robust in flavor as their wild counterparts, but they still add interest, texture, and flavor to many dishes. The fact that they're now cultivated doesn't mean the price is reasonable—it simply gives the consumer easier access to them. The following summary by no means lists all the wild and not-so-wild mushrooms found in markets, but it does include those most commonly available.

Chanterelle   A trumpet-shaped wild mushroom with a color that ranges from bright yellow to orange, the chanterelle has a delicate, nutty (sometimes fruity) flavor and a somewhat chewy texture. Fresh chanterelles are usually imported from Europe. They can also be found dried or canned in many large supermarkets. Although they're not widely cultivated, chanterelles are found growing in parts of the Pacific Northwest and along the East Coast. They're occasionally found fresh in markets during the summer and winter months.

Enoki   The cultivated variety of these crisply delicate mushrooms comes in clusters of long, spaghettilike stems topped with tiny, snow-white caps. In contrast, the wild form has orangey brown, very shiny caps. Enoki have an appealingly crunchy texture and mild—almost fruity—taste, unlike the bosky flavor of most mushrooms. They're generally used raw in salads and sandwiches. If cooked, they must be added to the dish at the last minute so as not to become tough. They're available fresh year-round (depending on the region) in Oriental markets and some supermarkets. They can also be purchased canned. Before using, enoki should be cut away from the mass at the base of the stems.

Matsutake   This dark brown Japanese wild mushroom has a dense, meaty texture; it can sometimes be tough. The matsutake has a wonderfully nutty, woodsy flavor. It's available fresh from late fall to mid-winter, usually only in Japanese markets or specialty produce stores. Canned matsutake are also available.

Morel   The morel is easy to recognize by its small (two to four inches high), honeycombed, cone-shaped cap. It can be rich tan to extremely dark brown in color. Its flavor is deliciously smoky, earthy, and nutty. In general, the darker the mushroom the stronger the flavor. Morels usually first appear in specialty produce markets in April and the season can last through June. Imported canned morels can be found in gourmet markets year-round.

Oyster (pleurote)   This fan-shaped mushroom grows both wild and cultivated in close clusters, often on rotting tree trunks in the wild. They're also called *oyster caps, tree mushrooms, tree oyster mushrooms, abalone mushrooms, pleurote,* and *summer oyster mushrooms.* The cap varies in color from creamy white to pale gray to dark brownish-gray. The flavor of raw oyster mushrooms is fairly robust and slightly peppery but becomes much milder when cooked. They're available in some areas year-round, particularly in specialty produce and Asian markets. Young oyster mushrooms (1½ inches in diameter and under) are considered the best. Also available are canned oyster mushrooms, which should be rinsed before using.

Porcini (Cèpe, Boletus, Steinpilze)   These members of the *Boletus* family are pale brown in color and can weigh from an ounce or two up to a pound. Their caps can be anywhere from one to ten inches across. Porcini have a smooth, meaty texture and pungent, woodsy flavor. In the United States, fresh porcini are sometimes available in specialty produce markets in late spring or autumn. Dried porcini are more readily available, usually in specialty markets.

Puffball   A firm, round, white mushroom which can range in size from about four ounces to a giant 50-pounder. It has a mild, nutty flavor. When young, the puffball's texture is smooth and firm. Fresh puffball mushrooms are available sporadically—usually from late spring to early autumn—in specialty produce markets.

Shiitake   Though originally from Japan and Korea, the shiitake is now being cultivated in the United States (where it's often called *golden oak*) in a number of states, including California, Pennsylvania, Vermont, Washington, and Virginia. The cap of the shiitake is dark brown, sometimes with tan striations, and it can be as large as eight to ten inches across. The average, however, is three to six inches. The meaty flesh has a full-bodied (some say steaklike) flavor. Both fresh and dried shiitakes are now available almost year-round in many supermarkets; they're most plentiful in spring and autumn.

Wood Ear (Tree Ear, Cloud Ear, Silver Ear)   These mushrooms have a slightly crunchy texture and a delicate, almost bland flavor that more often than not absorbs the taste of the more strongly flavored ingredients with which they are cooked. Oriental markets sell dried wood ears which, except for the albino varieties (silver ear), look like brownish black, dried chips. Upon reconstituting, they expand five to six times in size and vaguely resemble the shape of an ear.

✦✦✦✦✦ Okra

One of the many legends about okra is that Ethiopian slaves brought it to America's South, where it is still popular today. The slender green pods are ridged and have a tapered, oblong shape. Though it can grow to about 8 inches long, the okra found in markets is more likely to range from 1½ to 4 inches. Each pod is generously filled with tiny, white seeds that are soft and edible. When cooked, cut okra releases a viscous substance that serves to thicken any liquid in which it is cooked.

AVAILABILITY AND SELECTION: Although available fresh year-round in the South, the season for the rest of the country is from about May through October. When buying fresh okra look for firm, brightly colored pods less than four inches long. Larger pods may be tough and fibrous. Avoid those that are dull in color, limp or blemished.

STORAGE AND PREPARATION: Refrigerate okra in a plastic bag for up to five days. Wash, trim the stem ends, and cut (if doing so) just before cooking.

NUTRIENTS: Fresh okra contains fair amounts of potassium and vitamins A and C.

✦✦✦✦✦ Onions

The onion is prized around the world for the magic its pungent flavor and fragrance contributes to a multitude of dishes. There are two main classifications of onion—*green onions,* commonly known as *scallions* (see page 163), and *dry onions,* which are mature onions with a juicy flesh covered with dry, papery skin.

Dry onions come in a wide range of sizes, shapes, and flavors. Among those that are mild-flavored are the white or yellow *Bermuda onion,* available March through June; the larger, more spherical *Spanish onion,* which is usually yellow-skinned and in season from August to May; and the *red* or *Italian onion,* which is available year-round. The stronger-flavored *globe onions* can have yellow, red, or white skins. They range in size from 1 to 4 inches in diameter and in flavor from mildly pungent to quite sharp.

Among the special onion varieties are three exceedingly juicy specimens. The *Maui onion,* hailing—as the name implies—from the Hawaiian island of the same name, is sweet, mild, and crisply moist. It can range in color from white to pale yellow and is usually shaped like a slightly flattened sphere. It is in season from April to July. *Vidalia onions* are named for Vidalia, Georgia, where they thrive. At their best, these large, pale yellow onions are very sweet and juicy. They're usually available from May through June only in or near the region where they are grown or by mail-order. The state of Washington is the source of *Walla Walla onions,* named after the city of the same name. Large, round, and golden, they're in season from June to September but are usually available outside their growing area only by mail-order.

Tiny *pearl onions* are mild-flavored and about the size of a small marble. They can be cooked—they are often creamed—and served as a side dish or pickled and used as a condiment or garnish (as in the Gibson cocktail). *Boiling onions* are about 1 inch in diameter and mildly flavored. They're cooked as a side dish, used in stews, and pickled.

AVAILABILITY AND SELECTION: See individual onion listings above for seasonal availability. When buying onions, choose those that are heavy for their size with dry, papery skins and that show no signs of spotting or moistness. Avoid onions that are soft or sprouting.

STORAGE AND PREPARATION: Store onions in a cool, dry place with good air circulation for up to three months (depending on their condition when purchased). Humidity breeds spoilage in dry onions. Once cut, an onion should be tightly wrapped, refrigerated, and used within four days.

NUTRIENTS: Onions contain a fair amount of vitamin C and traces of other vitamins and minerals.

✦✦✦✦✦ Scallions ✦✦

The name *scallion* is applied to several members of the onion family including: a distinct variety called scallion, immature onions (also marketed as green or spring onions), young leeks, and sometimes the tops of young shallots. In each case the vegetable has a white base that has not fully developed into a bulb and green leaves that are long and straight. Both parts are edible. In true scallions the sides of the base are straight; the others usually have slightly curved sides, showing the beginnings of a bulb. All can be used interchangeably, although true scallions have a milder flavor than immature onions.

AVAILABILITY AND SELECTION: Scallions are available year-round but are at their peak during spring and summer. Choose those with crisp, bright green tops and a firm white base. Mid-sized scallions with long white stems are the best.

STORAGE AND PREPARATION: Store scallions, wrapped in a plastic bag, in the vegetable crisper section of the refrigerator for up to three days. Scallions can be chopped and used in salads, soups, and many other dishes for flavor. They can also be cooked whole as a vegetable much as you would cook leeks.

NUTRIENTS: Scallions are high in vitamin A, contain a moderate amount of vitamin C, and small amounts of calcium and potassium.

✦✦✦✦✦ Spinach   ✦✦✦

Popeye loved spinach because it's rich in the power-packing iron he needed when encountering his adversary, Bluto. Since spinach contains oxalic acid, which inhibits the body's absorption of calcium and iron, the truth is that its nutritional punch is somewhat diminished. It's this same oxalic acid that gives spinach its slightly bitter taste. Spinach has dark green leaves that, depending on the variety, may either be curled or smooth. *New Zealand spinach*—not a true spinach—has smaller, flat, spade-shape leaves that are often covered with a fine fuzz.

AVAILABILITY AND SELECTION: Fresh spinach is available year-round. Choose leaves that are crisp and dark green with a nice fresh fragrance. Avoid those that are limp, damaged, or spotted.

STORAGE AND PREPARATION: Like all greens, spinach should be washed as soon as you buy it. Loose spinach can be very gritty, so it must be thoroughly rinsed. The easiest way is to put it in a sink or large container full of cold water. Twist or cut the spinach leaves off just above the stem line and immerse in water. Swish the leaves around, then let them stand for a few minutes while the dirt sinks to the bottom. It may be necessary to rinse more than once. Thoroughly dry by using a salad spinner or by blotting with paper towels. Wrap in dry paper towels and seal in a plastic bag. Store in the refrigerator for up to five days.

NUTRIENTS: Spinach is a rich source of vitamin A, a very good source of iron and vitamin C, and contains a small amount of riboflavin.

✦✦✦✦✦ Squash ✦✦

Members of the far-flung squash family vary widely in size, shape, and color. There are two broad categories of squash, *summer squash* and *winter squash.* Summer squash varieties have thin, edible skins and soft seeds. The tender flesh has a high water content and mild flavor and doesn't require long cooking. The most widely available varieties of summer squash are crookneck, pattypan, and zucchini. Winter squash have hard, thick skins and seeds. The deep yellow to orange flesh is firmer than that of summer squash and requires longer cooking. Winter squash varieties include acorn, buttercup, butternut, hubbard, pumpkin, spaghetti, and turban.

AVAILABILITY AND SELECTION: Summer squash is best from early through late summer, although some varieties are available year-round in certain regions. Select the smaller specimens with bright-colored skins free of spots and bruises. Winter squash varieties are available year-round, though most are best from early fall through the winter. Choose winter squash that are heavy for their size and have a hard, deep-colored rind free of blemishes or moldy spots.

STORAGE AND PREPARATION: Summer squash is very perishable and should be refrigerated in a plastic bag for no more than five days. Winter squash does not require refrigeration and can be kept in a cool, dark place for a month or more, depending on the variety. Once the seeds are removed, winter squash can be baked, steamed, or simmered.

NUTRIENTS: Summer squash is high in vitamins A and C, as well as niacin. Winter squash is a good source of iron, riboflavin, and vitamins A (more than summer squash) and C.

✦✦✦✦✦ Sweet Potatoes ✦✦

The sweet potato is a large, edible root that is native to tropical areas of the Americas. There are many varieties of sweet potato but the two that are widely grown commercially are a pale sweet potato and a darker-skinned kind Americans erroneously call a yam (the true yam is not related to the sweet potato). The first has a thin, light yellow skin and a pale yellow flesh. Its flavor is not sweet and when cooked, its flesh is dry and crumbly, much like a white baking potato. The darker variety has a thicker, dark red-orange skin and a vivid orange, sweet flesh that cooks to a much moister texture.

AVAILABILITY AND SELECTION: Fresh sweet potatoes are available sporadically throughout the year, though not too readily during the summer months. When buying sweet potatoes choose those that are small- to medium-size with smooth unbruised skins.

STORAGE AND PREPARATION: Sweet potatoes don't store well unless the environment is just right, which means dry, dark, and around 55°F. Under perfect conditions they can be stored for three to four weeks. Otherwise, store in a cool, dark place and use within a week of purchase. Do not refrigerate. Sweet potatoes, particularly the pale variety, can be substituted for regular potatoes in most recipes.

NUTRIENTS: Sweet potatoes contain large amounts of vitamin A, a moderate amount of vitamin C, good potassium, and a smattering of minerals.

GINGER CREAM BEETS

Makes 4 servings

These beets can be cooked and julienned up to six hours in advance, then combined with the creamy ginger sauce at the last minute. The beets can be cooked on stovetop or in the microwave. The sauce, however, never quite develops in the microwave, so I've only given the conventional method for it.

1½ pounds small beets
 2 tablespoons butter
 1 shallot, minced
 1 tablespoon minced crystallized ginger
 1 tablespoon finely grated orange zest
 ¼ teaspoon ground allspice
 ¾ cup heavy whipping cream
    salt and freshly ground pepper
 3 tablespoons finely chopped toasted walnuts (optional)

1. Gently wash beets, being careful not to break the skin. Trim beets, leaving about 1 inch of both the stem and root end attached.

2. In a large saucepan, place beets in enough cold water to cover. Over medium heat, bring water to a boil. Reduce heat and simmer, uncovered, just until barely tender, 25 to 35 minutes.

♦ TIP ♦

Mince crystallized ginger slices a jarful at a time in a food processor fitted with a metal blade. If ginger begins to stick, add 1 or 2 tablespoons sugar and continue to process. Return minced ginger to jar; use as needed.

Microwave Method: In a deep 2-quart casserole, combine beets with 3 cups cold water. Cover and cook on HIGH for 17 to 20 minutes, or until tender, stirring once halfway through. Let stand for 2 minutes.

3. Drain cooked beets. Flush with cold running water. When cool enough to handle, trim remaining stem and root ends, then peel. Cut into ¼-inch julienne strips; set aside.

4. In a large skillet, heat butter over medium heat. Add shallot and ginger; sauté for 4 minutes. Stir in orange zest and allspice; sauté for 2 more minutes.

5. Reduce heat to low and stir in cream. Cook, uncovered, for 5 minutes. Salt and pepper to taste. Add beets and heat, stirring often, just until warmed through. Serve immediately, garnished with walnuts, if desired.

. . . .

BROCCOLI-CORN BEIGNETS WITH ROASTED GARLIC AIOLI

Makes about 48 (1½-inch) puffs

A New Orleans culinary legacy, the beignet (pronounced behn-YAY) is a sweet deep-fried pastry, popular both for breakfast and with afternoon coffee. This choux pastry (non-yeast) form of beignet is found in many New Orleans' cookbooks; it takes a break from tradition by being savory. The batter can be made the day before and deep-fried just before serving. After frying, the puffs can be kept warm in the oven, leftovers refrigerated and reheated the next day. Make the aioli the day before and refrigerate.

    Roasted Garlic Aioli (page 288)
1½ **tablespoons vegetable oil**
  1 **cup finely chopped broccoli florets**
  1 **cup fresh corn kernels (about 1 large ear)**
  ½ **cup finely chopped red bell pepper**
  8 **tablespoons (1 stick) butter, cut into 5 pieces**
  1 **small clove garlic, minced**
  1 **teaspoon sugar**
  ½ **teaspoon salt**

¼ teaspoon cayenne
1 cup all-purpose flour
4 large eggs
½ cup grated cheddar (about 2 ounces)
   about 3 quarts vegetable oil

1. Prepare the aioli; refrigerate.

2. In a wok or large skillet, heat 1½ tablespoons oil over high heat. Sauté broccoli, corn, and red peppers for 2 minutes; remove from heat.

3. In a medium saucepan, combine 1 cup water, the butter, garlic, sugar, salt, and cayenne. Bring to a boil over high heat.

Microwave Method: In a 4-cup glass measure, combine 1 cup water, the butter, garlic, sugar, salt, and cayenne. Cook on HIGH for 3 to 3½ minutes, or until water boils.

4. Remove water mixture from heat; add flour all at once, stirring rapidly with a wooden spoon until mixture leaves sides of container and forms a mound in the center. Let stand 5 minutes.

5. Add eggs, one at a time, beating until each egg is incorporated before the next one is added. Beat in cheese. Or turn mixture into a food-processor workbowl fitted with the metal blade. Use on/off pulses to process until dough is evenly distributed in bowl, about 5 seconds. Add eggs, all at once, then cheese, processing until smooth after each addition.

6. Stir in sautéed vegetables. (If a food processor was used to mix dough, return dough to pan or microwave container before adding vegetables.) Cover and refrigerate dough at least 3 hours; can be chilled overnight.

7. In a deep-fryer or heavy pot, heat 3 inches of oil to 375°F. on a deep-fat-frying thermometer. Preheat oven to 350°F. Line a large baking sheet with a double layer of paper towels; set aside.

8. Scoop up a heaping teaspoon of dough; use a second teaspoon to push it off into the hot oil. Fry about 8 beignets at a time, making sure not to overcrowd, until deep golden-brown, about 3 minutes. If beignets don't roll over by themselves, use a slotted spoon to turn them. The finished puffs should be no more than 1½ inches in diameter; larger than that, and they won't get done in the center. Keep deep-fat-frying thermometer in pan to make sure oil temperature is maintained. If it drops below 360°F., the dough will absorb too much oil.

9. Use a slotted spoon to remove beignets to lined baking sheet. Keep warm in oven while frying remaining dough. Serve hot with Roasted Garlic Aioli. Refrigerate leftover beignets; reheat in preheated 375°F. oven for 5 to 8 minutes.

. . . .

SWEET AND SASSY BRUSSELS SPROUTS STIR-FRY

Makes 4 to 6 servings

Sesame oil comes in two basic types. For this dish, I combine light sesame oil and Oriental sesame oil, which has a much stronger flavor and fragrance. Used alone, the darker sesame oil can overpower the other flavors in the dish.

For a five-minute final preparation, you can complete this dish through Step 2, and chop and refrigerate all the other ingredients the day before.

1 **teaspoon crushed red pepper**
1 **teaspoon chili powder**
1 **tablespoon, packed, light brown sugar**
3 **tablespoons dry sherry**
1 **pound Brussels sprouts**
3 **tablespoons sesame oil**
4 **scallions, white and green parts chopped separately**
½ **cup minced fresh red bell pepper or canned pimiento or roasted red pepper**
2 **tablespoons minced fresh gingerroot**
2 **large cloves garlic, minced**
2 **tablespoons toasted sesame seeds**

1. In a small bowl, combine the crushed red pepper, chili powder, brown sugar, and sherry; set aside.

2. Cut off a thin slice and cut an x in the stem end of each Brussels sprout; pull off any loose or pale leaves. In a large saucepan, cook Brussels sprouts in boiling water to cover for 10 minutes; drain. Rinse with cold water. Drain; blot dry with paper towels. When cool enough to handle, cut into ¼-inch slices; set aside. Brussels sprouts may be refrigerated at this point until ready to finish.

3. In a wok or large skillet, heat the oil over medium heat. Add chopped white scallions, red pepper, ginger-root, and garlic. Cook, stirring constantly, for 1 minute. Stir in flavored sherry, then the Brussels sprouts. Cook, tossing constantly, for 2 minutes, adding green scallions after 1 minute. Add sesame seeds; toss to combine. Serve hot.

. . . .

"NEW"-FASHIONED CREAMED CORN

Makes 6 servings

The flavors of tomatoes, leeks, and nutmeg bring this old-fashioned dish into the present. It's also "new"-fashioned since it uses only half the cream of the usual creamed corn, thereby keeping calories and cholesterol down.

about 5½ cups fresh yellow corn kernels (7 medium ears corn)
3 tablespoons vegetable oil
¼ cup finely chopped leeks, white part only
2 tablespoons all-purpose flour
¼ teaspoon freshly grated nutmeg
1 tablespoon sugar
1 teaspoon salt
1 cup heavy whipping cream
1 cup milk
1 medium tomato, seeded and chopped
white pepper

Up from the meadows rich with corn,
Clear in the cool September morn.
  —JOHN GREENLEAF
  WHITTIER

1. Use a sharp, firm-bladed knife to cut the kernels from each ear of corn. Stand the corn upright on a plate and move the blade down. Use the back of the blade to scrape what is left of the juice from the cobs. Set aside.

2. In a large heavy saucepan over medium-high heat, heat oil. Add the leeks; sauté just until leeks begin to soften. Stir in the flour and nutmeg; cook over low heat for 2 minutes. Stir in the sugar and salt.

3. Over low heat, gradually whisk in the cream and milk. Cook, stirring constantly, until mixture thickens. If desired, sauce may be covered and refrigerated overnight.

4. Just before serving, add corn and simmer, stirring several times, for 4 minutes. Add tomatoes and cook 1 more minute. If sauce has been refrigerated, reheat before adding corn and tomatoes. Season to taste with white pepper.

. . . .

ROASTED MARINATED EGGPLANT

Makes 4 to 6 side dish or first course servings

This versatile dish is just as good a starter as it is a side dish and every bit as wonderful hot as it is cold or at room temperature. It's perfect for company because it's made at least twelve hours in advance—the longer it sits in the marinade, the better it gets.

1½ pounds eggplant, unpeeled and cut lengthwise into
     ½-inch slices
     salt
¾ cup olive oil
⅓ cup balsamic vinegar
 1 tablespoon minced fresh oregano or 1 teaspoon
     dried oregano
 2 medium cloves garlic, minced
 2 teaspoons sugar
¼ teaspoon cayenne
     freshly ground pepper
½ cup grated Asiago
¼ cup finely chopped chervil or parsley

1. Lay the eggplant slices on paper towels; sprinkle with salt. Cover with more paper towels, then a large baking sheet. Weight baking sheet with something heavy, such as several 1-pound cans, a six-pack of soda, etc. Let eggplant drain 30 minutes.

2. Meanwhile, combine the olive oil, vinegar, oregano, garlic, sugar, and cayenne in a small bowl or measuring cup. Salt and pepper to taste. Pour marinade into a 17 x 11-inch jelly-roll pan or other large baking pan.

To eat is human; to digest, divine.
—MARK TWAIN

3. Thoroughly blot the eggplant with paper towels, wiping off any excess salt. Arrange the eggplant slices in the marinade, flipping each piece to coat both sides. Depending on the size of your pan, some slices may have to overlap.

4. Cover tightly with foil. Refrigerate for at least 12 hours, preferably 24, turning slices several times.

5. Turn a corner of the foil back from the pan. Hold surface of foil and drain off marinade into a screwtop jar. Save marinade to use in chilled eggplant variation or as a salad dressing. Remove foil entirely.

6. About 20 minutes before serving, preheat broiler. Position oven rack 5 to 6 inches from broiling unit.

7. Broil eggplant about 5 minutes on one side, or until surface begins to brown nicely. Flip slices and broil the other side, cooking only until eggplant is almost as brown as you want.

8. Remove eggplant; sprinkle with cheese. Return to broiler and continue to broil until cheese is melted, 1 to 2 minutes. Transfer to a warm platter. Sprinkle with chervil or parsley; serve immediately.

♦**VARIATIONS: Grilled Marinated Eggplant:**

1. Prepare the eggplant through step 5. At least 1 hour before grilling, soak 2 cups wood chips in water to cover. When ready, light fire in outdoor grill; just before grilling, sprinkle the wood chips over heat source.

2. Grill the eggplant slices over a medium fire until browned to your liking, 3 to 4 minutes. Turn and grill the second side in the same manner.

3. Transfer grilled eggplant to a platter; sprinkle with cheese and chervil or parsley. Serve warm or at room temperature.

Chilled Roasted or Grilled Marinated Eggplant: Do not top hot eggplant with cheese. Let eggplant cool to room temperature; cover and refrigerate for up to 3 days. Remove eggplant from refrigerator at least 30 minutes before serving. Just before serving, drizzle with leftover marinade, cheese, and chervil or parsley.

GOUDA GREEN BEANS

Makes 6 servings

My talented and beautiful sister, Tia Leslie, gave me this recipe, which has since become a favorite of mine. I changed it only slightly—adding sundried tomatoes and herbs. Besides its wonderful flavor, this dish is prized because it can be made a day in advance. Choose the slimmest green beans you can find.

1½ pounds fresh green beans, trimmed and cut into 2-inch lengths
 4 tablespoons vegetable oil
 1 small onion, finely chopped
 3 cups sliced mushrooms, (about ½ pound)
 ¼ cup chopped sundried tomatoes, commercial or homemade (page 289)
 1 large clove garlic, minced
 3 tablespoons all-purpose flour
 2 teaspoons minced fresh basil or ½ teaspoon dried basil, crumbled
 1 teaspoon minced fresh oregano or ¼ teaspoon dried oregano, crumbled
 1 teaspoon minced fresh tarragon or ¼ teaspoon dried tarragon, crumbled
 1 cup milk
 ⅓ cup dry sherry or additional milk
1½ cups grated Gouda cheese (6 ounces)
    salt and freshly ground pepper

1. Add the green beans to a large pot of boiling salted water. Once water returns to a boil, cook beans just until crisp-tender, 1½ to 2 minutes. Drain and rinse with cold water until beans are cool. Set aside to drain.

2. Preheat oven to 375°F. Lightly oil a 1½- to 2-quart casserole; set aside.

3. In a large skillet over medium-high heat, heat the oil. Add the onion; sauté for 3 minutes. Add the mushrooms, tomatoes, and garlic; sauté for 3 more minutes.

4. Reduce heat to medium-low. Stir in the flour, basil, oregano, and tarragon. Cook for 2 minutes.

5. Gradually stir in the milk, then sherry. Cook, stirring constantly, until mixture thickens, about 2 minutes. Stir in half the cheese; salt and pepper to taste.

6. Remove from heat. Stir in the beans. Turn into prepared casserole. Sprinkle top with the remaining cheese. If desired, cover and refrigerate for up to 24 hours. Let stand at room temperature for 1 hour before baking.

7. Bake, uncovered, for 30 minutes. If desired, place dish under broiler for 1 to 2 minutes to brown top at the end of the baking time. Serve hot.

. . . .

GARLIC-GRILLED OKRA

Makes 4 to 6 servings

Even if you're not an okra fan, you just might find yourself liking these garlicky, smoky pods because there's little evidence of okra's characteristic viscosity. Frozen okra can be used if the fresh is unavailable. Take a few extra minutes to make the Jalapeño Aioli (page 288); it's the perfect accompaniment for this dish.

⅓ **cup vegetable oil**
2 **tablespoons red wine vinegar**
3 **medium cloves garlic, minced**
½ **teaspoon salt**
¼ **teaspoon cayenne**
1 **pound fresh or thawed frozen okra, stem ends lightly trimmed**

1. In a 13 x 9-inch baking pan, combine all the ingredients except the okra. Add the okra, toss to thoroughly coat pods. Cover and refrigerate at least 3 hours or overnight.

2. At least 1 hour before grilling, soak 2 cups wood chips in water to cover. When ready, light fire in outdoor grill. Just before grilling, sprinkle soaked chips over heat source.

3. Use tongs to place okra pods crosswise over grids of grill. Cover and cook over medium-high heat about 3 minutes, or until lightly browned. Turn okra; grill an additional 2 to 3 minutes, or until lightly browned. Serve hot or at room temperature.

SAUTÉ OF PEAS, FENNEL, WILD MUSHROOMS, AND HAM

Makes 6 servings

This easy sauté goes together quickly. If fresh peas aren't in season, use frozen petite peas—they're sweet and succulent, and a lot easier than shelling your own. Just be sure to buy the *petite* peas, which are more tender than the larger varieties.

2 **small fennel bulbs (about 1 pound)**
2 **tablespoons vegetable oil**
½ **teaspoon fennel seeds**
3 **tablespoons butter**
1 **large shallot, finely chopped**
3 **cups chopped wild mushrooms, such as shiitakes, chanterelles, or morels, or cultivated mushrooms (about ½ pound)**
2 **cups fresh or frozen petite peas (10-ounce package)**
6 **ounces smoked ham, cut into ¼-inch dice (about 1¼ cups)**
   salt and freshly ground pepper

1. Trim the root ends of the fennel bulbs and cut off stems. Reserve 4 to 6 of the greens for garnish. Cut fennel into ⅜-inch chunks.

2. In a large skillet, heat the oil over medium-high heat. Add the fennel and fennel seeds. Sauté, stirring often, for 5 minutes. Add ¼ cup water; cover and cook just until fennel is crisp-tender, about 8 minutes. Transfer fennel to a colander to drain.

3. In the same skillet, heat the butter over medium-high heat. Add the shallot and mushrooms. Sauté, stirring often, just until mushrooms begin to brown, 3 to 5 minutes.

4. If using frozen peas, place in a colander while mushrooms are cooking. Rinse with running lukewarm water to thaw, tossing peas with your fingers. Blot peas dry with a paper towel.

5. Add the ham, peas, and fennel to the mushroom mixture. Sauté, stirring often, just until peas are tender, about 3 minutes. Salt and pepper to taste. Serve immediately.

SZECHUAN SPINACH SAUTÉ

Makes 4 servings

Hot-pepper oil is available in Oriental markets and the gourmet section of many supermarkets. It's great for all kinds of stir-frys, and adds zest to salad dressings.

1 **tablespoon hot-pepper oil or ½ tablespoon** *each* **hot-pepper oil and sesame oil**
2 **medium cloves garlic, minced**
1 **small fennel bulb, root trimmed and stalks removed, diced**
2 **pounds fresh spinach, trimmed, washed, and dried**
1 **cup sliced radishes**
1 **to 1½ tablespoons toasted sesame seeds**
  salt and pepper

1. In a nonreactive wok or very large skillet, combine the oil and garlic. Cook over medium-high heat just until garlic begins to sizzle. Add the fennel; cook 3 minutes, stirring often.

2. Add the spinach; cook just until greens begin to wilt. Add the radishes and sesame seeds; toss and cook 1 minute. Salt and pepper to taste. Serve immediately.

. . . .

ORIENTAL SPAGHETTI SQUASH STIR-FRY

Makes 4 to 6 main course servings

I prepare everything for this dish in advance. I cook the spaghetti squash in the microwave oven, chop and refrigerate the vegetables and sausage (the vegetables in the food processor, the sausage by hand), and even measure out the oil, soy sauce, and other ingredients. That way I can throw together this stir-fry in less than ten minutes.

Lop chong is a smoky, slightly sweet Chinese sausage similar to pepperoni in texture. It's available in specialty meat markets and Chinese markets. Any other hard, smoked Chinese sausage can be substituted. If you don't live near a Chinese market, either substitute your favorite hard, smoked sausage, or prepare your stir-fry vegetarian style.

Spaghetti squash is a creamy-yellow, watermelon-shaped squash, so called because when cooked, the yellow-gold flesh separates into spaghettilike strands. It is available year-round with a peak season from early fall through winter.

I cook the squash several hours, or as much as a day, ahead so I don't have to handle it while it's hot. I think the easiest way to cook this squash is in the microwave, but you can choose whatever method suits you best.

1　**medium spaghetti squash (4 to 4½ pounds)**
¾　**pound broccoli**
1　**to 2 tablespoons hot-pepper oil**
2　**to 3 tablespoons Oriental sesame oil**
1　**large onion, finely chopped**
½　**pound lop chong or other Chinese sausage or a dry smoked sausage, thinly sliced**
4　**star anise**
1　**tablespoon minced fresh gingerroot**
1　**large red bell pepper, chopped**
2　**large cloves garlic, minced**
¼　**cup light soy sauce**
¼　**pound snow peas or sugar snap peas, washed, dried, and stems removed from snow peas**
⅓　**cup packed basil leaves, washed, dried, and finely chopped**
⅓　**cup chopped scallions, green part only**
½　**cup dry-roasted peanuts**
　salt and freshly ground pepper

1. Use any of the following three methods to prepare the spaghetti squash.

Microwave Method: Use a large carving fork to pierce squash in 8 evenly spaced places. Place the squash on a microwavesafe plate or shallow dish. Cover loosely with plastic wrap. Cook on HIGH for 10 minutes. Use oven mitts or a dish towel to pick up squash and turn it over. Cover loosely again with plastic wrap. Cook on HIGH for 9 more minutes. Let stand in oven for 5 minutes. Test squash for doneness by piercing with a fork.

Oven Method: Position oven rack in center of oven; preheat oven to 375°F. Lightly oil a medium baking sheet;

place squash in center of sheet. Bake about 45 minutes, or until a fork can easily pierce squash.

Stovetop Method: Place whole squash in a large pot. Cover with water. (If squash is too large for your deepest pot, cut the squash in half lengthwise and discard seeds. Place halves, cut side down, in pot; add water to a depth of 2 inches.) Bring water to a boil. Reduce heat to medium and boil gently, covered, until a fork can easily pierce the squash, 25 to 30 minutes for whole squash, 15 to 20 minutes for squash halves.

2. Either cool the squash to room temperature or cut it in half while still hot. Whole squash can be cooled to room temperature, wrapped in plastic wrap, and refrigerated overnight, if desired. Cutting the squash in half lengthwise will give you shorter strands than if you cut it crosswise. Use a spoon to scrape out seeds. Use a fork to pull out the strands of squash. Transfer strands to a plate; set aside.

3. Cut broccoli tops into small florets; set aside. You should have about 2 heaping cups of florets.

4. In a very large wok or skillet over high heat, heat 4 tablespoons oil. (The amount of each oil is up to you: 2 tablespoons of hot-pepper oil will give the dish a nice glow). Add the onion, sausage, star anise, and gingerroot. Sauté, stirring often, until onions begin to soften, about 3 minutes.

5. Add the red pepper, garlic, and broccoli. Sauté for 5 minutes, stirring often. Remove the star anise. Stir in soy sauce, then the snow peas and squash; sauté 2 more minutes. Remove from heat. Add the basil, scallions, and peanuts; toss to combine. Salt and pepper to taste. Serve immediately.

. . . .

SPICED SQUASH IN SAUSAGE SHELLS

Makes 8 to 12 side dish servings

This dish takes time but isn't at all difficult; it can be made in stages and in advance. For simpler vegetarian fare, the spiced squash can be baked by itself in a 1½-quart oiled casserole for 30 to 40 minutes, or until the center is set.

2 to 2¼ **pounds acorn or butternut squash**
2 to 3 **slices whole wheat or white bread**
3 **large eggs**
1 **pound bulk sausage**
2 **tablespoons butter, softened**
¼ **cup half-and-half**
2 **tablespoons pure maple syrup**
2 **teaspoons grated orange zest**
¼ **teaspoon ground cinnamon**
¼ **teaspoon freshly grated nutmeg**
  salt and freshly ground pepper

> The right food always comes at the right time. Reliance on out-of-season foods makes the gastronomic year an endlessly boring repetition.
> —ROY ANDRIES DE GROOT

1. Cut the squash in half. (For greater ease in cutting squash, microwave on HIGH for 1½ minutes, or until just warm to the touch.) Use a spoon to scrape out the seeds and membranes.

2. Preheat oven to 375°F. Lightly oil a baking pan. Place squash, cut side down, on pan and bake for about 40 minutes, or until fork tender.

Microwave Method: Line a 12 x 7-inch baking dish or the bottom of the microwave oven with wax paper. Arrange the squash, cut side down, on the wax paper. Cook on HIGH for 6 minutes. Rotate dish a half turn, or reverse squash halves. Cook on HIGH for 5 to 6 more minutes, or until the squash is fork tender. Remove squash from oven; set aside to cool.

3. If microwave method was used to cook squash, preheat oven to 375°F. Lightly oil 12 large muffin cups (2¾ inches across top); set aside.

4. While the squash is cooking, place the bread in a food-processor workbowl fitted with the metal blade. Process until finely crumbled. Or, crumble bread by hand. In a medium bowl, combine 1 cup of the bread crumbs, 1 egg, and sausage. Use your fingers or a wooden spoon to thoroughly blend ingredients. Divide mixture evenly among the prepared muffin cups. Use your fingers or the back of a spoon to press sausage evenly over the bottom and up the sides of the muffin cups.

5. Bake for 10 minutes, or until the sausage begins to brown. Remove from oven. Carefully pour off excess fat, being careful not to let the sausage cups fall out.

6. While sausage shells are baking, use a spoon to scrape squash away from skin; turn into a medium bowl. Add the butter; stir to melt. Lightly beat the remaining 2 eggs. Add eggs and remaining ingredients to squash. Whisk well to combine. Spoon squash mixture into sausage shells. If desired, dish may be covered and refrigerated overnight at this point. If refrigerated, let stand at room temperature 1 hour before baking.

7. Bake for 30 minutes, or until squash is slightly puffy and a knife inserted in the center comes out almost clean.

8. Loosen sausage shells from the pan with a knife. Serve hot.

. . . .

HAM AND SWEET POTATO RÖSTI

Makes 4 servings

In Switzerland *Rösti* means "crisp and golden," which is just how this dish turns out. The classic *Rösti* (pronounced ROOSH-tee) is made with white potatoes. This variation on a theme pairs sweet potatoes with ham and scents the dish with orange zest and nutmeg. The darker-skinned variety of sweet potato—often mislabeled as yam—has an orangey flesh that gives this dish a beautiful color. The pale-skinned sweet potato works just as well, though, as do regular baking potatoes. For added snap, substitute spicy-hot tasso, a Cajun cured-pork specialty, for the ham.

CHUTNEY SOUR CREAM (optional):

1 cup sour cream
2 tablespoons finely chopped chutney

Rösti:

 1 **pound sweet potatoes or yams, peeled**
 1 **tablespoon, packed, light brown sugar**
1½ **tablespoons red wine vinegar**
 ½ **teaspoon freshly grated nutmeg**
 ¼ **teaspoon cayenne**
 1 **tablespoon finely grated orange zest**
 ½ **cup minced smoked ham or tasso**
 2 **tablespoons finely chopped chives**
   salt and freshly ground pepper
 3 **tablespoons butter**
 3 **tablespoons olive or vegetable oil**

1. Combine the sour cream and chutney, if desired. Cover and refrigerate for 1 hour before serving. May be stored in refrigerator for up to 5 days.

2. Using a food processor fitted with the shredding disc or the coarse side of a hand grater, grate the potatoes. Turn into a large bowl of cold water. Drain potatoes well; pat dry.

3. Drain and dry the bowl. Add the brown sugar, vinegar, nutmeg, and cayenne; stir to combine. Add the potatoes, orange zest, ham, and chives; toss to combine. Salt and pepper to taste.

4. Heat 2 tablespoons each of the butter and oil in a heavy 9- to 10-inch skillet over medium-low heat. Add the potato mixture, using a pancake turner to spread it evenly over the bottom of skillet; press down firmly. Cook without stirring for 15 to 20 minutes, or until a golden-brown crust forms on the bottom.

5. Use a wide spatula to loosen potato cake from bottom and sides of pan. Gently slide it out onto a large plate. Place a second large plate on top; flip so cooked side is up.

6. Add the remaining 1 tablespoon each butter and oil to skillet; heat 1 minute. Gently ease potato cake back into skillet. Cook for 15 more minutes, or until bottom is golden-brown.

7. Loosen cake from bottom and sides of pan. Place upside-down serving plate over skillet and invert onto

....

W hat I say is that, if a fellow really likes potatoes, he must be a pretty decent sort of fellow.

—A. A. MILNE

....

plate. Serve hot, accompanied by Chutney Sour Cream, if desired.

. . . .

ZUCCHINI "NOODLE" TOSS

Makes 4 servings

So thin you can see light through them, these "noodles" are a different approach to the ever-popular zucchini. Be sure the zucchini you select are small and firm, with vibrantly colored skins. Older, larger specimens will have soft, seedy insides.

2 pounds zucchini, unpeeled (about 4 medium)
3 tablespoons olive oil
1 medium shallot, minced
½ medium red bell pepper, seeded and minced
1 teaspoon celery seed
1 large clove garlic, minced
1½ to 2 teaspoons lemon zest
1 tablespoon minced fresh oregano or 1 teaspoon dried oregano, crumbled
1 tablespoon minced fresh basil or 1 teaspoon dried basil, crumbled
   salt and freshly ground pepper
½ cup freshly grated Parmesan (2 ounces)
3 sprigs basil (optional)

1. Wash and dry the zucchini. Use a vegetable peeler to shave it lengthwise into paper-thin strips; set aside.

2. In a large skillet, heat the oil over medium heat. Add the shallots; sauté just until they begin to soften, about 5 minutes. Add the red bell pepper, celery seed, garlic, and lemon zest; sauté 3 more minutes.

3. Add the zucchini, oregano, and basil. Cook, stirring constantly, just until zucchini is warmed through, about 2 minutes. Remove from heat. Salt and pepper to taste.

4. Transfer to a warm serving bowl; sprinkle with Parmesan. Garnish with basil sprigs, if desired. Serve immediately.

Fish and Shellfish Show-offs

Fish are no longer struggling to swim upstream these days when it comes to acceptance in the American diet. Consumers have finally discovered that not only is fish easy and quick to cook, but the wide selection available

makes finding one you
with the modern-day
foods that taste good,
It's an excellent source
vitamins, and minerals
potassium, and phos-
the added bonus of
page 196), which are
coronary health. Both
water fish are low in
compared to meat—
Specialty fish markets
of fish and shellfish.
highest turnover, which
absolute must with fish.
when shopping for fish
that in some regions
than fresh fish. That's
minute it's caught, then
the fishing boat returns
your fishmonger to rec-

> The bivalve mollusk is
> deemed a treat
> Toward which treat-lovers
> hustle,
> Yet it's not the scallop
> itself they eat,
> But the scallop's adductor
> muscle.
> My craving for pot is
> none of the time,
> And for alcohol, sporadic,
> But I cannot conceal from
> the scallop that I'm
> An adductor muscle addic.
> —"The Scallop,"
> Ogden Nash

like easy. In addition,
emphasis on nutritious
fish is a natural choice.
of protein, B-complex
including calcium, iron,
phorus. And then there's
the Omega-3 oils (see
particularly beneficial to
saltwater and fresh-
sodium content and—
also low in calories.
have the best selection
They also have the
assures freshness, an
Though the keynote
is to buy fresh, it's a fact
frozen fish is "fresher"
because it's iced the
deep-frozen as soon as
to the plant. Rely on
ommend the freshest

fish available. (See page 190 for more information on the subject.)

Fish and shellfish find their way into salads, soups, stews, mousses, fritters —you name it. They can be prepared countless ways, including baking, broiling, deep-frying, grilling, microwaving, panfrying, poaching, sautéing, and steaming. The cooking method is usually dictated by the type of fish. Lean fish can easily be dried out by dry-heat methods like baking, which is better suited for high-fat fish.

Considering all its advantages—cooking ease, nutrition, and the many kinds available—there's only one thing left to say: How can you miss with fish?

. . . .

CALICO SALMON SAUTÉ

Makes 6 servings

As brilliantly hued as a Matisse painting, this is a multi-colored dish of yellow corn, green peppers, pink salmon, red tomatoes, and jade-green watercress. Be sure to use yellow corn—it adds color to the mix and better complements the salmon because it's not as sweet as white corn.

Calico Salmon Sauté also makes a wonderful salad. Prepare as directed and either cool to room temperature or refrigerate until cold, toss with your favorite vinaigrette, and serve on a bed of greens.

¼ **cup olive oil**
2 **cups fresh corn kernels (about 2 large ears corn)**
½ **cup chopped leeks, white part only**
1 **medium green bell pepper, seeded and chopped**
2 **pounds skinless salmon fillet, cut into ¾- to 1-inch cubes**
2 **tablespoons fresh lemon juice**
2 **tablespoons dry white wine**
2 **cups packed watercress leaves, chopped**
24 **tiny cherry tomatoes, halved and seeded**
   salt and freshly ground pepper

1. Heat the oil in a large skillet over high heat. Add the corn, leeks, and green pepper; sauté 1 minute. Add the salmon, lemon juice, and wine; cook 2 minutes, stirring often. Salmon should be almost done.

2. Add the watercress and tomatoes; cook 1 minute, or just until warmed through. Salt and pepper to taste. Serve immediately.

♦**NOTE:** To remove corn kernels from the cob, begin by cutting a small piece off the tip so that it's flat. Holding the stem end, stand the cob upright on its flat end. Set it on a plate and use a firm-bladed, very sharp knife to cut downwards, removing the corn three or four rows at a time. To get the "milk" of the corn, use the back of the blade to scrape what is left of the juice from the cobs.

Seed the cherry tomatoes by sticking your thumb or finger into the tomato halves and flicking out the seeds.

✦✦✦✦✦✦✦ FISH AND SHELLFISH—WHAT'S THE DIFFERENCE? ✦✦✦✦✦✦✦

All fish can be classified into two very broad categories—fish and shellfish. In the most basic terms, fish have fins, backbones, and gills, while shellfish have shells of one form or another.

Fish are divided into two groups, freshwater and saltwater. Because salt water provides more buoyancy than fresh water, saltwater fish, such as cod, flounder, and tuna, have thicker bones. Freshwater fish, like catfish, perch, and trout, have a light skeletal framework with lots of minuscule bones.

Fish can also be classified as flatfish and roundfish. Flatfish are shaped like an oval platter, the top side being dark and the bottom light in color. Both eyes are on the dark side of the body. Flounder, halibut, and true sole are all flatfish. Roundfish, such as grouper, rockfish, and salmon, have a rounder body, with eyes on both sides of the head.

Further, fish are divided into three categories based on fat content—lean, moderate-fat and high-fat. The oil in lean fish is concentrated in the liver, rather than being distributed throughout the flesh. The fat content of lean fish is less than 2½ percent and the flesh is mild and lightly colored. Fish in the lean category include black sea bass, brook trout, cod, croaker, flounder, haddock, hake, halibut, pollock, ocean perch, red snapper, rockfish, smelts, and tilefish.

Moderate-fat fish usually have less than 5 to 10 percent fat and include bluefish, striped bass, sturgeon, swordfish, tuna, and whiting. High-fat fish are those with more than 10 percent fat content. Some of the more popular high-fat fish are herring, butterfish, mackerel, rainbow trout, king salmon, shad, and yellowtail. The more even distribution of fat in moderate- and high-fat fish gives their flesh a darker color, firmer texture, and more distinctive flavor.

Shellfish is a broad term for all aquatic animals that have a shell of some kind, whether crustaceans or mollusks. Crustaceans have elongated bodies and jointed, soft, crustlike shells. Crustaceans include crabs, crayfish, lobster, and shrimp.

Mollusks are invertebrates with soft bodies covered by a shell of one or more pieces. They're divided into three groups. Gastropods (also called univalves) all have a single shell and single muscle. Gastropods include abalone, limpet, periwinkle, snail, and whelk. Bivalves are soft-bodied mollusks that have two shells hinged together by a strong muscle. Bivalves include clams, mussels, oysters, and scallops. Cephalopods have tentacles attached to the head, and ink sacs, which serve to evade predators. The most common cephalopods are octopus, squid, and cuttlefish.

HUSHPUPPY-
FRIED
CATFISH

Makes 4 servings

Not too many years ago, catfish could be found readily in markets and on menus only in the South. Thankfully, those days are gone, with catfish farms producing an abundance of this sweet, firm-fleshed fish for wide distribution. You can substitute grouper, halibut, snapper, or turbot in this recipe.

1½ cups Cajun Tartar Sauce (page 291)
 ½ cup fine white cornmeal
 ¾ cup all-purpose flour
 ½ teaspoon baking soda
  1 teaspoon salt
 ½ teaspoon ground cayenne
1½ cups buttermilk
  1 large egg, lightly beaten
 ⅓ cup finely chopped chives or scallions, green parts only
      about 3 cups vegetable oil
1½ pounds catfish fillets, cut into 1-inch chunks

> Food is meant to tempt as well as nourish, and everything that lives in water is seductive.
> —JEAN-PAUL ARON

1. Prepare Cajun Tartar Sauce. Cover and refrigerate.

2. In a shallow medium bowl, combine the cornmeal, ¼ cup of the flour, the baking soda, salt, and cayenne. Stir in the buttermilk, egg, and chives, mixing only until dry ingredients are moistened. Let stand, uncovered, at room temperature for 20 minutes.

3. In a heavy deep skillet, pour oil to a depth of 1¼ inches. Over medium-high heat, bring oil to 375°F. Keep a deep-fat-frying thermometer in pan to make sure oil temperature is maintained. If it drops below 360°F., the batter will absorb too much oil.

4. Preheat oven to 300°F. Line a large baking sheet with a double layer of paper towels; set aside.

5. Place remaining ½ cup flour in a medium paper or plastic bag. Add catfish chunks; shake bag to coat fish. Shake excess flour from fish; set on a sheet of wax paper.

6. Stir the batter. Dip fish chunks in batter, allowing any excess to drip off. Fry fish in batches, being careful not to crowd, until golden brown on each side, 2 to 3 minutes.

7. Place fried fish on the lined baking sheet. Keep warm in oven while frying remaining fish.

8. Serve hot with Cajun Tartar Sauce.

. . . .

CRISPY HALIBUT WITH PUMPKIN-SEED TARTAR SAUCE

Makes 4 servings

This broiled fish has a crunchy coating made with ground, toasted pumpkin seeds. The halibut can also be fried in a small amount of olive oil, though some of the crispy coating is lost with this method. Sunflower seeds can be substituted for the pumpkin seeds.

1 cup Pumpkin-seed Tartar Sauce (page 291)
1 cup hulled pumpkin seeds, toasted and cooled
4 halibut fillets (about 6 ounces each)
⅓ cup olive oil
  salt and pepper

1. Prepare Pumpkin-seed Tartar Sauce; set aside at room temperature.

2. Place rack 8 inches from heat source. Preheat broiler for 10 minutes. Line a baking sheet with aluminum foil.

3. In a blender or food processor fitted with the metal blade, process pumpkin seeds using on/off pulses until ground medium-coarse. If grinding seeds in a blender, use low speed, scraping larger seeds toward the middle as necessary.

4. Place ground pumpkin seeds in a shallow dish; set aside. Place halibut fillets on a piece of wax paper. Brush one side of each fillet with oil; salt and pepper to taste. One by one, dip oiled side of fillet into ground seeds. Brush uncoated side with oil; salt and pepper to taste. Spear fillet with fork; coat second side with ground seeds. Repeat with remaining fillets.

5. Place fillets on prepared baking sheets. Broil 4 minutes. Turn and continue to broil 4 to 5 minutes, or just until fish is opaque. Top each serving with a dollop of Pumpkin-seed Tartar Sauce. Serve immediately.

F or my part, I mind my belly most studiously and very carefully; for I look upon it that he who does not mind his belly will hardly mind anything else.
—SAMUEL JOHNSON

. . . .

✦✦✦✦✦✦✦✦✦ BUYING AND STORING FISH AND SHELLFISH ✦✦✦✦✦✦✦✦✦

Guidelines for buying fish depend on what form the fish is in when purchased.

FRESH WHOLE FISH: Look for bright, clear, full eyes (cloudy or sunken eyes indicate stale fish); shiny, brightly colored skin; a fresh, mild odor; firm flesh that clings tightly to the bones and springs back when pressed with your finger; and red to bright pink gills, free from any slime or residue.

Whole fish comes either ungutted or drawn, that is, its entrails and sometimes its gills have been removed. Dressed fish has also had the scales removed. *Whole-dressed* usually refers to the whole fish; *pan-dressed* to a fish with head, tail, and fins removed.

FISH FILLETS AND STEAKS: Choose those with a fresh odor, firm texture, and moist appearance. Fillets are a boneless, lengthwise cut from the sides of a fish. They are usually single pieces, though butterfly fillets (both sides of the fish connected by the uncut strip of skin on the belly) are also available. Fish steaks are cross-section cuts from large, dressed fish. They're usually ⅝ to 1 inch thick and contain a small section of the backbone.

FROZEN FISH: Make sure it's solidly frozen. Frozen fish should be tightly wrapped in an undamaged, moisture- and vaporproof material, and should have no odor. White, dark, icy, or dry spots indicate damage through drying or deterioration. Avoid frozen fish that you suspect was thawed and refrozen.

SHELLFISH: In general, shellfish should smell of the sea with no hint of ammonia. Mollusks (clams, mussels, and oysters) can be bought either in the shell or shucked. Scallops are usually sold shucked. Because bacteria form quickly in dead shellfish, it's important that it be alive when you buy it in the shell. Make sure the shells are tightly closed. If a shell is slightly open, give it a light tap—if it doesn't snap shut, the mollusk is dead and should be discarded. To test a soft-shell clam, lightly touch its neck; if it moves, it's alive. Shucked clams, mussels, oysters, and scallops should be plump and in clear liquid.

Crabs, crayfish, and lobsters must be alive when purchased fresh. To make sure, pick up the lobster—if the tail curls under the body it's alive. This test is especially important with lobsters that have been stored on ice because they're so sluggish it's sometimes hard to see movement.

STORING FISH: Fresh fish and shellfish should immediately be stored, tightly wrapped, in the coldest part of the refrigerator, and used the same day as purchased. Never store ungutted fish. Frozen fish can be stored in a moisture- and vaporproof wrapping in the freezer for up to six months. Thaw in the refrigerator for 24 hours (for a one-pound package) before cooking. Quick-thawing can be accomplished by placing the wrapped, frozen fish in cold water, allowing one hour to thaw a one-pound package. Never refreeze fish.

CANNED FISH: Canned tuna, salmon, and sardines will generally keep for about a year stored at 65°F. or less. However, since you don't know under what conditions canned goods were stored before you got them, it's best to buy only what will be used within a few months.

GRILLED SWORDFISH WITH CUCUMBER-CORN SALSA

Makes 4 servings

The mild-flavored, moderately fat flesh of the swordfish is firm, dense and meatlike, making it one of the most popular fish in the United States. It's perfect for grilling. Serve it with a cool Cucumber–Corn Salsa (page 285).

1½ cups Cucumber–Corn Salsa
½ cup olive oil
¼ cup fresh lime juice
2 large cloves garlic, minced
2 tablespoons minced cilantro
½ teaspoon salt
½ teaspoon freshly ground pepper
4 swordfish steaks, 1 inch thick

1. At least 3 hours in advance, make the Cucumber–Corn Salsa and refrigerate. Remove salsa from refrigerator 30 minutes before serving.

2. In a large shallow bowl, combine all remaining ingredients except the swordfish. Add fish, turning to coat well. Cover and refrigerate 3 hours.

3. At least 1 hour before grilling, soak 2 cups wood chips in water to cover. When ready, light fire in outdoor grill. Just before grilling, sprinkle wood chips over heat source. Brush grill lightly with vegetable oil.

4. Grill fish steaks, uncovered, over a hot fire, basting with marinade, until cooked through, about 5 minutes on each side. Serve hot, accompanied with Cucumber–Corn Salsa.

♦ TIP ♦

Rolling a lemon, orange, or lime between your palm and the countertop will result in more juice when the fruit is squeezed.

SESAME MONKFISH

Makes 4 servings

This low-fat, firm-textured fish has a mild, sweet flavor that's often compared to that of lobster. Indeed, shellfish are an important part of the monkfish diet. Depending on where it's marketed, it's also called angler, lotte, bellyfish, frogfish, and sea devil. The monkfish is extremely ugly and very large. Its prodigious size is what prompted Julia Child to pronounce monkfish the "Sydney Greenstreet of the ocean." The only edible portion of this impressive fish is the tail, which is suitable for almost any method of cooking.

```
1   cup Toasted Sesame Butter (page 304)
4   monkfish fillets (6 to 8 ounces each)
1   large tomato, peeled, seeded, and chopped
¼   cup finely chopped onion
2   teaspoons finely chopped lemon zest
2   teaspoons Oriental sesame oil
2   teaspoons minced fresh gingerroot
    salt and freshly ground pepper
3   tablespoons toasted sesame seeds
1½  tablespoons finely chopped chives
```

1. Make Toasted Sesame Butter. Cover and refrigerate until 30 minutes before serving.

2. Arrange rack 6 inches below broiler unit. Preheat the broiler. Lightly oil a medium baking sheet.

3. Arrange the monkfish fillets 3 inches apart on the baking sheet; set aside.

4. In a medium bowl, combine all the remaining ingredients except the sesame seeds and chives. Spoon ¼ of the mixture over each fillet, spreading to cover surface.

5. Broil until fish is cooked through and topping is lightly charred, 6 to 8 minutes.

6. Sprinkle top of cooked fish with sesame seeds and chives. Serve immediately, passing Toasted Sesame Butter on the side.

. . . .

GRILLED FENNEL- STUFFED SNAPPER

Makes 4 servings

Though there are about 250 species of snapper, by far the best known and most popular is the red snapper, so named because of its reddish-pink skin and red eyes. Its mild, sweet flesh is firm-textured and lean. I prefer leaving the tail on for this preparation, but I'm not fond of my food staring back at me so—to paraphrase the Queen in *Alice in Wonderland*—I say "Off with their heads!"

1 **medium fennel bulb**
2 **medium oranges**
   about 3 tablespoons olive or vegetable oil
2 **shallots, chopped**
1 **teaspoon fennel seed, chopped**
   salt and freshly ground pepper
4 **small snapper, dressed (about 1¼ pounds each)**

1. At least one hour before grilling, soak 2 cups wood chips in water to cover. When ready, light a fire in an outdoor grill.

2. While fire is heating, trim a thin slice off the base of the fennel bulb. Remove fennel stems; set aside 4 sprigs of the feathery greens for a garnish. Finely chop fennel bulb and remaining greens (but not stems), keeping chopped bulb and greens separate. Set aside.

3. Use a citrus zester or a grater to remove zest from 1 orange. Squeeze and strain the juice of 1 orange. Set zest and juice aside. Cut 4 thin slices from the second orange. Cut each slice from the outer edge to the center. Twist slice to form an S. Set aside for a garnish.

4. In a large skillet over medium-high heat, heat 2 tablespoons of the oil. Add the shallots, fennel seed, and chopped fennel bulb; sauté 5 minutes. Add orange zest and juice. Cook over medium-high heat, stirring often, until juice has reduced to about 1 tablespoon, about 5 minutes. Remove from heat; stir in chopped fennel greens. Salt and pepper to taste.

5. While fennel is sautéing, rinse the fish and pat dry with paper towels. Brush outside of fish with olive oil; salt and pepper to taste. Spoon fennel mixture into the cavity of each fish, being careful not to overstuff.

6. If using wood chips, sprinkle over heat source. Brush grill lightly with oil.

7. Grill fish either directly on the grill or in an oiled hinged fish basket over a hot fire for about 4 minutes on each side, or until fish turns opaque. Turn fish carefully, so that none of the filling spills out. Serve hot, garnished with reserved fennel greens and twisted orange slices.

✦✦✦✦✦✦✦✦✦✦✦✦✦✦✦ WHEN IS IT DONE? ✦✦✦✦✦✦✦✦✦✦✦✦✦✦✦✦

The most common error when preparing fish is to overcook it. The old guideline "cook until it flakes" has done more to turn people off fish than almost anything else. The very fact that the fish can be flaked signals that it's overdone. Fish is at its best at the point when it turns opaque. A basic guideline when cooking fish is ten minutes per inch of thickness. This timing will vary, depending on the density of the fish, how fatty it is, and whether or not it's been boned. To test, stick the tip of a knife into the flesh at its thickest point and check for opacity. Don't forget that fish will continue to cook by the residual heat—even after it's removed from the heat.

GRILLED TUNA FAJITAS

Makes 4 to 6 servings

Though this recipe calls for grilling, the tuna can also be broiled (two minutes on each side) or sautéed. Swordfish may be substituted for the tuna. Make sure the fish steaks are about the same thickness so they cook evenly.

- ½ cup plus 2 tablespoons vegetable oil
- ⅓ cup fresh lime juice
- ⅓ cup fresh lemon juice
- ¼ cup finely chopped cilantro
- 3 large cloves garlic, minced
- 1½ teaspoons chili powder
- ¾ teaspoon ground cumin
- ½ teaspoon crushed dried red pepper
- 2 medium onions, thinly sliced
- 2 medium green bell peppers, thinly sliced
- 1½ pounds tuna steaks
  salt and pepper

8 **large flour tortillas**
2 **cups grated Monterey Jack (about 8 ounces)**
1½ **cups Avocado Salsa (page 286)**
  sour cream
  additional chopped cilantro

1. In a large shallow bowl, combine ½ cup oil, the lime and lemon juices, cilantro, garlic, chili powder, cumin, and crushed red pepper. Add onions and peppers; toss to coat. Cover and refrigerate 2 hours.

2. Using a slotted spoon, remove the onions and peppers from the marinade; cover and refrigerate vegetables.

3. Cut the tuna steaks horizontally in half (no thinner than ¼ inch). Place the pieces in the marinade, turning to coat. Cover and refrigerate at least 2 hours.

4. At least 1 hour before grilling, soak 2 cups wood chips in water to cover. When ready, light fire in outdoor grill.

5. Remove the tuna from the refrigerator. Strain off marinade; salt and pepper tuna to taste. Just before grilling tuna, sprinkle soaked wood chips over heat source. Brush grill lightly with vegetable oil. Grill tuna over medium-hot coals a scant 1 minute per side. Remove from grill. Let stand until cool enough to handle, then cut into thin strips.

6. Meanwhile, in a large skillet, heat 2 tablespoons oil. Sauté marinated onions and peppers until onions are golden. Remove from heat.

7. Position rack 6 inches from broiling unit. Preheat broiler.

8. Arrange 4 tortillas on each of 2 large baking sheets. Divide tuna strips evenly among the tortillas; top with grilled onions and peppers, then grated cheese.

9. Broil until cheese is bubbly and begins to brown. Fold each tortilla in half. Serve hot, accompanied with Avocado Salsa, sour cream, and chopped cilantro.

· · · · · · · · · · ·

◆◆◆◆◆◆◆◆◆◆◆◆◆ THE MAGIC OF OMEGA-3 OILS ◆◆◆◆◆◆◆◆◆◆◆◆◆

Omega-3 oils are fatty acids found in the flesh of all sea creatures. These unsaturated oils have been found to be particularly beneficial to coronary health as well as to brain growth and development. Among the fish that are particularly good sources of Omega-3 oils are sardines, herring, mackerel, bluefish, tuna, salmon, pilchard, butterfish, and pompano.

High cooking temperatures can destroy almost half the Omega-3 in fish, but microwave cooking doesn't appear to have an adverse effect on it. Canned tuna packed in water is a quick and easy way for many people to get their Omega-3 oils, but it's worth noting that combining it with the fat in mayonnaise offsets any positive effects.

◆◆◆

FLOUNDER BAKED IN GINGERED BASIL CREAM

Makes 6 servings

Flounder is prized for its fine texture; its lean flesh is elegantly offset with this creamy ginger-basil sauce. Sanddab, sole, and turbot can be substituted for flounder. Gingerroot Rice (page 138) is the perfect accompaniment.

6 flounder fillets (6 to 8 ounces each)
   about 1 tablespoon vegetable oil
1½ cups Crème Fraîche (page 301), or heavy whipping cream
3 tablespoons finely chopped basil
1½ teaspoons minced fresh gingerroot
1½ teaspoons minced lemon zest
   salt and freshly ground pepper
6 sprigs basil or lemon slices for garnish

1. Preheat oven to 450°F. Lightly oil a large shallow baking dish.

2. Lightly brush both sides of fillets with oil; arrange in baking dish; set aside.

3. In a small bowl, combine the Crème Fraîche, basil, gingerroot, and lemon zest. Salt and pepper to taste. Pour over fish fillets. Cover tightly with foil. Bake just until fish turns opaque, about 7 minutes.

Microwave Method: Place fillets in a shallow microwave-safe baking dish. Pour sauce over fish. Cover tightly with plastic wrap; pierce center of wrap with a fork. Cook on HIGH for 6 to 6½ minutes, or until fish is almost done, rotating a half turn after 3½ minutes. Let stand, covered, for 1 minute.

4. Garnish fish with basil sprigs or lemon slices; serve immediately.

. . . .

OYSTERS ROCKEFELLER BEIGNETS

. . . .

*Makes 6 main course or
8 to 12 appetizer servings*

Two New Orleans traditions combine in these light, crispy bites—the ethereal beignet and oysters Rockefeller. Though Pernod, a licorice-flavored liqueur, is traditional in oysters Rockefeller, other similar liqueurs such as ouzo or Galliano can be substituted. You can also substitute milk; increase the anise seed then to ¾ teaspoon.

It's very important that as much liquid as possible is squeezed from the spinach before it goes into the batter. I use my hands to wring out the spinach, then wrap it in a double layer of paper towel and squeeze it again.

Serve these savory beignets as a main course accompanied by tossed greens and hot bread spread with fennel butter (See Herb Butter, page 306).

½ cup thawed frozen chopped spinach (10-ounce package)
⅓ cup finely chopped scallions, white and green parts
⅓ cup finely chopped fresh fennel
1½ tablespoons vegetable oil
¾ cup milk
¼ cup Pernod
 8 tablespoons (1 stick) butter, cut into 5 pieces
 1 small clove garlic, minced
½ teaspoon anise seed
½ teaspoon salt
½ teaspoon cayenne
 1 cup all-purpose flour
 4 large eggs, at room temperature
12 large or 18 medium shucked oysters, washed, drained, and chopped
    about 3 quarts vegetable oil

1. Squeeze as much water as possible from spinach. Set aside.

2. In a large skillet over medium-high heat, sauté the scallions and fennel in oil until tender, about 5 minutes. Add the spinach; sauté for 3 minutes.

3. In a medium saucepan, combine the milk, Pernod, butter, garlic, anise seed, salt, and cayenne. Bring to a boil over high heat.

Microwave Method: In a 4-cup glass measuring cup, combine the milk, Pernod, butter, garlic, anise seed, salt, and cayenne. Cook on HIGH for 3 to 3½ minutes, or until mixture comes to a boil.

4. Remove from heat; add the flour all at once, stirring rapidly with a wooden spoon until mixture leaves sides of container and forms a mound in the center. Let stand 5 minutes.

5. Add the eggs, one at a time, beating until each egg is incorporated before adding the next one, or turn the mixture into a food-processor workbowl fitted with the metal blade. Use on/off pulses to process until batter is evenly distributed in bowl, about 5 seconds. Add eggs all at once; process until smooth.

6. Stir in the oysters and sautéed vegetables. (If a food processor was used, return batter to pan or microwave container before adding vegetables and oysters.) Cover and refrigerate for at least 3 hours; can be chilled overnight. For a quick chill, place the batter in the freezer for 45 to 60 minutes.

7. Preheat oven to 350°F. Line a large baking sheet with a double layer of paper towel; set aside.

8. In a deep-fat fryer or heavy pot, heat 3 inches of oil to 375°F. on a deep-fat-frying thermometer.

9. Scoop up a heaping teaspoon of batter; use a second teaspoon to push it off into the hot oil. Fry about 8 beignets at a time, making sure not to overcrowd, until deep golden-brown, about 3 minutes. If beignets don't roll over by themselves, turn them with slotted spoon. The finished puffs should be no more than 1½ inches in diameter; if any larger, they won't get done in the center. Keep the deep-fat-frying thermometer in the pan to make sure oil temperature is maintained. If it drops below 360°F., the batter will absorb too much oil.

10. Use a slotted spoon to remove beignets to the lined baking sheet. Keep finished puffs warm in oven while frying remaining batter. Serve hot. Refrigerate leftover beignets; reheat in preheated 375°F. oven for 5 to 8 minutes.

. . . .

SPICED TOMATO– ORANGE SCALLOPS

Makes 4 to 6 main course or 6 to 8 first course servings

The flavors of tomato and orange intermingle wonderfully in this dish. It has a gorgeous red-gold color that's the perfect visual foil for the pale scallops. For all its complex taste, the sauce is quick and easy to make—and can be made ahead for last-minute finishing. It also goes with such simply broiled or grilled fish as salmon, snapper, and swordfish.

Serve scallops over Cinnamon Rice (page 136), accompanied by tossed greens dressed with Orange–Curry Vinaigrette (page 107).

   2 **shallots, finely chopped**
   2 **tablespoons olive oil**
   2 **tablespoons all-purpose flour**
  ½ **teaspoon ground cinnamon**
  ¼ **teaspoon freshly grated nutmeg**
  ¼ **teaspoon ground cumin**
  ¼ **teaspoon ground cayenne**
  ¾ **cup fresh orange juice**
1¼ **pounds vine-ripened tomatoes, peeled and coarsely**
      chopped, or 1½ cups canned Italian tomatoes, drained
      and chopped
   2 **pounds sea or bay scallops, cleaned, rinsed, and drained**
      about 2 tablespoons shredded orange zest (optional)
      additional freshly grated nutmeg (optional)

1. In a large skillet over medium-high heat, sauté shallots in oil just until they begin to soften. Add the flour, cinnamon, nutmeg, cumin, and cayenne. Cook, stirring often, for 3 minutes.

2. Reduce heat to medium. Stirring constantly, gradually add the orange juice, blending until mixture is combined. Stir in the tomatoes. Cook over medium heat for 5 minutes. If desired, sauce may be covered and set aside at room temperature until ready to finish the dish, up to 3 hours, or refrigerated for up to 3 days. Bring sauce back to a simmer before adding scallops.

3. Add the scallops. Cook, stirring constantly, just until scallops turn white, 2 to 4 minutes. Serve immediately. If desired, garnish with shredded orange zest and a sprinkling of freshly grated nutmeg.

. . . .

SHOW-OFF SHRIMP AND SCALLOPS

Makes 4 servings

I know—Scotch with shellfish does sound like an odd duo. But, oh, what magic on the tastebuds! I haven't the foggiest where this recipe originated—I've been working with a hand-scribbled recipe all these years, liberally revised from the looks of all my changes. Though I try to suggest stand-ins for liquor in my recipes, there simply is no substitution for the Scotch and wine here. I've tried it without, but the dish just doesn't have the same mysteriously husky flavor without the spirits.

1 medium lemon
2 tablespoons butter
1 medium shallot, minced
1 medium clove garlic, minced
½ pound medium shrimp, peeled and cleaned
½ pound bay scallops or sea scallops cut into bite-size pieces
3 cups thinly sliced mushrooms (about ½ pound)

1 **teaspoon fresh minced tarragon or ¼ teaspoon dried tarragon, crumbled**
⅓ **cup Scotch whisky**
½ **cup dry white wine**
1 **cup Crème Fraîche (page 301), or heavy whipping cream**
3 **tablespoons finely chopped parsley**
   salt and freshly ground pepper

1. Finely grate the lemon zest. Squeeze 1½ tablespoons lemon juice. Set aside zest and juice.

2. In a large skillet over medium-high heat, melt the butter. When butter sizzles, add the shallot. Cook until soft, 3 to 5 minutes. Add the garlic; cook for 1 more minute. Add the shrimp and scallops. Sauté, stirring constantly, just until shrimp is almost cooked through, about 1½ minutes. Use a slotted spoon to transfer shrimp and scallops to a plate; set aside.

3. Add the mushrooms, tarragon, Scotch, wine, lemon juice, and lemon zest. Increase heat to high. When bubbles form around edge of pan, continue to cook for 3 minutes.

4. Remove from heat and gradually stir in the Crème Fraîche and 2 tablespoons of the parsley. Cook over medium-low heat until mixture thickens slightly, about 3 minutes.

5. Add shrimp and scallops. Heat just until warmed through. Garnish with remaining parsley. Serve immediately.

· · · · · · · · · · ·

♦ TIP ♦

Never cook with any wine or spirit you wouldn't drink! Cooking—and the process of reducing a sauce —will bring out the worst in an inferior potable.

JAMBALAYA FRITTERS WITH CREAMY CREOLE SAUCE

Makes 6 servings

This light, crispy variation on the Cajun jambalaya theme is complemented with a Creamy Creole Sauce (page 292). Make the sauce the day before to let the flavors mingle and develop. Don't worry if the fritters are misshapen— that's the way they should look.

2 cups Creamy Creole Sauce
2 tablespoons plus about 2 cups vegetable oil
1 small onion, finely chopped
½ cup finely chopped green bell pepper
1 large clove garlic, minced
½ teaspoon chili powder
2 teaspoons finely chopped fresh thyme or ½ teaspoon dried thyme
¼ teaspoon ground cloves
¼ teaspoon ground allspice
⅛ teaspoon cayenne
½ cup finely chopped smoked ham
1½ cups cooked, finely chopped shrimp, oysters, or crab, or a combination
1½ cups cooked long-grain white rice
2 tablespoons minced parsley
1½ cups all-purpose flour
2 teaspoons baking powder
4 large eggs
½ cup milk
 salt and freshly ground pepper

1. Make Creamy Creole Sauce the day before, if possible. If refrigerated, reheat before serving.

2. In a large saucepan, heat 2 tablespoons oil over medium-high heat. Sauté the onion and pepper until onion is almost soft, about 4 minutes. Add the garlic, chili powder, thyme, cloves, allspice, and cayenne; sauté for 2 more minutes. Remove from heat. Stir in ham, seafood, rice, and parsley; set aside.

3. In a medium bowl, combine the flour and baking powder; set aside. In a second medium bowl, combine 2 whole eggs and 2 egg yolks; place remaining 2 egg whites in the small bowl of an electric mixer and set aside. Lightly beat eggs and egg yolks. Blend milk into egg mixture. Gradually add to flour, stirring constantly until smooth. Add batter to rice mixture and stir to combine. Set aside.

4. In a heavy deep skillet, pour oil to a depth of ½ inch. Over medium-high heat, bring oil to 375°F. Keep deep-fat-frying thermometer in pan to make sure oil temperature is maintained. If it drops below 360°F., the batter will absorb too much oil.

5. Preheat oven to 400°F.

6. When oil has almost reached 375°F., beat egg whites with ¼ teaspoon salt until stiff but not dry. Stir ⅓ of the whites into the rice mixture. Gently fold in remaining whites. Salt and pepper to taste.

7. Drop tablespoons of batter into the hot oil, pushing the spoon down into the center of each fritter to make a hole. That will help the fritters cook evenly. Don't use more than a tablespoon of batter at a time or the fritters won't get done in the center. Fry fritters until deep golden brown on both sides, about 1 to 1½ minutes total.

8. Use a slotted spoon to transfer fritters to paper towels to blot off excess oil. Transfer to a baking sheet and keep warm in oven. Be sure to bring oil back to 375°F. before frying each batch of fritters. Serve hot with Creamy Creole Sauce.

. . . .

Meat and Poultry Pleasers

. . . .

There's no doubt about it, meat consumption today is taking a backseat to other entree choices such as fish, vegetables, and grains. However, there's one inescapable truth about meat: When you crave a thick steak or a big, juicy hamburger, absolutely nothing else will do. Fortunately for meat lovers, state-of-the-art breeding methods mean that leaner pork and beef are now readily available.

As for the venerable bird, Brillat-Savarin once said, "Poultry is for the cook what canvas is for the painter." That's just one of the reasons why Americans so love poultry. It's also versatile, nutrition- and calorie-wise, and very economical. But poultry wasn't always as reasonably priced as it is today. Before World War II, only chicken farmers and the affluent could manage even the proverbial Sunday chicken. Aren't we lucky that times have changed?

MEATS

Because each meat has its own idiosyncrasies regarding the way it's cooked, I've included tips and guidelines with each recipe. In the following pages, I discuss each type of meat, including selection and storage guidelines.

✦✦✦✦✦ Beef

Beef comes from cattle of all ages. *Baby beef* is the lean, tender but not too flavorful meat of a seven- to ten-month-old calf.

Government inspectors check all meat sold in the United States for wholesomeness. Beyond that, meat packers can request and pay for their meat to be graded by the U.S. Department of Agriculture (USDA). The grading is based on three factors: conformation (the proportion of meat to bone), finish (proportion of fat to lean), and overall quality. Beginning with the best quality, the eight USDA grades for beef are: *prime*, *choice*, *good*, *standard*, *commercial*, *utility*, *cutter*, and *canner*. The meat's grade is stamped within a purple shield (a harmless vegetable dye is used for the ink) at regular intervals on the outside of each carcass.

Prime beef has the most marbling (the lacy network of fat that weaves throughout the meat) and is generally aged the longest. Because it's the best, it's also the most expensive. Prime is rarely seen at the retail level except at specialty meat markets. Most of it is reserved for fine restaurants. The less expensive *choice* beef is what we find in supermarkets and other retail markets. It has less marbling but is still quite tender and flavorful. Beef graded *good,* though less juicy and flavorful, is still acceptable for many preparations. It can often be found under a market's own label. The lower grades are generally used only for sausages and in cured and canned meats.

Ideally, beef is at its best—both in flavor and texture—at 18 to 24 months. The meat at that age is an even rosy red color. If the animal is over two and a half years old, it is usually classified as *well-matured beef* and though more full-flavored, the meat begins to toughen and darken to a purplish red. Slow, moist-heat cooking, however, will make it palatable.

Beef Selection: Choose bright red meat that is well marbled. The flesh should be firm, the fat a rich, creamy color. Leaner cuts won't have the even marbling, but they are lower in calories. Choose tender cuts such as porterhouse, sirloin, and tenderloin for quick-cooking methods like grilling and pan-frying. The larger cuts, like standing rib roasts and top round, are suitable for roasting. Less tender cuts like chuck and rump require moist-heat cooking such as stewing and braising.

Beef Storage: If the meat will be cooked within six hours of purchase, it may be left in its plastic-wrapped package. Otherwise, remove the packaging and store either unwrapped in the refrigerator's meat compartment or loosely wrapped with wax paper in the coldest part of the refrigerator, for up to two days for ground beef and stew meat, three days for other cuts. Let the air circulate and keep the meat's surface somewhat dry, to inhibit bacterial growth. Cooked meat should be wrapped airtight and stored in the refrigerator. Ground beef can be wrapped airtight and frozen for up to three months, solid cuts up to six months.

◆◆◆◆◆ Pork ◆◆

Today's pork is leaner (a third fewer calories) and higher in protein than that consumed just ten years ago. Most pork in the marketplace today is cured—like bacon and ham—while the remainder is termed fresh. Though pork generally refers to swine under a year old, most pork today is slaughtered at between six and nine months, producing leaner, more tender meat.

Slaughterhouses can (but usually don't) request and pay for their pork to be graded by the USDA. Beginning with the best, the grades are: 1, 2, 3, 4, and utility, based on the proportion of fat to lean. Whether graded or not, all pork sold for intrastate commerce is subject to state or federal inspection for wholesomeness, insuring that the slaughter and processing of the animal was done under sanitary conditions. Pork shipped interstate must be federally inspected.

Thanks to improved feeding techniques, trichinosis in fresh pork is now also rarely an issue. Normal precautions should still be taken, however, such as washing anything (hands, knives, cutting boards, etc.) that comes in contact with raw pork and never tasting uncooked pork. Cooking it to an internal temperature of about 140°F. will kill any trichinae. To allow a safety margin for thermometer inaccuracy, most experts recommend an internal temperature of from 150° to 170°F., which will still produce juicy, tender results. The 175° to 185°F. temperature recommended in many cookbooks produces overcooked meat.

Pork Selection: Though available year-round, fresh pork is more plentiful—and the prices lower—from October to February. Look for pork that is pale pink with a small amount of marbling and white (not yellow) fat. The darker pink the flesh, the older the animal.

Pork Storage: Fresh pork that will be used within six hours of purchase may be left in its store packaging. Otherwise, remove the packaging and wrap loosely with wax paper. Store in the coldest part of the refrigerator for up to two days. Wrapped airtight, pork can be frozen from three to six months, with the larger cuts having longer storage capabilities than ground meat or chops.

♦♦♦♦♦ Lamb ♦♦♦

The term lamb refers to a sheep less than one year old, known for its tender meat. Baby lamb and spring lamb are both milk fed. *Baby lamb* is customarily slaughtered at between six and eight weeks old. *Spring lamb* is usually three to five months old and must be killed between March and the first full week in October. *Regular lamb* is slaughtered under a year of age. Lamb between one and two years is referred to as *yearling lamb*, over two years it's called *mutton.* The latter two categories have a strong flavor and less tender flesh.

There are five USDA grades for lamb based on the proportion of fat to lean. Beginning with the best, they are: *prime, choice, good, utility,* and *cull.* Most retail cuts are graded choice.

Lamb Selection: When purchasing lamb, let color be the guide. In general, the darker the color, the older the animal. Baby lamb will be pale pink, regular lamb pinkish red. No matter the grade or type, always choose lamb that is nicely marbled.

Lamb Storage:　Refrigerate ground lamb and small lamb cuts loosely wrapped for up to three days. Roasts can be stored up to five days. Ground lamb can be freezer-wrapped and frozen up to three months; solid cuts up to six months.

✦✦✦✦✦ **Veal**　✦✦✦

The delicate flavor and fine texture of veal have appealed to diners for centuries. Veal is often cooked by moist-heat methods to compensate for its lack of natural fat. It's easy to overcook and dry out, so careful attention must be paid during preparation.

Though there are no precise age standards for veal, the term is generally used to describe a young calf from one to three months old. *Milk-fed veal* comes from calves up to twelve weeks old who have not been weaned from their mother's milk. Their delicately textured flesh is firm and creamy white with a pale grayish-pink tinge. *Formula-fed veal* can come from calves up to about four months old, fed a special diet of milk solids, fats, various nutrients, and water. The meat from formula-fed veal is not as rich or delicate as milk-fed veal because butterfat is missing from the diet. The term *Bob veal* applies to calves younger than one month old. Their pale shell pink flesh is quite bland and the texture soft. In all true veal, the animals haven't been allowed to eat grains or grasses, either of which would cause the flesh to darken.

Calves between six and twelve months old are called *baby beef.* The meat is coarser and stronger-flavored than veal, and from pink to light red in color. True veal is usually plentiful in the spring and late winter. At other times of the year, calves over three months old are often sold as veal. The USDA grades veal in six different categories. From the highest to lowest grade they are: prime, choice, good, standard, utility, and cull. The last three grades are rarely sold in retail outlets.

Veal Selection:　When choosing veal, let color be your guide. The flesh should be creamy white—barely tinged with grayish pink—and the fat white. Meat that's pink turning red means the so-called veal is older than it should be. Veal's texture should be firm, finely grained, and smooth.

Veal Storage:　Veal can be stored in the same manner as beef.

POULTRY

The term poultry refers to any domesticated bird used as food. Today there are many varieties of poultry, the most popular in the United States being chicken, turkey, and duck.

✦✦✦✦✦ Chicken ✦✦

The chicken can be prepared in almost any way imaginable, including baking, broiling, barbecuing, roasting, frying, poaching, braising, and stewing. Boning chicken will shorten any cooking time but will also slightly diminish the flavor. White meat and chicken without skin have fewer calories.

Chicken falls into several classifications. The *broiler-fryer* can weigh up to three and a half pounds and is usually around two and a half months old. These chickens, as the name implies, are best when broiled or fried. The larger and more flavorful roasters have a higher fat content and therefore are perfect for roasting and rotisserie cooking. They usually range from three and a half to five pounds and can be up to eight months old. *Stewing chickens* (also called hens, boiling fowl, and fowl) usually range in age from ten to eighteen months and can weigh from three to six pounds. Their age makes them more flavorful but also less tender, so they're best cooked with moist heat, as in stewing or braising. A *capon* is a rooster that is castrated when quite young (usually before eight weeks), fed a fattening diet, and brought to market before it's ten months old. Ranging from four to ten pounds, capons are full-breasted with tender, juicy, flavorful meat that is particularly suited to roasting.

Free-range chickens are the elite of the poultry world in that—instead of the mass-produced birds' allotted one square foot of space—each range chicken has double that area indoors plus the freedom to roam outdoors. They're fed a special vegetarian diet free (according to most range chicken breeders) of antibiotics, animal byproducts, hormones, and growth enhancers. The special diet and freedom of movement gives the free-range chicken a fuller, more chickeny flavor, and firmer flesh. But the amenities make them much more expensive than mass-produced chickens. Free-range chickens average 4½ pounds and are usually around ten to twelve weeks old.

The government grades chicken quality with USDA classifications A, B, and C. The highest grade is A, and is generally what is found in markets. Grade B chickens are less meaty and well finished. Grade C is usually reserved for scrawny turkeys. The grade stamp can be found within a shield on the package wrapping, or sometimes on a tag attached to the bird's wing.

Salmonella bacteria are present on most poultry (though only about four percent of salmonella poisonings are chicken-related). To avoid any chance of bacterial contamination, it's important to handle raw chicken with care. The first rule is never to eat chicken in its raw state. After cutting or working with raw chicken, thoroughly wash utensils, cutting tools, cutting board, and your hands. Cooking chicken to 170°F. (the juices will be yellow and the meat opaque) will kill any lurking bacteria. Don't let any raw juices come in contact with cooked chicken.

Chicken Selection: Chicken is available in markets throughout the year either fresh or frozen, whole or cut into parts. The neck and giblets (liver, gizzard, and heart) are either packaged separately and placed in a whole bird's body cavity or sold individually. Choose a meaty, full-breasted chicken with plump, short legs. The skin—which can range from cream-colored to yellow, depending on the breed and the chicken's diet—should be smooth and soft. Avoid chickens with an off odor or with skin that's bruised or torn. Smoked chicken is also available, as is canned boned chicken.

Chicken Storage: Store chicken in the coldest part of the refrigerator. If packaged tightly in plastic, loosen the packaging or remove it and loosely rewrap chicken in wax paper. Remove and store separately any giblets from the body cavity. Refrigerate raw chicken up to two days, cooked chicken up to three days. For maximum flavor, freeze raw chicken no longer than two months; cooked chicken up to a month.

✦✦✦✦✦ Turkey ✦✦✦

Most U.S. turkeys raised today are from the White Holland variety, which has been bred to produce a maximum of white meat. Although male (tom) turkeys can reach 70 pounds, those over 20 pounds are becoming less and less available. The female (hen) turkey usually weighs from 8 to 16 pounds. Gaining in popularity is a smaller version of both sexes (sometimes called a fryer-roaster), which weighs in at between five and eight pounds. The trend toward these compact turkeys is the result of both smaller families and the desire of turkey producers to make turkey everyday rather than exclusively holiday fare.

Turkeys are available fresh and frozen year-round. They're sold both whole and as separate parts—such as breasts or drumsticks. Some whole turkeys have a built-in plastic thermometer that pops up when the turkey is done. Self-basting turkeys have been injected with butter or vegetable oil. Smoked turkey—whole or parts—is also available, as is canned boned turkey. Turkey is very similar to chicken in many regards, including USDA grading.

Turkey Selection and Storage: The guidelines for turkey selection and storage are the same as for chicken.

✦✦✦✦✦ Duck ✦✦✦

Today's domestic ducks are all descendants of one of two species—the mallard or the muscovy duck. Comprising about half the domesticated ducks in the United States are the white-feathered, full-breasted Long Island ducks, known for their dark, succulent flesh. These direct descendants of the Peking duck (a variety of mallard) are all the progeny of three ducks and a drake brought from Peking on a clipper ship in 1873. Besides Long Island, the locations most widely known for the cultivation of superior ducks are Peking, China, and Rouen, France.

Since most ducks are marketed while still quite young and tender, the words duck and duckling are interchangeable. Broilers and fryers are less than eight weeks old; roasters no more than sixteen weeks old. Domestic ducks can weigh between three and six pounds; the older ducks are generally larger.

USDA grades ducks A, B, and C. The highest grade is A; this is generally what is found in markets. Grade B ducks are less meaty and well finished; grade C ducks are generally used for commercial purposes. The grade stamp can be found within a shield on the package wrapping or sometimes on a tag attached to the bird's wing.

Duck Selection: Fresh duck is available from late spring through early winter, but generally only in regions where ducks are raised. Almost 90 percent of ducks that reach market are frozen and are available year-round. When buying fresh duck, choose one with a broad, fairly plump breast; the skin should be elastic, not saggy. For frozen birds, make sure the packaging is tight and unbroken.

Duck Storage: Fresh duck can be stored, loosely covered, in the coldest section of the refrigerator for two to three days. Remove and store separately any giblets from the body cavity. Frozen duck should be thawed in the refrigerator. It can take from 24 to 36 hours, depending on the size of the bird. Do not refreeze duck once it's been thawed.

. . . . :

PLUM DELICIOUS STEAK

Makes 4 servings

It's your choice whether to sauté or grill these steaks. The Plum Barbecue Sauce is also delicious with pork tenderloin (see variation following the recipe).

1⅓ cups Plum Barbecue Sauce (page 293)
4 New York strip or sirloin tip beef steaks, trimmed of excess fat (about 8 ounces each, 1 inch thick)
2 tablespoons vegetable or olive oil

1. Mix the ingredients of Plum Barbecue Sauce in a shallow pan or bowl large enough to hold the steaks (do not cook sauce). Place the steaks in the marinade, turning

to coat both sides. Cover and marinate at least 6 or up to 12 hours. Turn several times while marinating.

2. About an hour before cooking steaks, transfer them from the marinade to a plate. Cover with plastic wrap and set out at room temperature for 30 to 60 minutes. Refrigerate them if you do not intend to cook them within an hour; bring to room temperature for 30 to 60 minutes before cooking.

3. Pour marinade into a small saucepan and cook as directed on page 293. Cover and set over very low heat to keep warm until ready to serve steaks.

4. Heat the oil in a large skillet over medium-high heat. Sauté the steaks for about 3 minutes per side for medium-rare.

To grill steaks: At least 1 hour before grilling, soak 2 cups wood chips in water to cover. When ready, light a fire in the grill. Just before grilling, sprinkle wood chips over heat source. Grill 4 minutes on each side for medium-rare.

5. Serve steaks hot, topped with Plum Barbecue Sauce.

♦ **VARIATION: Plum Delicious Pork Tenderloin:**
 1. Prepare the Plum Barbecue Sauce; set aside.
 2. Preheat oven to 400°F.
 3. Rub 1½ pounds of pork tenderloin (two ¾-pound pieces) all over with salt, pepper, and olive oil. Do not marinate. In a large ovenproof skillet or sauté pan over high heat, sear tenderloin until browned on all sides.
 4. Transfer to oven. Roast, uncovered, until internal temperature reaches 150° to 160°F., on a meat thermometer (according to personal preference), about 15 to 20 minutes.

To grill meat: Omit pan-browning. Grill tenderloin over a medium-hot fire for 15 to 20 minutes, turning every 4 to 5 minutes to ensure even cooking. Check internal temperature (160°F.) with a meat thermometer.

 5. Let tenderloin stand 5 minutes before carving into ½-inch slices. Serve with Plum Barbecue Sauce.

. . . .

GRILLED BOURBON-GLAZED FLANK STEAK

Makes 4 servings

Flank steak is at its best when cooked rare to medium-rare; overcooking it will toughen it to the point of inedibility. Try the marinade with grilled pork chops; it's wonderful!

½ cup bourbon
½ cup V 8 juice or spicy tomato juice
¼ cup dark corn syrup
3 tablespoons vegetable oil
2 medium cloves garlic, crushed
1 teaspoon coarsely ground pepper
½ teaspoon salt
¼ teaspoon ground allspice
1½ pounds flank steak, about ½-inch thick

1. In a shallow glass or ceramic pan large enough to hold the steak, combine all the ingredients except the steak; stir well.

2. Use a sharp knife to trim all visible fat from the steak. If necessary, pound steak so that it's ½ inch thick all over. Score steak in a diamond pattern on each side, cutting about ⅛ inch deep.

3. Dip the meat in marinade to coat one side. Flip steak onto uncoated side in marinade. Cover tightly with plastic wrap; refrigerate overnight or at least 8 hours. Best if marinated 24 hours. Once or twice during marinating time, either turn steak over or spoon marinade over surface. Or place the meat and marinade in a large plastic bag, seal tightly, and refrigerate, turning several times.

4. At least 1 hour before grilling steak, soak 2 cups wood chips in water to cover; remove meat from refrigerator. When ready, light a fire in the grill.

5. Drain the marinade into a small saucepan. Bring to a boil; cook 3 minutes. Cover and keep warm over low heat.

6. Just before grilling, sprinkle soaked wood chips over heat source. Brush grid of grill lightly with vegetable oil. Grill steak over high heat for 3 to 5 minutes per side. Carve immediately, cutting diagonally across the grain into thin slices. Drizzle marinade over steak slices; pass remaining sauce on side.

'Tis not the meat, but 'tis the appetite
Makes eating a delight.
—SIR JOHN SUCKLING

MEAT AND MASHED POTATOES LOAF

....

Makes 8 to 10 servings

Meatloaf—in all its homey splendor—is back in a big way. The real surprise here is a layer of cheddared mashed potatoes sandwiched inside. The potatoes should be much stiffer than you'd normally make them because the meat juices will soften them during the baking process.

This recipe purposely makes a huge meatloaf—how else would there be leftovers for sandwiches? I like it even better cold than hot because the potatoes firm up and the loaf is easier to slice. Try it spread with Cranapple–Apricot Chutney (page 295) sandwiched between slices of sourdough wheat bread.

1   pound baking potatoes (2 to 3 medium), peeled and cut into eighths
¼ to ½ cup heavy whipping cream or half-and-half
½   teaspoon freshly grated nutmeg
½   teaspoon cayenne
2   cups grated sharp cheddar (8 ounces)
    salt and freshly ground pepper to taste
1   cup packed dried apple pieces (about 2½ ounces)
2   large cloves garlic
1   medium onion, cut into sixths
2   pounds ground chuck
½   cup chopped walnuts
1   cup fresh or unthawed frozen corn kernels (2 medium ears fresh)
2   large eggs
1   teaspoon ground allspice
1¼ teaspoons salt
⅓   cup additional finely chopped walnuts for garnish (optional)

1. Place potatoes in a medium saucepan and cover with cold water. Bring to a boil. Reduce heat to medium-low; cover and cook until potatoes are tender, 20 to 30 minutes. Drain potatoes.

2. Return potatoes to pan if using an immersion blender. If using electric mixer, transfer potatoes to mixer bowl. Add ¼ cup of the cream and ⅛ teaspoon *each* nutmeg and cayenne. Beat potatoes until smooth, adding

more cream, if necessary. Potatoes should be quite stiff. Fold in 1 cup of the grated cheese; salt and pepper to taste. Set aside.

3. In a food processor fitted with the metal blade, finely chop the apples; turn out into a large bowl and set aside.

4. Leave metal blade in food processor. With the machine running, drop garlic into the workbowl; process until garlic is chopped and clinging to sides of bowl. Scrape down sides of food processor bowl. Add onion; process until finely chopped. Turn out into bowl with apples.

5. Add the ground chuck, walnuts, corn, eggs, allspice, salt, the remaining cup of grated cheese, and remaining ⅜ teaspoon each nutmeg and cayenne. Mix well to thoroughly combine (your hands will do the best job).

6. Position oven shelf in the center of the oven. Preheat oven to 400°F. Lightly oil a 15 x 10-inch jelly-roll pan.

7. Form half of the meatloaf mixture into an oval 8½ inches long by 6 inches wide in the middle of the pan. Flatten the top of the oval. Form an even layer of the mashed potatoes on top of the meat, to within 1 inch of edges. Cover with remaining meatloaf mixture, sealing edges of meatloaf to enclose potatoes as much as possible. The size of the final oval will be about 10 x 7 inches.

8. If desired, sprinkle top of meatloaf with ⅓ cup walnuts; lightly press into surface. Bake meatloaf for 60 minutes. Drain off fat; let stand 15 to 20 minutes before serving.

. . . .

PORK TENDERLOIN WITH PEANUT- SERRANO SAUCE

Makes 4 servings

The peanut-serrano sauce tastes fresh because it's only warmed, not cooked. It can be served barely warm or at room temperature and makes an unusual but very good sauce for pasta.

The heat of chili peppers can vary. Taste a tiny piece of one to see if you want to increase or decrease the amount. Removing the seeds and membrane will lower the heat. Wear rubber gloves or wash your hands with soap after working with chilies. The pepper-flower garnish is easy and quick and adds sparkle to the dish.

5 serrano or jalapeño chili peppers for garnish (optional)
1 cup dry-roasted peanuts
1 medium clove garlic
2 serrano or 3 jalapeño chili peppers, seeds removed and coarsely chopped
1 cup firmly packed cilantro leaves
1 cup plus 3 tablespoons olive oil
   salt and freshly ground pepper
1½ pounds pork tenderloin, cut into 8 slices
   about 5 sprigs cilantro for garnish (optional)

1. To make a pepper-flower garnish, if desired, cut each pepper 5 to 6 times from the tip to within ⅜ inch of the stem end. Carefully cut out seeds and membrane. Place peppers in a medium bowl filled with ice water; refrigerate for about 4 hours, or until peppers open like a flower. Drain well and blot dry with paper towels before using.

2. In a large ungreased skillet over medium-high heat, cook the peanuts, stirring often, until lightly browned. Remove from heat; set aside.

3. Meanwhile, fit the food processor with the metal blade. With the machine running, drop the garlic through the feed tube; process until garlic is chopped and clinging to sides of bowl. Without stopping machine, add the chili peppers; process until clinging to sides of bowl.

4. Scrape garlic and peppers down from sides of bowl. Add cilantro and peanuts. Process until mixture is finely ground, stopping and scraping down sides of bowl as necessary.

5. Turn peanut mixture into a small saucepan. Add 1 cup olive oil; stir to combine. Salt and pepper to taste; set aside.

6. Flatten each tenderloin slice until about 1 inch thick. Heat the remaining 3 tablespoons oil in a large skillet over medium-high heat. Add the tenderloin slices; cook 3 to 4 minutes on each side. While the second side of meat is cooking, heat the peanut-serrano sauce over medium-low heat just until warm. Overcooking will cause sauce to thicken too much.

7. Arrange the cooked tenderloin slices on a warm serving plate. Stir sauce; drizzle over meat. If desired, garnish with pepper flowers and/or sprigs of cilantro. Serve remaining sauce on the side.

· · · · · · · · · · ·

SON-OF-A-GUN STEW

Serve this hearty stew with Russian black bread and icy mugs of beer, and you have the comfort formula for a cold winter's eve.

Makes 8 servings

1½ cups dark beer (12-ounce can)
6 ancho chili peppers
¼ cup vegetable oil
3 medium onions, chopped
1 pound chorizo
1½ pounds boneless chuck steak, cut into 1½-inch cubes
1½ pounds boneless pork shoulder or butt, excess fat removed, cut into 1½-inch cubes
2 teaspoons ground cumin
2 teaspoons dried oregano, crumbled
¼ cup all-purpose flour
1½ pounds yams or sweet potatoes, peeled and cut into 1-inch cubes
8 medium cloves garlic, minced
3 cups canned ready-cut tomatoes or chopped canned Italian-style tomatoes, with juice (2 14½-ounce cans)
3 cups canned yellow hominy, drained (2 15-ounce cans)
⅓ cup red wine vinegar
1 tablespoon Worcestershire sauce
½ to 1½ cups homemade beef stock or canned beef broth salt and cayenne
½ cup chopped scallions, green part only
⅓ cup chopped cilantro
1½ cups shredded Monterey Jack (optional)

1. Pour the beer into a small saucepan; add the ancho chili peppers. Bring to a boil. Remove from heat; cover and let stand 15 minutes to soften chilies.

2. In a Dutch oven or other large pot with a lid, heat the oil over high heat. Add the onions; sauté for 3 minutes. Squeeze chorizo from casings into pan. Add beef and pork. Sauté meats, stirring often and crumbling sausage as it cooks, until they begin to brown, 10 to 15 minutes.

3. Sprinkle cumin, oregano, and flour over meat. Sauté, stirring constantly, for 3 minutes.

4. Meanwhile, remove chili peppers from beer. Cut in half; remove stems, seeds, and membranes. (Wash your hands with soap after working with chilies to avoid irritation.) Place the chilies, ⅓ cup of the beer, and the garlic in a blender jar or a food-processor workbowl fitted with the metal blade. Process until chilies are pureed.

5. Slowly stir the chili puree, then the remaining beer into meat mixture. Add the sweet potatoes, tomatoes and their juice, hominy, vinegar, Worcestershire, and ½ cup of the beef stock. Stir well. Bring to a boil. Reduce heat to low; cover and cook for 1 hour, adding additional beef broth, if desired, for a thinner stew.

6. Defat stew, if necessary. Season to taste with salt and cayenne. Garnish with scallions and cilantro. Pass cheese, if desired, to stir into stew.

♦**NOTE:** The ancho chili pepper is the dried form of the *poblano*. It's from three to five inches long and has a dark reddish-brown color. The flavor of the ancho ranges from mildly spicy to hot. It can be found in Latin markets as well as many supermarkets.

. . . .

BRAZILIAN STUFFED PORK LOIN

Makes 8 servings

A black bean and rice stuffing with orange, chili powder, and cinnamon perfumes a pork loin with flavors that epitomize Brazilian cuisine. Make sure your butcher cuts the pocket all the way through the loin so you can stuff it from both ends. The sauce can be made and the loin stuffed the day before, then refrigerated for last-minute preparation. In that case, remove the loin from the refrigerator at least an hour before roasting. Leftovers make great sandwiches on French bread.

about 5 tablespoons olive oil
1 large red onion, finely chopped
2 green bell peppers, seeded and finely chopped
3 large cloves garlic, minced
3½ cups canned ready-cut tomatoes or chopped canned Italian-style tomatoes, with juice (2 14½ ounce cans)
1¼ cup golden raisins
½ cup fresh orange juice
2 teaspoons finely grated orange zest
2 tablespoons plus 1 teaspoon chili powder
1 teaspoon ground cinnamon
about 1½ teaspoons salt
1½ cups cooked long-grain white rice (½ cup raw rice)
1 cup cooked black turtle beans (about ⅓ cup uncooked)
4 regular slices bacon, cooked until crisp and finely crumbled
1 boneless pork loin, with a pocket cut lengthwise all the way through the center (4 to 4½ pounds)

1. In a large skillet over medium-high heat, heat 3 tablespoons of the oil until hot. Add the onion; cook 5 minutes. Add the green peppers; cook an additional 3 minutes. Stir in 2 cloves minced garlic and cook 2 more minutes.

2. Add the tomatoes and their juice, the raisins, orange juice, orange zest, 2 tablespoons of the chili powder, ½ teaspoon of the cinnamon, and 1 teaspoon of the salt. Bring to a boil. Reduce heat to medium-low and cook, uncovered, until sauce thickens, 15 to 20 minutes. Stir occasionally during that time. When sauce is done, remove from heat and cover.

3. Position the oven rack in the middle of the oven. Preheat oven to 350°F.

4. In a medium bowl, combine the rice, beans, bacon, and ⅔ cup of the sauce. Set aside.

5. If necessary, use a long knife with a thin blade to increase the width of the pocket; it should come to within ½ inch of the sides. Use a long-handled wooden spoon to stuff the pocket with the rice-bean mixture, working from both ends. Pack pocket full of stuffing. Use metal skewers to secure both ends.

6. In a small bowl, combine 1 tablespoon olive oil and remaining 1 clove minced garlic, 1 teaspoon chili powder, ½ teaspoon cinnamon, and ½ teaspoon salt. Blend well to form a paste. Rub all over the surface of pork loin. Place the pork loin in a shallow roasting pan.

7. Roast, uncovered, for 45 minutes, lightly brushing the surface with remaining oil once or twice. Remove pork from oven and spoon about ½ cup sauce over top. Continue to roast another 45 minutes, or until pork reaches an internal temperature of 160°F. on a meat thermometer. (When testing temperature, be sure probe is inserted in meat, not in the filling.)

8. Remove roast from oven and let stand 15 minutes before carving. Reheat remaining sauce and serve alongside the roast.

◆ TIP ◆

Allowing roasts and other large cuts of meat to rest for 15 minutes after they're cooked sets the juices and makes the meat easier to carve.

· · · · · · · · · · ·

POSOLE
POT PIE

Makes 4 to 6 servings

Posole (pronounced poh-soн-leh, and also spelled *pozole*) is a Mexican hominy-and-pork soup that originated in Jalisco. It's always been one of my favorites, which led to its recreation in the guise of a pot pie crowned with a crisp cornmeal crust. This dish veers away from the classic in that the meat is grilled instead of simmered, chicken broth is used in lieu of pork broth, and both chorizo and chayote are used. (I've given alternative methods of preparing the meat in case you can't grill it.) The meat can be prepared the day before and added to the pot-pie filling just before baking.

Chayote (chy-oн-tay), a food of the Aztecs and Mayas, is a gourdlike fruit about the size and shape of a large pear. Its crisp flesh is similar to that of pattypan squash (which can be substituted). In this recipe, the chayote is cooked just until crisp-tender; it adds a nice contrast to the other ingredients. In some parts of the United States, chayote is known as mirliton, and in France it's called *christophène*. See page 63 for information on chorizo.

½ pound chorizo
1 boneless pork loin, pork shoulder end, or pork butt (1½ pounds)
about ½ cup olive oil
1 Cornmeal Crust (recipe follows)
1 small onion, finely chopped
1 large chayote, seeded and cut into ⅜-inch dice (about ½ pound)
2 medium cloves garlic, minced
1 jalapeno chili pepper, seeded and minced
½ teaspoon dried oregano
½ teaspoon ground cumin
⅔ cup all-purpose flour
3 cups homemade chicken stock or canned chicken broth
1 cup finely chopped unpeeled tomatillos, husks removed (about 6 ounces)
3 cups canned hominy, well drained (2 15-ounce cans)
2 to 3 tablespoons finely chopped cilantro
1 egg white mixed with 1 teaspoon water for glaze

1. At least 1 hour before grilling meat, soak 2 cups wood chips in water to cover. When ready, light a fire in the grill. Use indirect method of grilling. Just before grilling, sprinkle chips over the heat source.

2. Use a fork to pierce each sausage in several places. Cut pork loin or butt in half crosswise; brush with olive oil. Place sausages and pork in center of grill over drip pan. Cover and grill 10 minutes. Turn sausages and grill an additional 5 minutes; transfer to a plate. Continue to grill pork 5 more minutes. Turn and grill 10 to 15 minutes, or until meat reaches an internal temperature of between 155° and 170°F. Remove to plate; cool to room temperature. Cut cooled chorizo into ⅜-inch dice; shred pork, discarding excess fat.

Alternate Method: In a medium skillet, sauté chorizo over medium heat, crumbling the sausage as it cooks. Drain off fat; set crumbled sausage aside. Place pork in a large pot and cover with water. Bring to a boil. Reduce heat and simmer for 40 minutes. Remove meat from broth; set aside.

3. Prepare Cornmeal Crust; refrigerate for 30 minutes. On a lightly floured surface, roll dough out in the shape of your dish but 2 inches larger. Form a raised edge by folding ½ inch under on all sides of crust. Refrigerate until ready to use.

4. Preheat oven to 375°F. Position an oven rack in center of oven. Lightly oil a shallow 3-quart casserole.

5. In a large skillet heat about ⅓ cup oil over medium-high heat. Add the onion and chayote; sauté just until onion softens. Add the garlic, jalapeño, oregano, cumin, and flour; sauté for 2 minutes. Reduce heat to medium. Gradually add the chicken stock, whisking constantly, and cook until mixture is thickened. Stir in the tomatillos, hominy, cilantro, pork, and chorizo. Cook 5 minutes. (If pork was simmered instead of grilled, the pork broth, fat removed, may be substituted for chicken broth.)

6. Turn mixture into prepared pan. Position rolled-out crust on top of filling. Use the tines of a fork to press raised edge of dough against sides of dish to seal in filling.

Cut 3 to 4 slits, ½ inch long, in the center of the dough. Brush surface with egg-white glaze.

7. Bake 30 minutes, or until crust is golden brown. Serve hot.

CORNMEAL CRUST:

  1 **cup all-purpose flour**
  ½ **cup fine yellow cornmeal**
  1 **tablespoon brown sugar**
  ½ **teaspoon salt**
  8 **tablespoons (1 stick) cold butter, cut into 8 pieces**
  1 **to 3 tablespoons ice water**

1. In a medium bowl, combine the flour, cornmeal, brown sugar, and salt. Use a pastry cutter or 2 knives to cut in butter until mixture resembles coarse crumbs. Add 1 tablespoon of the ice water; stir only until the dough begins to hold together. Add more water only if necessary.

Food-Processor Method: Place the flour, cornmeal, brown sugar, and salt in the food processor workbowl fitted with the metal blade; process 1 second. Add butter; process in quick on/off pulses until mixture resembles coarse crumbs. Add 1 tablespoon of the ice water; process with quick on/off pulses only until the dough begins to hold together. Add more water only if necessary.

2. Form dough into a disc, ½-inch thick. Wrap in plastic wrap and refrigerate for 30 minutes. Dough may be made in advance and refrigerated for up to a week. If dough has been chilled for over 30 minutes, remove from refrigerator 30 minutes before rolling out.

. . . .

ITALIAN SAUSAGE SPOONBREAD

Makes 4 servings

Unlike the usual puddinglike spoonbread, this lighter version is a cross between a soufflé and a pudding. Cooking the spoonbread in the microwave rather than the oven produces a slightly moister spoonbread. It also deflates a bit more than the baked version.

You can either fry the sausage or use the microwave oven. To microcook the sausage, place it in a shallow, 2-quart casserole and cook on HIGH for about 5 minutes, rotating dish halfway through. Finely crumble the sausage after it cools.

1   cup buttermilk
4   large eggs, separated, at room temperature
2   tablespoons vegetable oil
½   teaspoon salt
½   teaspoon sugar
⅛   to ¼ teaspoon cayenne
½   cup yellow cornmeal
1   teaspoon baking soda
½   pound sweet Italian sausage, cooked and finely crumbled
1   cup grated cheddar (4 ounces)
¼   teaspoon cream of tartar

1. Preheat oven to 350°F. Lightly oil a shallow, 2-quart baking dish.

2. In a medium bowl or 2-cup measure, combine the buttermilk and egg yolks.

3. In a large saucepan over high heat, bring 1 cup water, the oil, salt, sugar, and cayenne to a boil. Whisking rapidly, gradually add the cornmeal. Cook, stirring constantly, about 1 minute, or until thick. Remove from heat; gradually whisk in buttermilk mixture. Return pan to medium-high heat, stirring constantly until mixture becomes very thick and begins to pull away from side of pan. Remove from heat; stir in baking soda. Blend in sausage and cheese.

4. Beat the egg whites with cream of tartar until stiff but not dry. Gently fold whites, one-third at a time, into sausage mixture. Turn into prepared baking dish.

5. Bake 30 to 35 minutes, or until top is golden brown

♦ TIP ♦

Cooking should be enjoyable—an adventure, not a trauma. Never point out kitchen mishaps when they can be handled with style and flair. If your corn soufflé flops, call it corn pudding and act as if that's how it's supposed to look. It will still be delicious, and no one will know the difference!

and a metal skewer inserted in the center comes out almost clean.

Microwave Method: Lightly oil a shallow 2-quart baking dish. In a medium bowl or 4-cup measure, combine the buttermilk and egg yolks; set aside. In a 2-quart glass measure or deep microwavesafe bowl, combine 1 cup water, the oil, salt, sugar, cayenne, and cornmeal. Microwave on HIGH for 2 minutes. Stir well; cook on HIGH for another 30 seconds. Whisk in buttermilk mixture. Cook on HIGH for 4 minutes, whisking once halfway through. Stir in baking soda; blend in sausage and cheese. Beat egg whites with cream of tartar until stiff but not dry. Gently fold whites, one-third at a time, into sausage mixture. Turn into prepared baking dish. Cook on MEDIUM (50% power) about 8 minutes, or until spoonbread just begins to pull away from side of dish. Rotate dish after 4 minutes of cooking. If a browned top is desired, place spoonbread under broiler for 2 to 3 minutes.

. . . .

GRILLED LAMB STEAKS WITH FENNEL AND HAZELNUTS

Makes 4 servings

Many people shy away from fennel, thinking it has a strong anise or licorice taste. In reality, the flavor of fennel is much more delicate than either of those aromatics and, when cooked, becomes even lighter and more elusive. I always make a double batch of the fennel-hazelnut garnish; leftovers are great tossed with greens the next day.

This dish takes all of ten minutes to prepare if you chop and sauté the fennel mixture while the lamb is grilling. I use the food processor to chop the hazelnuts and fennel (in that order, so the bowl doesn't have to be washed). The fennel can also be shredded, but in that case, you have to reduce the cooking time by several minutes. It should be tender-crisp.

One-inch-thick lamb chops can be substituted for the lamb steaks; the timing will be the same. Take care not to overcook the lamb. The flavor and texture are far superior when the meat is at least slightly pink in the center.

4   8-ounce lamb steaks, 1 inch thick
    salt and freshly ground pepper
1   small fennel bulb (about 8 ounces)
2   tablespoons olive oil
1   large clove garlic, minced
1½ tablespoons grated lemon zest
4   tablespoons lemon juice
½   cup dry white wine
½   cup toasted hazelnuts

1. At least 1 hour before grilling the lamb, soak 2 cups wood chips in water to cover. When ready, light a fire in the grill. Just before grilling, sprinkle the chips over the heat source.

2. Trim all but ¼ inch fat from lamb. Slash the remaining fat at 1-inch intervals. Lightly salt and pepper both sides of the lamb steaks. Grill 3 to 4 minutes per side for rare; 4 to 5 for medium-rare.

3. Meanwhile, trim a thin slice off the base of the fennel bulb. Remove fennel stems; set aside 4 strips of the greens for garnish. Chop fennel (including remaining greens) into large pea-size pieces.

4. Heat the oil in a large skillet over high heat. Sauté the fennel, stirring often, for 2 minutes. Add the garlic, lemon zest, lemon juice, and wine. Cook over high heat, stirring often, for 3 to 5 minutes, or until the liquid is reduced by half. Add the hazelnuts; stir to combine.

5. Spoon fennel-hazelnut mixture over grilled lamb steaks; garnish with reserved fennel greens. Serve immediately.

. . . .

CITRUS-CREAM VEAL SCALOPPINE

Makes 4 servings

Fragrant with ginger and citrus, this dish is company special. The candied zest garnish can be made the day before.

1 small orange
1 small lemon
½ cup sugar
  about ⅓ cup orange juice
½ cup plus 2 tablespoons all-purpose flour
½ teaspoon ground ginger
½ teaspoon ground allspice
  salt and freshly ground pepper
1½ pounds veal scallops, pounded thin
4 tablespoons olive or vegetable oil
1 medium shallot, minced
1 medium clove garlic, minced
2 tablespoons minced crystallized ginger
½ cup homemade chicken stock or canned chicken broth
¾ cup half-and-half

♦ TIP ♦

Save time by having your butcher bone meat and chicken, cut meat for stew, or cut pockets in roasts and thick chops.

1. Use a citrus zester, vegetable peeler, or small sharp knife to remove the zest from the orange and lemon. If not using a zester, cut zest into thin slivers.

2. In a small saucepan, combine the zest, sugar, and ½ cup water. Bring to a boil. Cover and reduce heat; simmer, without stirring, for 15 minutes. Strain off syrup. Place candied zest on a wax paper–lined plate; set aside.

3. Meanwhile, preheat oven to 250°F.

4. Juice the orange and lemon. Add enough additional orange juice to equal ¾ cup; set aside.

5. Combine ½ cup flour, ground ginger, and allspice on a large plate. Add salt and pepper to taste. Dredge veal scallops in flour, shaking off excess.

6. In a large skillet, heat 2 tablespoons of the oil over medium-high heat. Add the scallops, in batches if necessary, and sauté for 1 minute on each side. The veal won't brown, so don't overcook. Transfer scallops to a serving platter; place in warm oven.

7. Add the remaining oil to skillet. Sauté the shallot over medium-high heat for 2 minutes. Stir in the garlic, ginger, and remaining 2 tablespoons flour. Continue to cook, stirring often, about 3 minutes.

8. Use a whisk to gradually blend in the juices, chicken broth, and half-and-half. Reduce heat to medium-low. Cook, stirring constantly, until sauce is thickened. Salt and pepper to taste.

9. Pour sauce over veal scallops; garnish with candied citrus zest. Serve immediately.

. . . .

CHUNKY PEANUT CHICKEN

Makes 4 servings

Leslie Bloom, a talented food writer and close friend, created this recipe for her book *Chicken on the Run*. I've made only a couple of changes in Leslie's original (we food writers can never leave a recipe alone!). I've substituted scallions for white onions—a personal idiosyncrasy, as I like the added color—used cayenne pepper in lieu of Tabasco, and garnished the dish with dry-roasted peanuts. Either Gingerroot Rice (page 138) or Toasted Orzo Pilaf (page 123) would make a suitable accompaniment.

8 teaspoons Worcestershire sauce
4 tablespoons vegetable oil
4 skinless and boneless chicken breast halves, cut into 1-inch pieces
1 cup homemade chicken stock or canned chicken broth
2 tablespoons minced fresh tarragon or 2 teaspoons dried tarragon, crumbled
3 medium cloves garlic, minced
1 teaspoon ground cumin
¼ cup chunky peanut butter
2 tablespoons tomato paste
¼ teaspoon cayenne
½ cup chopped scallions, green parts only
  salt and freshly ground pepper
⅓ cup dry-roasted peanuts (optional)

A gourmet challenged me to
   eat
A tiny bit of rattlesnake
   meat,
Remarking, "Don't look
   horror-stricken,
You'll find it tastes a lot like
   chicken."
It did.
Now chicken I cannot eat.
Because it tastes like
   rattlesnake meat.
     —"Experiment
       Degustatory,"
       OGDEN NASH

1. In a large bowl, combine 4 teaspoons of the Worcestershire sauce and 1 tablespoon of the oil. Add chicken; toss to coat. In a 1-cup measure, combine the chicken stock with tarragon. Let chicken and broth stand 30 minutes at room temperature.

2. In a wok or large skillet, heat the remaining 3 tablespoons oil over medium-high heat. Sauté chicken 1 minute, or until lightly browned. Reduce heat to medium; add garlic and cumin. Sauté, stirring constantly, 2 minutes. Use a slotted spoon to transfer chicken to a large plate.

3. In same pan over medium heat, combine the peanut butter, tomato paste, cayenne, and remaining 4 teaspoons Worcestershire sauce. Whisking constantly, gradually add chicken stock. Cook, stirring often, until sauce thickens slightly. If the sauce gets too thick, thin with a little chicken stock.

4. Return chicken to pan; add scallions. Heat just until chicken is warmed through. Salt and pepper to taste. Serve immediately, garnished with dry-roasted peanuts, if desired.

. . . .

CHICKEN-APPLE SAUSAGE

Makes about 1¾ pounds

Why pay a premium for specialty sausages like this when it's so easy to make your own? Ground chicken and turkey are readily available in supermarkets now, and the food processor makes combining the ingredients a snap. You can also make the sausage by hand, mixing the ingredients together in a large bowl with your hands. Compared to most commercial sausages, this one is very low in fat. If you're frying the sausage, it may be necessary to oil the pan. The low fat content will also cause the sausage to become dry if overcooked.

This fragrant sausage has countless uses—cook and toss it with pasta or rice, such as Cinnamon Rice (page 136), form it into patties and cook it for a breakfast meat, make burgers with it, add it to meatloaf, use it in stuffings, as for the Baked Apples With Walnut–Sausage Stuffing (page 36). The list goes on and on.

1 **cup packed dried apple pieces or slices (about 3½ ounces)**
2 **medium cloves garlic**
2 **slices whole wheat bread, torn into quarters**
¼ **cup coarsely chopped scallions or chives, green parts only**
1 **cup chopped toasted walnuts (optional)**
1 **pound ground chicken or turkey**
1 **teaspoon sweet Hungarian paprika**
1 **teaspoon salt**
¾ **teaspoon freshly ground pepper**
½ **teaspoon ground allspice**
½ **teaspoon ground coriander**
¼ **teaspoon freshly grated ground nutmeg**

1. In a food processor fitted with the metal blade, finely chop the apples. Turn out onto a piece of wax paper or into a small bowl; set aside.

2. Leave the metal blade in food processor and start machine. Drop in the garlic through feed tube; process until garlic is chopped and clinging to sides of bowl. Scrape down sides of food processor bowl.

3. Add the bread; process until ground medium-fine.

4. Add scallions and walnuts. Use quick on/off pulses to chop until nuts are medium-fine.

5. Distribute ground chicken evenly in food processor bowl; add remaining ingredients. Use on/off pulses to process just until mixture is combined. Stop machine and use a rubber spatula to push meat down into blade. Add apples; process until sausage reaches a medium-fine texture.

6. Turn sausage out onto a large sheet of plastic wrap. To test sausage for seasoning, pinch off a small amount (about 2 teaspoons) and sauté in a lightly oiled skillet until done. Or place the same amount of sausage on a small plate and microwave on HIGH for about 1 minute. Taste sausage and adjust seasonings as desired.

7. Form sausage into a mound or into a log 8½ inches long by 2½ inches in diameter; wrap well with plastic wrap. Refrigerate at least 3 hours to let flavors mingle and develop. May be refrigerated for up to 3 days, frozen up to 6 months.

8. Form the sausage into patties or cut the sausage log into ½-inch slices and cook over medium heat until nicely browned, about 3 minutes per side. Or use the sausage in stuffing, meatloaf, and the like.

. . . .

CRISPY DUCK WITH ONION- ORANGE MARMALADE

Makes 4 to 6 servings

For deliciously crisp skin, first let the bird dry overnight in the refrigerator, then roast the duck in a very hot oven. The whole unpeeled garlic cloves roasted in the cavity subtly flavor the duck. The cooked garlic is extremely mild and buttery-soft. It's wonderful spread on dark bread. For a change of pace, accompany the duck with Cranapple–Apricot Chutney (page 295) instead of the Onion–Orange Marmalade.

1½ cups Onion–Orange Marmalade (page 296)
  2 ducks, thawed if frozen (about 5 pounds each)
     salt and freshly ground pepper
  2 large oranges, cut into sixths
 20 medium to large cloves garlic, unpeeled

1. The day before, make the Onion–Orange Marmalade and begin preparing the duck. Remove the giblets from the cavities; pull excess fat out of cavity and neck areas. Rinse ducks; thoroughly blot all moisture with a paper towel. Use a fork to prick the skin (but not the flesh) all over at ½-inch intervals. Rub ducks generously inside and out with salt and pepper. Place them, breast side down, on a rack set over a baking pan. Refrigerate, uncovered, overnight to let skin dry out.

2. The next day, remove ducks from refrigerator 2 hours before roasting. Stuff each duck cavity with 6 orange wedges and 10 garlic cloves.

3. Preheat oven to 500°F.

4. Place the ducks, breast side down, on a baking rack in a shallow roasting pan. The pan and rack should be large enough to hold the ducks without crowding. Roast for 30 minutes; draining fat from pan as necessary. Reduce oven heat to 425°F.

5. Turn ducks breast side up. Continue roasting, draining fat from pan as necessary, for 30 to 40 minutes, or until done to your liking. To test, pierce a thigh; if juices run slightly pink, meat will be on the pink side; clear juices mean meat is well done. The skin should be deep golden brown.

6. Remove from oven. Let duck stand for 15 minutes. Use kitchen shears or a sharp knife to cut ducks in quarters. First cut along breast bone, then along both sides of back bone, removing as much bone as is easily possible.

7. Serve duck immediately, garnished with garlic cloves, and accompanied with Onion–Orange Marmalade, slightly warmed or at room-temperature.

. . . .

TROPICAL TURKEY CUTLETS

Makes 4 servings

Pounded very thin, turkey cutlets have been known to masquerade as veal scaloppine. Fortunately, they can be easily found in most supermarkets.

The coconut-orange sauce works as well with chicken or pork, so if you prefer, substitute chicken breasts pounded ¼ inch thick, or slices of pork tenderloin. Marinating the meat overnight gives it a delicate, velvety texture. Serve the cutlets with Gingerroot Rice (page 138).

1¼ **cups Coconut–Citrus Sauce (page 294)**
1½ **pounds turkey cutlets, pounded until ¼-inch-thick**
    salt and white pepper
 2 **tablespoons vegetable oil**
 4 **sprigs mint (optional)**

1. Make the Coconut–Citrus Sauce through Step 1. Add turkey cutlets, turning to coat both sides with marinade. Cover and refrigerate overnight, turning cutlets once or twice during that time.

2. At least 30 minutes before cooking the cutlets, transfer them from the marinade to a plate. Salt and pepper cutlets to taste. Cover with plastic wrap and set aside. If cutlets won't be cooked within the hour, refrigerate until 30 minutes before cooking.

3. Turn marinade into a small saucepan and cook as directed on page 294. Cover and set over very low heat to keep warm until ready to serve.

4. Heat the oil in a large skillet over medium-high heat. Sauté turkey cutlets for 2 minutes each side.

5. Reduce heat to medium-low. Stir sauce and pour over cutlets. Cook for 2 more minutes. Serve hot, garnished with mint sprigs, if desired.

. . . .

♦ ♦ ♦

♦ ♦ ♦

Bread Basket

· ·

There are few things that can bring on a smile more quickly than homemade bread. Then there's the sense of accomplishment and satisfaction you get from baking it. Yet for some reason, the difficulty and mystery of breadmaking has long been exaggerated. And there's been a "yeast mystique" that has intimidated would-be bakers for decades. Non-sense! There's absolute-ly nothing mysterious about making bread. To-day, with bread-mixing and kneading aids like food processors and heavy-duty mixers with dough hooks, even a beginner can bake bread successfully the first time out. Breadmaking should be an adventure. Once you know a few basics you'll be baking with ease and flair.

> "A loaf of bread,"
> the Walrus said,
> "Is what we chiefly need."
> —Lewis Carroll

Bread can be divided into four basic categories: yeast breads, which are leavened with yeast and require kneading to stretch the flour's gluten; batter breads, yeast-leavened breads that are beaten instead of kneaded; quick breads, which use baking powder, baking soda, or eggs for leaveners, and require gentle mixing; and unleavened breads like matzo, which are quite flat because they contain no leavening at all.

In the following pages, you'll find a small battery of breads, including yeast breads that are kneaded (Wild Rice Breadsticks and Toasted Sunflower-seed Bread) and one that is beaten (Amaretto–Almond Batter Bread). And there are breads that use baking powder and/or baking soda as leaveners (Quick Chinese Scallion Bread and Piña Colada Bread). Check the breakfast chapter too, where you'll find scones and muffins.

✦✦✦✦✦✦✦✦✦✦✦✦✦✦ ABOUT FLOUR AND LEAVENERS ✦✦✦✦✦✦✦✦✦✦✦✦✦✦

FLOUR   The most commonly used flour in breadmaking is wheat flour, which contains a protein called gluten. When dough is kneaded or beaten, gluten forms the elastic network that holds in the carbon dioxide gas created by the leavener. The gas bubbles cause the gluten to stretch and expand, forming the bread's framework. The less gluten (protein) in the flour, the weaker the elasticity. And without a strong elastic network, the gas bubbles will escape into the air rather than leavening the bread.

Look on the flour package label under Nutritional Information to select a high protein (good gluten-developing) flour. Flours with 12 to 14 grams of protein per cup are best for yeast breads; those with 9 to 11 grams are better for quick breads and pie crusts. Characteristics of flour vary greatly, making it impossible to give a precise amount of flour for each recipe. Flour will absorb less liquid on hot, humid days than in dry weather because it will have already absorbed some of the moisture from the atmosphere. Your best guideline is to add only enough flour to keep the dough from being too sticky to work with. A dough that is slightly tacky to the touch will yield a much nicer loaf than one that is too dry.

Sifting flour isn't necessary. The recipes in this book use the "stir and spoon" method. Simply stir the flour to loosen it, then spoon it into your measuring cup and level it off with the flat edge of a knife. Don't shake or pack the flour down into the cup before leveling. (Measure other dry ingredients using the same method.)

All-purpose flour is made from a blend of high-gluten hard wheat and low-gluten soft wheat. It's a fine-textured flour milled from the inner part of the wheat kernel, and contains neither the germ (the sprouting section) or the bran (the outer husk). By law in the United States, all flours not containing wheat germ must have niacin, riboflavin, and thiamin added. Most all-purpose and bread flours are labeled *enriched*, indicating that these nutrients have been added.

All-purpose flour comes bleached and unbleached. They can be used interchangeably. I prefer unbleached flour, which is what I used in testing the following recipes. Having avoided the hazards of cosmetic chemical bleaching, it is sturdier and has retained more of its nutrients. All-purpose flour is suitable for most kinds of baking including quick and yeast breads, biscuits, muffins, cookies, and cakes.

Bread flour is a specially formulated flour high in protein, usually about 14 grams per cup. It is about 99.8 percent unbleached flour, with a small amount of malted barley flour (to improve yeast activity), and ascorbic acid (vitamin C) or potassium bromate to make the gluten more elastic and improve the dough's gas retention. I use bread flour in all yeast breads because it gives a hearty loaf with a firm crumb. It's readily available in supermarkets.

Whole wheat flour is a light brown flour that tastes of the grain. It has a higher fat content than all-purpose or bread flour because it's milled from the whole kernel and contains the germ.

Store flour in air-tight containers. All-purpose and bread flours can be kept at room temperature for up to six months. Temperatures above 75°F. invite bugs and mold. Flours containing part of the grain's germ (such as whole wheat flour) turn rancid quickly because of the oil in the germ. Purchase such flours in small quantities and store, tightly wrapped, in the refrigerator for six months, in the freezer for a year. Always bring chilled flours to room temperature before using.

LEAVENING AGENTS   Simply stated, leavening agents are what make bread rise. The most commonly used leaveners are yeast in yeast breads, baking powder and baking soda in quick breads, biscuits, and muffins.

Yeast is a living organism that thrives on the natural sugar in starch. When combined with moisture and warmth, yeast begins to ferment, converting the flour's starchy nutrients into alcohol and carbon dioxide gas. Gas bubbles trapped in the gluten's elastic meshwork makes the dough rise. Oven heat kills the yeast and evaporates the alcohol. This causes the gas to expand in a final burst of energy called oven-spring, and raises the dough.

Active dry yeast is packaged in ¼-ounce envelopes or jars or sold in bulk. Compressed fresh yeast is packaged in .06-ounce cakes. One package of dry yeast is equal to one scant tablespoon of dry yeast or one cake of compressed yeast. Active dry yeast was used for the recipes in this book because of its higher reliability and ease in storing.

Active dry yeast comes in two forms, regular and quick-rising. They may be used interchangeably. Bread made with quick-rising yeast rises in a third to half the time of that made with regular dry yeast. All active dry yeast has been dehydrated. Its cells are alive but dormant. The cells become active again when mixed with a warm liquid. Dry yeast should be stored in a cool, dry place, but can be kept in the refrigerator or freezer. Properly stored, it's reliable when used by the expiration date stamped on the envelope. Bulk dry yeast, available at health-food stores, is a bit risky because you don't know how old it is or under what conditions it has been stored. The best way to check any yeast to be sure it's still alive is to proof it (see The Proof's in the Yeast, page 249).

Compressed fresh yeast is moist and extremely perishable. It must be refrigerated and used within one or two weeks, or by the date indicated on the package. It can be frozen; defrost it at room temperature and use it immediately. Always proof compressed yeast to be sure it's still alive.

The temperature of the liquid in which yeast is dissolved is very important. Too much heat will kill it, too little will slow its growth. Dissolve dry yeast in liquids at 105° to 115°F.; compressed yeast at 95°F. Don't try to guess the temperature of the liquid. Until you're an experienced baker, use an accurate thermometer for accurate readings of warm liquids.

Baking soda or *bicarbonate of soda,* when combined with a liquid acid ingredient, such as buttermilk, yogurt, or molasses, produces carbon dioxide. Because baking soda reacts immediately when moistened, it should always be mixed with the dry ingredients in the recipe before any liquid is added. The immediate rising speed of baking soda (and baking powder) makes it important to have the oven preheated and pans greased before combining ingredients.

Baking powder contains baking soda, an acid such as cream of tartar, and a moisture-absorber such as cornstarch. When mixed with a liquid, baking powder releases carbon dioxide gas. Single-acting baking powder immediately releases gas into the batter. The more commonly used double-acting baking powder releases gas twice—when a liquid is mixed with it and when the batter is exposed to oven heat. Double-acting baking powder is used in the bread recipes in this book.

Baking powder is perishable and should be kept in a cool, dry place. Always check the date on the bottom of the can when you buy it. If you're unsure of your baking powder's power, combine a teaspoon of it with one-third cup hot water. If it bubbles enthusiastically, use it.

Too much baking powder or soda gives bread a crumbly, dry texture and bitter undertaste. It can also make the batter overrise, causing the bread to fall. Too little baking powder or soda produces a bread with a heavy, gummy texture.

✦✦

PIÑA COLADA BREAD

Makes 1 loaf

Like its namesake, the popular Caribbean drink, this bread is heady with rum and flavored with pineapple and coconut. Piña Colada (PEEN-yuh koh-LAH-duh) Bread is wonderful for gift giving, great when spread with softened cream cheese for a sandwich, and makes delicious breakfast toast.

1½ **cups shredded coconut**
2¾ **cups all-purpose flour**
  2 **teaspoons baking powder**
  ½ **teaspoon baking soda**
  1 **teaspoon salt**
  ¾ **cup sugar**
  1 **large egg, at room temperature**
  1 **cup unsweetened pineapple juice, at room temperature**
  ½ **cup light rum or ½ cup milk plus ½ teaspoon rum extract**
  1 **teaspoon pure vanilla extract**
  2 **tablespoons vegetable oil**

1. Preheat oven to 350°F. Generously grease a 9 x 5-inch loaf pan; set aside.

2. Spread the coconut in a single layer on an ungreased baking sheet. Toast in preheated oven, stirring often, until golden brown, 4 to 6 minutes. Set aside to cool.

3. In a large bowl, stir together the flour, baking powder, baking soda, salt, sugar, and all but ¼ cup of the toasted coconut; set aside.

4. In a medium bowl, lightly beat the egg. Stir in the pineapple juice, rum, vanilla, and oil. Gradually add to flour mixture, stirring just until the dry ingredients are moistened.

5. Turn into prepared pan; smooth top. Sprinkle with the remaining ¼ cup coconut.

6. Bake 55 to 60 minutes, or until a wooden pick inserted in the center comes out clean. Let stand in pan 10 minutes before turning out onto a rack to cool. Wrap in plastic wrap and store at room temperature for up to 5 days. Or wrap and refrigerate up to 10 days; double-wrap and freeze up to 6 months.

♦ TIP ♦

A good serrated bread knife is worth its weight in gold! Don't ruin your freshly baked bread with the wrong knife.

BAKED HUSHPUPPIES

Makes 12 hushpuppies

Legend has it that this bread was so named because Southern cooks, to keep hungry dogs from begging for food while dinner was being prepared, used to toss scraps of fried batter to the pets with the admonition, "Hush, puppy!" This quick, delicious baked version is not only lower in calories than the fried bread, but also a lot less messy to prepare. Though baked in muffin cups, these hushpuppies won't look like regular muffins. Instead, their tops will be crinkled and funny looking—the result of dropping the batter into hot oil.

    6 tablespoons vegetable oil
1¾ cups fine yellow cornmeal
    ¾ cup all-purpose flour
    1 tablespoon baking powder
    1 teaspoon baking soda
    1 teaspoon salt
    ⅛ to ¼ teaspoon cayenne
1½ cups buttermilk, at room temperature
    1 large egg, at room temperature
    ½ cup chopped scallions, both white and green parts

♦ TIP ♦

Buttermilk powder is a boon for those who don't have a carton of buttermilk sitting in the fridge. For each cup of fresh buttermilk needed, mix ¼ cup buttermilk powder with the dry ingredients and add 1 cup water to the liquids. Keep the opened can of powder in the refrigerator.

1. Preheat oven to 425°F. for 15 minutes. Place 1 teaspoon oil in each of 12 standard muffin cups, 1 or 1½ inches deep. Turn pan to coat sides of cups; place in oven to preheat 10 minutes.

2. In a medium bowl, combine the cornmeal, flour, baking powder, baking soda, salt, and cayenne; set aside. In a 2-cup measure, combine the buttermilk, egg, and remaining 2 tablespoons oil. Mix to combine. Add to flour mixture along with the scallions, stirring only until dry ingredients are moistened.

3. Remove muffin pan from oven. Working quickly, use a ¼-cup measure to fill each of the 1-inch-deep muffin tins, a ⅓-cup measure for the 1½-inch-deep muffin tins. Batter will bubble in the hot oil.

4. Return filled muffin tin to oven. Bake 12 to 15 minutes, or until golden brown. Serve hot.

♦ **VARIATION: Hushpuppy Crisps:** Preheat oven to 350°F. Use a serrated knife to cut leftover hushpuppies into ¼-

inch slices; arrange on a large ungreased baking sheet. Bake 5 minutes, or until browned on the bottom. Remove from oven; turn over slices. Bake an additional 5 minutes, or until nicely browned. Cool 5 minutes before serving with soups or salads or as a snack.

. . . .

QUICK CHINESE SCALLION BREAD

Makes 6 servings

This bread can be whipped up quickly to accompany salads, like Spicy Asian Noodle Salad (page 99), or soups, like Smoked Tomato Soup (page 83), or for a satisfying snack. If you have two large skillets, fry two breads at a time so they are as hot as possible.

2 cups all-purpose flour
1 teaspoon baking powder
½ teaspoon baking soda
½ teaspoon salt
½ teaspoon freshly ground pepper
½ cup plus 1 tablespoon cool water
1 tablespoon Oriental sesame oil
  about ½ cup vegetable oil
½ to ⅔ cup chopped scallions, equal amounts white and green parts

1. In a food processor fitted with the plastic or metal blade, combine the flour, baking powder, baking soda, salt, and pepper. Process 10 seconds to combine. With machine running, add water, processing just until mixture forms crumbs, 20 to 30 seconds. Add the sesame oil, 1 tablespoon of the vegetable oil, and the scallions. Turn on machine; process until dough forms a ball, then process an additional 30 seconds.

Manual Method: In a medium bowl, combine the flour, baking powder, baking soda, salt, and pepper. Stir in the water, then the sesame oil, 1 tablespoon of the vegetable oil, and the scallions. Turn out onto a lightly floured surface. Knead dough until smooth and resilient, about 3 minutes.

2. Form dough into a ball and wrap in plastic wrap. Set aside to rest for 15 minutes.

3. Place dough on a lightly floured surface and divide into 3 equal pieces. Roll each piece into a 9-inch circle. Cover with a dish towel.

4. Preheat oven to 375°F. Pour 1½ tablespoons vegetable oil into a large skillet. (If possible, work with 2 skillets at a time.) Heat over medium-high heat until very hot.

5. Fry scallion rounds until nicely browned on the bottom, 1½ to 2 minutes. Use a fork to flip bread; fry other side until browned. (Second side won't brown as evenly as the first.) Blot fried bread on paper towels; sprinkle with salt, if desired. Place on a baking sheet and keep warm in oven until remaining dough is fried. Cut each round into 6 wedges. Serve warm.

- - - - - - - - - - -

> ◆ TIP ◆
>
> Cooling quick breads in the pan for 10 minutes before transferring to a rack to cool allows bread to set.

POLENTA-CHEESE CRACKERS

Makes 2 dozen (2½-inch-square) crackers

These crispy cornmeal crackers make delicious accompaniments to soups and salads, and they're also great simply eaten as snacks.

1⅓ **cups polenta (coarse cornmeal), or regular yellow cornmeal**
½ **teaspoon salt**
⅛ **teaspoon cayenne**
1⅓ **cups boiling water**
2½ **tablespoons olive oil or vegetable oil**
1 **cup grated fontina, cheddar, Swiss, or Monterey Jack**
1 **tablespoon minced fresh herbs, such as oregano, basil, or chervil, or 1 teaspoon dried herbs, crumbled**

1. Position oven rack in middle of oven. Preheat oven to 325°F. Lightly oil a 15- x 10-inch jelly-roll pan; set aside.

♦ TIP ♦

A ruler, an oven thermometer, and a thermometer for reading liquid temperatures should be in every baker's *batterie de cuisine*.

2. In a medium bowl, stir together the polenta, salt, and cayenne. Gradually add the boiling water and oil, stirring until well combined. Stir in the cheese and herbs.

3. Use your fingers, a rubber spatula, or the back of a spoon to press the mixture evenly over the bottom of the prepared pan. Use a pointed knife to score polenta into 24 squares, cutting 6 strips crosswise, 4 lengthwise.

4. Bake 60 to 70 minutes, or until deep golden brown. The edges will brown faster than the center. Remove from oven and immediately cut through scoring to separate crackers. Cool to room temperature before serving.

. . . .

TASSO– CHEESE CORNBREAD STICKS

Makes 24 (3¾ x 1¼-inch) pieces

Tasso, a Louisiana specialty, is a smoked, spicy-hot cured pork. Because of its highly seasoned flavor, tasso is generally used as a flavoring. If you don't like its assertive spiciness, substitute the Cajun sausage, andouille (pronounced an-DOO-ee or ahn-DWEE), or your favorite smoked sausage.

The traditional way to serve this cornbread is hot from the oven. My preference, however, is to make it the day before and then recrisp the individual sticks. Serve with soups, stews, or salads or just eat them as a snack.

    4 tablespoons vegetable oil
 1½ cups fine yellow cornmeal
  ½ cup all-purpose flour
    2 teaspoons baking powder
  ½ teaspoon baking soda
  ½ teaspoon ground cumin
  ½ teaspoon salt
    2 large eggs, at room temperature
    1 cup milk, at room temperature
    1 medium clove garlic, minced
    1 teaspoon Tabasco or other hot sauce
 1¼ cups grated cheddar (about 5 ounces)
  ¼ pound tasso, andouille, or other smoked sausage, minced and fried until crisp

1. Pour 1 tablespoon of the oil onto the bottom of a 15 x 10-inch jelly-roll pan; spread over bottom and sides. Place pan in oven; preheat oven to 400°F.

2. In a large bowl, stir together the cornmeal, flour, baking powder, baking soda, cumin, and salt; set aside.

3. In a medium bowl or 2-cup glass measure, lightly beat the eggs. Stir in the milk, garlic, Tabasco, and remaining 3 tablespoons oil. Add milk mixture, 1 cup of the cheese, and all but ¼ cup of the tasso into flour mixture, stirring just until dry ingredients are moistened.

4. Remove pan from oven. Pour in batter, spreading evenly. Sprinkle top with reserved tasso.

5. Bake 10 minutes. Remove from oven; sprinkle with remaining ¼ cup cheese. Return to oven and bake 5 more minutes, or until deep golden brown.

6. Remove from oven; let stand in pan 5 minutes. Use a tomato knife or other serrated knife to cut cornbread into 24 fingers (each about 3¾ x 1¼ inches), cutting 8 strips lengthwise and 4 strips crosswise. Serve warm. For crispy corn sticks, let the cornbread cool completely in pan on a rack. Cut as directed.

7. May be covered and refrigerated for up to 2 days. To recrisp, arrange cornbread sticks, 1 inch apart, on 2 large baking sheets. Bake in a preheated 425°F. oven for 5 to 10 minutes, or until crisp and lightly browned.

♦ TIP ♦

Using up leftover savory breads and cornbreads in stuffings is an easy and delicious way to enhance their flavor.

GREASING PANS

In this book the term "grease a pan" refers to coating the container with a thin film of shortening, unsalted butter or margarine, or vegetable oil (regular or spray). Too much fat can create overbrowning; salted fats can cause baked goods to stick to the pan. If you don't want to use your fingers to grease a pan, a crumpled piece of paper towel will do just as well. "Grease and flour" means sprinkling a greased pan with a small amount of flour, then tapping and rotating the container until the entire surface is coated with flour. Invert the pan over the sink and shake it gently to remove excess flour.

BLUE CHEESE BAGUETTES

Makes 3 baguettes

For a real treat, split these baguettes lengthwise, spread with Blue Cheese Butter (page 245), and pop under the broiler for a few minutes. Or cut the bread into thin rounds, toast, and spread with pâté for an appetizer. Or layer thin slices of tomato on halved baguettes, sprinkle with crumbled blue cheese, and broil until the cheese melts.

1 package active dry yeast or quick-rising yeast (1 scant tablespoon)
1 teaspoon sugar
¾ cup warm water (110°F.)
3 tablespoons unsalted butter, melted
1 teaspoon salt
¼ teaspoon white pepper
3 to 3½ cups bread flour or all-purpose flour
1 cup crumbled Roquefort or other blue cheese (4 ounces)
1 egg white mixed with 2 teaspoons water for glaze

1. In a 1-cup measure, dissolve yeast and sugar in warm water. Let proof until foamy, about 5 minutes. Pour mixture into a food-processor workbowl fitted with the plastic blade or the large bowl of an electric mixer.

2. *Food Processor Method:* Add the butter, salt, pepper, and 3 cups of the flour. Process until mixture holds together, about 1 minute. Scrape down sides of bowl; add cheese. Process 1 more minute. Dough should be elastic and soft, but not sticky. If necessary, add a small amount of additional flour. Process 30 seconds, or until flour is incorporated. Turn dough out onto a lightly floured work surface; knead about 1 minute, or until smooth and elastic.

Electric Mixer or Manual Method: Add the butter, salt, pepper, and 1 to 1½ cups of the flour. Beat at medium speed for 2 minutes or beat 200 vigorous strokes by hand. Change to dough hook(s) or turn dough out onto a lightly floured surface. Add cheese and enough of the remaining flour to make a soft dough. Knead dough 4 to 6 minutes, or until smooth and elastic, adding only enough flour to prevent sticking.

3. Form dough into ball; place in a lightly oiled medium

♦ TIP ♦

Baking breads at lower temperatures results in crusts that are thicker and chewier; higher temperatures yield thinner, crisper crusts.

bowl. Cover bowl with a slightly damp towel; set in a warm draft-free place. Let rise until doubled in bulk, about 1 hour (about 40 minutes for quick-rising yeast).

Micro-rise Method: Cover with damp towel; microwave at 10% power for 10 minutes, rotating bowl after 5 minutes. Let rest in microwave oven for 5 minutes. Microwave at 10% power until doubled in bulk, 5 to 10 minutes.

4. Punch dough down; knead 30 seconds. Cover and set aside for 5 minutes. Grease 2 large baking sheets; set aside.

5. Divide dough into 3 equal pieces. Shape each piece into a 12-inch baguette, slightly tapered at the ends. Place 2 baguettes well apart on one baking sheet, 1 baguette on the other. Cover with dry towels and set in a warm draft-free place. Let rise until doubled in bulk, 30 to 45 minutes (20 to 30 minutes for quick-rising yeast).

6. Preheat oven to 375°F. Use a very sharp knife to cut 3 diagonal slashes in tops of loaves, about ½ inch deep. Brush baguettes with egg glaze.

7. Bake 20 to 30 minutes, or until bread sounds hollow when tapped on the bottom with your fingertips. Cool on racks.

✦✦✦✦✦✦✦✦✦✦✦✦✦✦✦✦ KNEADING BREAD ✦✦✦✦✦✦✦✦✦✦✦✦✦✦✦✦

Kneading is a technique used to mix and work a dough in order to form it into a cohesive, pliable mass. During kneading, the gluten in the flour forms a network of strands that stretches and expands. It's this gluten framework that enables the dough to hold in the gas bubbles formed by a leavener, thereby making the bread rise. Kneading can be done either by hand or by machine. Mechanical kneading is usually accomplished in a large mixer equipped with a dough hook (some machines have two hooks) or a food processor with a plastic blade. Special breadmaking machines mix, knead, rise, and bake bread all in a single container. Kneading by hand is done with a pressing-folding-turning action performed by pressing down into the dough with the heels of both hands, then pushing away from the body. The dough is folded in half, given a quarter turn, and the process is repeated. Depending on the dough and the method used, kneading time can range anywhere from 5 to 20 minutes. Well-kneaded dough is smooth and elastic.

✦✦✦✦✦✦ HOW MUCH HAS IT RISEN?—THE FINGER-POKE METHOD ✦✦✦✦✦✦

Yeast dough should rise to double its original bulk. To test it after the first rise, poke two fingers into the dough. Don't be timid—jab them in a good half inch. If the indentations stay, the dough is ready. The finger-poke method is only good for the first rise. After the dough is shaped into loaves and risen for the second time, you won't want to ruin the bread by poking holes in the center. Instead, simply look to see whether or not the dough has doubled in bulk.

✦✦

WILD RICE BREADSTICKS

Makes about 4 dozen breadsticks

These crunchy-crisp breadsticks are great with soups or salads, with before-dinner drinks, or as a snack.

1 **package active dry yeast or quick-rising yeast (about 1 scant tablespoon)**
½ **teaspoon sugar**
1 **cup warm water (110°F.)**
½ **cup olive oil or vegetable oil**
1 **teaspoon salt**
¼ **teaspoon freshly ground pepper**
3 **to 3½ cups bread flour or all-purpose flour**
1 **recipe Puffed Wild Rice (page 141)**
1 **egg white mixed with 1 teaspoon water for glaze**

1. In a 1-cup measure, dissolve the yeast and sugar in warm water. Let proof until foamy, about 5 minutes. Turn mixture into either a food-processor workbowl fitted with the plastic blade or the large bowl of an electric mixer.

2. *Food Processor Method:* Add the oil, salt, pepper, and 3 cups of the flour to the yeast in the food processor. Process until mixture holds together, about 1 minute. Scrape down sides of bowl; add Puffed Wild Rice. Process 1 additional minute. Dough should be elastic and soft but not sticky. If necessary, add a small amount of additional flour and process 30 seconds, or until flour is incorporated. Turn dough out onto a lightly floured work surface; knead about 1 minute, or until smooth and elastic.

Electric Mixer or Manual Method: Add the oil, salt, pepper, and 2 cups of the flour to the bowl. Beat at medium speed for 2 minutes or beat 200 vigorous strokes by hand. Change to dough hook(s), or turn dough out onto a lightly floured surface. Add Puffed Wild Rice and enough of the remaining flour to make a soft dough. Knead dough 6 to 8 minutes, or until smooth and elastic, adding only enough flour to prevent sticking.

3. Form dough into ball; place in a lightly oiled medium bowl. Cover bowl with a slightly damp towel; set in a warm draft-free place. Let rise until doubled in bulk, about 1 hour (about 40 minutes for quick-rising yeast).

Micro-rise Method: Cover with damp towel; microwave at 10% power for 10 minutes, rotating bowl halfway through. Let rest in microwave oven for 5 minutes. Microwave at 10% power until doubled in bulk, 5 to 10 minutes.

4. Punch dough down; knead 30 seconds. Divide dough in half; cover and set aside for 5 minutes. Grease 2 large baking sheets; set aside.

5. Working with half of the dough at a time, roll or pat dough into a 12 x 6-inch rectangle. Cut crosswise into 24 strips, ½ inch wide. Arrange, ½ inch apart, on prepared baking sheets, twisting strips slightly and stretching them to 8 inches. Repeat with second half of dough. Brush bread sticks with egg glaze. Cover lightly with wax paper; let rise 20 minutes in a warm draft-free place.

6. Preheat oven to 350°F. Bake 20 to 25 minutes or until golden brown. Cool on racks.

◆**VARIATIONS: Pepper Sticks:** Add 1 teaspoon freshly ground pepper with the flour in Step 2. Before baking, brush breadsticks with egg glaze; sprinkle with cracked pepper and, if desired, coarse salt.

Seeded Breadsticks: Add 1 to 1½ teaspoons poppy seed, caraway seed, sesame seed, dill seed, or crushed fennel seed with the flour in Step 2. Omit Puffed Wild Rice. Before baking, brush breadsticks with egg glaze; sprinkle with type of seed used in dough.

Italian Breadsticks: Add ¼ cup freshly grated parmesan, 1 medium crushed garlic clove, ¾ teaspoon *each* dried basil and dried oregano, and ¼ teaspoon freshly ground pepper with the flour in Step 2. Omit Puffed Wild Rice. Before baking, brush breadsticks with egg glaze; sprinkle lightly with additional parmesan or coarse salt.

Cheesy Breadsticks: Add ⅔ cup grated cheddar, Swiss, or Parmesan cheese with the flour in Step 2. Omit Puffed Wild Rice. Before baking, brush breadsticks with egg glaze; sprinkle lightly with additional cheese.

Beer Sticks: Substitute 1 cup full-flavored dark beer for water. Pour beer into a 2-cup measure; stir vigorously and let sit 15 minutes at room temperature to flatten slightly. Heat beer to 110°F. Dissolve yeast in beer; omit sugar. Before baking, brush breadsticks with egg glaze; sprinkle with your topping of choice.

❖❖❖❖❖❖❖❖❖❖❖ THE DOUGH ALSO RISES—BUT WHERE? ❖❖❖❖❖❖❖❖❖❖❖

Yeast doughs need a warm place in which to rise. Begin by covering the bowl containing the dough with a slightly damp towel to retain the natural moisture. Ideally, dough should rise at temperatures of 80° to 85°F., but will rise at temperatures up to 100°F. without killing the yeast.

Dough rises nicely inside a gas oven warmed only by the pilot light. Or, an electric oven that's been heated at 200°F. for one minute and then turned off. (To be on the safe side, check with an oven thermometer to be sure it's not too hot.) If you're doing laundry, a good rising spot is on top of the washer or dryer. The room will be warm and humid—yeast's favorite atmosphere. Or, run the dryer for a minute on the heat cycle, then turn it off and place the dough inside. You can also set your dough over a pan of hot water on the bottom shelf of a closed oven. Or bring two cups of water to a boil in your microwave oven to create a warm, moist atmosphere. Turn off the power; set the dough inside and close the door. (Also see Micro-Rising Bread Dough, page 253.)

You'll find all kinds of other places in your house where your bread dough can incubate. Just be sure the place is draftfree. Drafts are enemies of yeast and will cause dough to rise unevenly and slowly.

❖❖

◆◆◆◆◆◆◆◆◆◆◆◆◆◆◆ THE PROOF'S IN THE YEAST ◆◆◆◆◆◆◆◆◆◆◆◆◆◆◆

Proofing yeast simply means checking to be sure it's alive by combining it with a small amount of sugar and warm liquid. Because of the reliability of today's active dry yeast, proofing isn't always necessary. It does, however, give yeast a head start. If the expiration date on the package has passed, or if you're unsure of the yeast in any way, proof it before using. Because of its perishability, compressed fresh yeast should always be proofed.

To proof yeast, dissolve yeast and one teaspoon sugar in the warm liquid called for in the recipe; let stand for five to ten minutes. If the mixture begins to swell and bubble, the yeast is alive and well. If you see no activity, discard the mixture and begin again with new yeast. There's absolutely no way to revive dead yeast.

◆◆

TOASTED SUNFLOWER-SEED BREAD

Makes 2 loaves

This hearty loaf is loaded with toasted sunflower seeds, which add crunch and flavor. It makes great sandwiches, particularly avocado, tomato, and bacon. Don't use the food processor for this recipe unless it's a heavy-duty machine. The volume is too much for small machines or those with only standard power.

1¾ cups plus about ⅓ cup dry-roasted or toasted hulled
    sunflower seeds
  2 packages active dry yeast or quick-rising yeast, about 2
    scant tablespoons
  1 teaspoon sugar
  1 cup warm water (110°F.)
  ¼ cup honey
  ¼ cup vegetable oil
  1 cup plain yogurt, at room temperature
  1 large egg, at room temperature
  1 large egg yolk, at room temperature
1½ teaspoons salt
  5 to 5½ cups bread flour or all-purpose flour
1½ cups whole wheat flour
  1 egg white mixed with 2 teaspoons water for glaze

    1. In a blender or food processor fitted with the metal blade, process ½ cup of the sunflower seeds until ground very fine; set aside.

◆ TIP ◆

When you add ingredients at room temperature to yeast doughs and quick bread batters, their rising and baking times are speeded up.

2. In a 1- or 2-cup glass measuring cup, dissolve the yeast and sugar in warm water. Let proof until foamy, about 5 minutes. Turn mixture into a food-processor workbowl fitted with the plastic blade or the large bowl of an electric mixer. Add the honey, oil, yogurt, egg, egg yolk, and salt.

3. *Food Processor Method:* Add 5 cups bread or all-purpose flour, the whole wheat flour, and ground sunflower seeds to the food-processor workbowl. Process until mixture begins to hold together, about 30 seconds. Scrape down sides of workbowl. Add the remaining 1¼ cup whole sunflower seeds; process until dough begins to form a ball, about 1 minute. Don't process so much that the dough becomes hot. Turn dough out onto a lightly floured work surface and knead about 1 minute, or until

✦✦✦✦✦✦✦✦✦✦ HIGH-ALTITUDE ADJUSTMENTS FOR BAKING ✦✦✦✦✦✦✦✦✦✦

At altitudes above 3,500 feet flour tends to be drier and absorb more liquid than at lower altitudes. Therefore, slightly more liquid or less flour may be required for a dough or batter to reach the proper consistency. Leavening must also be adjusted so baked goods don't overrise. Likewise, sugar adjustments are necessary in order to prevent a porous crumb with a heavy crust.

No recipe adjustment is suggested for yeast doughs—however, letting the dough rise twice before the final pan rising allows it to develop a fuller flavor. Increasing the baking temperature by 25°F. will help set the crust faster so bread will not overrise during the oven-spring that takes place the first ten to fifteen minutes of baking.

Ingredient	Altitude		
	3,000 Feet	5,000 Feet	7,000 Feet
Reduce baking powder:			
For each teaspoon, decrease	⅛ tsp	⅛ to ¼ tsp	¼ tsp
Reduce sugar:			
For each cup, decrease	0 to 1 Tbsp	0 to 2 Tbsp	1 to 3 Tbsp
Increase liquid:			
For each cup, add	1 to 2 Tbsp	2 to 4 Tbsp	3 to 4 Tbsp

smooth and elastic. If dough is very sticky, knead enough of the remaining ½ cup flour to make it manageable.

Electric Mixer or Manual Method: Add 2½ to 3 cups (depending on how heavy-duty your mixer is) bread or all-purpose flour to the ingredients in the bowl. Beat at medium speed for 2 minutes or beat 200 vigorous strokes by hand. Add whole wheat flour, ground sunflower seeds, the remaining 1¼ cup whole sunflower seeds, and enough remaining bread or all-purpose flour to make a soft dough. Change to dough hook(s) or turn dough out onto a lightly floured surface. Knead dough 8 to 10 minutes, or until smooth and elastic, adding only enough flour to prevent sticking.

4. Form dough into ball; place in a large, lightly oiled bowl. Cover bowl with a slightly damp towel; set in a warm draft-free place. Let rise until doubled in bulk, about 1 hour (about 40 minutes for quick-rising yeast).

Micro-rise Method: Cover with damp towel; microwave at 10% for 10 minutes, rotating bowl halfway through. Let rest in microwave oven for 5 minutes. Microwave at 10% power until doubled in bulk, 5 to 10 minutes.

5. Punch dough down; knead 30 seconds. Divide dough in half. Cover and set aside for 5 minutes. Generously grease 2 loaf pans, 8 x 4 inches or 9 x 5 inches. Sprinkle 2 tablespoons sunflower seeds over bottom and sides of each pan.

6. Form into loaves; place in prepared pans. Cover with a dry towel and set in a warm draft-free place. Let rise until doubled in bulk, 30 to 45 minutes (20 to 25 minutes for quick-rising yeast).

7. Preheat oven to 375°F.

8. Cut 3 diagonal slashes, ½ inch deep, in the top of each loaf. Brush with egg-white glaze. Sprinkle about 2 teaspoons sunflower seeds over each loaf.

9. Bake 30 to 35 minutes, or until bread sounds hollow when you turn it out and tap it on the bottom. Cool completely on racks before cutting.

♦**NOTE:** If the bottom crust of your bread is not as crisp or brown as you'd like, remove bread from pan and place

♦ TIP ♦

Because glass bakeware conducts and retains heat better than metal, reduce the oven temperature by 25°F. when using glass pans.

directly on oven rack for the final 5 minutes of baking. Cooling bread on a rack prevents the bottom crust from becoming soggy.

✦✦✦✦✦✦✦✦✦✦✦✦✦ MICRO-RISING BREAD DOUGH ✦✦✦✦✦✦✦✦✦✦✦✦✦

Dough can rise in a microwave oven in about a third the regular time of conventional methods. However, any form of quick rising means the dough won't have as much time to develop its full flavor. *You must have a microwave oven with 10% power.* If your power levels don't go that low, or your microwave oven only has low, medium, and high settings, forget micro-rising—your dough will simply turn into a half-baked lump.

TO RISE ENOUGH DOUGH FOR TWO STANDARD-SIZE LOAVES IN A MICROWAVE   Set a cup of hot water at the back corner of your microwave oven. Place the dough in a large, greased, microwavesafe bowl. Cover with a damp towel. Set the power level at 10% power; turn on for ten minutes. Let the dough rest in microwave oven for five minutes. Microwave at 10% power for five to ten minutes longer, or until the dough has doubled in bulk.

The second rising—after the dough is shaped into loaves—will take about 10 minutes, but the loaves must be in glass baking dishes. Refer to your owner's guide for specific information on rising bread in your microwave oven.

✦✦✦

AMARETTO- ALMOND BATTER BREAD

Makes 2 medium loaves

Years ago I won a cooking contest with this recipe, which features one of my favorite types of bread—batter bread. This yeast bread relies on vigorous beating rather than kneading to stretch the gluten. Either an electric mixer or a food processor can replace elbow grease and muscle for the beating process. This type of bread begins as a batter so thick a wooden spoon can stand up in it. The texture is a little coarser than kneaded bread, but the flavor is wonderful. Serve this bread with Amaretto Butter (page 308) for an extra-special treat.

1	cup golden raisins
⅓	cup Amaretto or other almond-flavored liqueur
2	packages active dry yeast or quick-rising yeast (2 scant tablespoons)
1	teaspoon plus 2 tablespoons sugar
½	cup warm water (110°F.)
⅔	cup milk, at room temperature
6	tablespoons butter, melted
½	cup mild honey or Lyle's Golden Syrup
2	large eggs, at room temperature
1	teaspoon salt
2	teaspoons pure vanilla extract
1½	tablespoons finely grated lemon zest (1 large lemon)
4¼ to 4¾	cups bread flour or all-purpose flour
2	cups toasted finely chopped almonds

1. In a small bowl, combine the raisins and liqueur. Cover with plastic wrap. Microwave on HIGH for 30 seconds; let stand, covered, for 10 minutes. Or combine the raisins and liqueur in a small saucepan. Bring liquid to a boil. Remove from heat; cover and let stand for 15 minutes.

2. In a 1-cup glass measuring cup, dissolve the yeast and 1 teaspoon sugar in warm water. Let proof until foamy, about 5 minutes.

3. Turn mixture into either a food-processor workbowl fitted with the plastic blade or the large bowl of an electric mixer. Add the milk, butter, honey, eggs, salt, vanilla, lemon zest, and 2½ cups of the flour.

4. *Food Processor Method:* Process for 2 minutes. Turn batter into a large bowl. Stir in 1 cup of the almonds, the raisins and liqueur, and enough remaining flour to make a stiff batter.

Electric Mixer or Manual Method: Use electric mixer fitted with beater to beat at medium speed for 4 minutes (or beat 400 vigorous strokes by hand). Stir in 1 cup of the almonds, the raisins and liqueur, and enough remaining flour to make a stiff batter.

5. Cover bowl with a slightly damp towel; set in a warm draft-free place. Let rise until doubled in bulk, about 1½ hours (about 1 hour for quick-rising yeast).

Micro-rise Method: Cover with damp towel; microwave at 10% power for 10 minutes, rotating bowl a half turn after 5 minutes. Let rest in microwave oven for 5 minutes. Microwave at 10% power until doubled in bulk, about 10 minutes.

6. Generously grease two 8 x 4-inch loaf pans. Sprinkle bottom and sides of pans with ½ cup almonds.

7. Stir batter down; divide equally between the 2 pans. Butter your fingers and a 12-inch square of wax paper. Smooth top of batter with your buttered fingers. Sprinkle tops of loaves with the remaining ½ cup of almonds, pressing lightly into the surface. Sprinkle each loaf with 1 tablespoon sugar. Cover with buttered wax paper.

8. Let rise in a warm draft-free place until doubled in bulk, about 1 hour (40 minutes for quick-rising yeast).

9. Preheat oven to 350°F.

10. Bake 40 to 45 minutes, or until bread sounds hollow when tapped on the bottom. Remove loaves from pans and cool on racks. Bread may be sliced and eaten as soon as cool. Wrap tightly and store leftovers at room temperature for up to 1 week. Or double-wrap and freeze for up to 3 months.

· · · · · · · · · · ·

> **♦ TIP ♦**
> If you find that your bread is beginning to brown too fast, cover it with a tent of aluminum foil.

The Sweet Life

....

One of my earliest and fondest childhood memories is that of standing on tiptoes, eyes level with the kitchen tabletop, gazing in silent fascination as my mother formed magical swirls in a frosting as white and fluffy as a summer cloud. With the tip of a teaspoon and a flick of her wrist, she created wondrous peaks and valleys in the frosting. My taste buds tingled with anticipation. The thought of waiting until after dinner for such a creation was made bearable only by the bribe of licking the beaters.

My love affair with sweets has not dimmed in passion since I was a tot. And why should it? Was there ever a dish so completely designed to give pure pleasure as dessert? It teases, it contents, it soothes, it delights. It gives a meal a satisfying sense of completion. A fine dessert hints at luxury and indulgence as few other courses can.

Bas-reliefs in the tombs of Egyptian pharaohs show that bakers were making pies at least 30 centuries ago. But it wasn't until the fourth century B.C. that Persia and Arabia began cultivating sugar cane. The western world wasn't introduced to it until the Moors conquered the Iberian peninsula in the ninth century. Slowly but surely, sweet seduction spread throughout the world.

For centuries, desserts were luxuries only the affluent could afford because sugar—referred to in times past as "white gold"—was scarce, and therefore expensive. Early sugar wasn't the granulated, alabaster substance we know today. It came in the form of large, solid loaves or blocks, ranging from off-white to light brown in color. Chunks of the rock-hard sucrose had to be chiseled from the main mass and ground to a powder with a mortar and pestle. Sugar is no longer scarce or expensive, and we may indulge in sweet conceits whenever we wish.

The word "dessert" comes from *desservir*, French for "to clear away." Indeed, the table is usually cleared to make way for the grand finale of the meal. Dessert is an integral part of a menu and should be planned so that its flavors both complement and harmonize with those of the other dishes served. Any dessert—whether a simple, down-home ending like Warm Spiced Apples with Caramel Whipped Cream, or a showstopping extravaganza like the Tunnel-of-Fudge Cheesecake—should have inherent elegance and be presented with pride. For this reason, it's especially important to buy the very best ingredients for your desserts. Cheap substitutions and imitation products always betray their value in the final taste test.

One of my favorite ways to entertain a large group is to serve a simple, single-course meal like Black and White Chili (page 147) with warm loaves of homemade bread, then follow it with an elaborate dessert buffet. The sweets might range from little tempters like Maple–Pecan Shortbread and Double Chocolate Filigree Cookies, to large show-stoppers like Black Bottom Lemon Torte and White Chocolate Truffle Torte. Camembert–Pear Tart, served with Spiced Crème Fraîche, and Cappuccino Poundcake could be offered for those who prefer their desserts less sweet. The delighted gasps when guests first see such a spectacular array of desserts is ample reward for time spent in the kitchen preparing this sweet treasure trove.

The little eye-pleasing finishing touches you give your desserts can be the simple difference between a good and a spectacular one. A garnish doesn't have to be time-consuming or elaborate, but it should reflect the flavor of the dessert it adorns. It can be as simple as a single fresh strawberry atop the Pepper–Berry Fool, or as sensationally showy (but easy to create) as Chocolate Leaves crowning the Tunnel-of-Fudge Cheesecake.

On the following pages, you'll find many recipes that can be made ahead. None of them are difficult, nor do they require special skills to recreate. Read the recipe carefully before beginning to be sure you have the necessary equipment and ingredients on hand. Don't expect to substitute one size pan for another, skim milk for cream, or cocoa powder for chocolate and have the dish turn out the same. It's equally important to follow a recipe's instructions. If cheesecake directions call for overnight refrigeration, don't try to get by with a three-hour chill. The results may be passable, but the cheesecake won't have the proper creamy texture and may fall apart when you try to cut it.

A dessert should be an event, a celebration, a personal statement. A truly wonderful dessert—whether simple or elaborate—should dazzle the eye, excite the mind, and delight the palate. It should be the quintessential *pièce de résistance* and end a meal with style and grace.

SPICED MELON COUPE

Makes 6 to 8 servings

The combination of melon and ice cream is always refreshing. Particularly this melon, which has been steeped in a spiced orange–mint marinade. Coupes are traditionally served in stemmed, wide, deep bowls. However, large balloon wine glasses or pretty glass bowls will do just as well.

¾ cup chopped fresh mint leaves
3 (3-inch) cinnamon sticks, broken in half
15 whole allspice berries
15 whole cloves
2½ cups fresh orange juice
½ cup dark rum
½ cup sugar
4½ tablespoons finely julienned lemon zest
6 cups melon balls, such as cantaloupe, honeydew, Crenshaw, and so on
1 to 1½ quarts French vanilla ice cream
6 to 8 sprigs mint

1. Combine the chopped mint and spices in the center of a triple-layered, 6-inch circle of cheesecloth. Bring edges of cheesecloth up to center; tie securely with string. Place bag in a medium saucepan; add the orange juice, rum, sugar, and lemon zest. Bring to a boil. Reduce heat; simmer, uncovered, 40 minutes.

2. Remove bag of spices. Turn marinade into a shallow 2-quart dish; refrigerate or freeze until cool.

3. Add the melon, stirring to coat with marinade. Cover and refrigerate 12 to 24 hours, stirring occasionally.

4. To serve, place 1 or 2 scoops of ice cream in each of 6 to 8 coupe dishes, balloon wine glasses, or pretty glass bowls. Top each serving with melon balls and some of the marinade, including lemon zest. Garnish with mint sprigs.

PEPPER–BERRY FOOL

Makes 4 servings

Fool is an early American dessert (by way of England) composed of crushed gooseberries and whipped cream. This updated low-calorie version substitutes strawberries for gooseberries, and lemon yogurt for most of the whipped cream. The real surprise comes from the pizzazz added by freshly ground pepper.

2 pints strawberries
2 cups lemon yogurt
¼ to ½ teaspoon freshly ground pepper
½ cup heavy whipping cream, whipped until stiff

1. Reserve 4 of the prettiest strawberries for garnish. Hull and chop the remaining berries.

2. In a medium bowl, use a fork to thoroughly crush 1 cup of the berries. Stir in the yogurt and pepper. Fold in whipped cream and remaining chopped berries.

3. Spoon into 4 stemmed glasses; garnish each serving with a whole strawberry. Cover and refrigerate for at least 3 hours.

. . . .

CARAMEL BRÛLÉ WHIPPED CREAM

Makes about 1½ cups

Brûlé (broo-LAY) is the French word for "burned," and this topping has the wonderful burnt-caramel flavor of the classic dessert, *crème brûlée*. It can be made on the stovetop or in the microwave—both ways are easy. Caramel Brûlé Whipped Cream is equally good over fresh fruit (particularly apples, peaches, and pears), plain poundcake, chocolate cake, or pudding.

½ cup sugar
⅛ teaspoon salt
1 teaspoon pure vanilla extract
1 cup heavy whipping cream

1. In a small, heavy saucepan, combine the sugar, 2 tablespoons water, and salt; stir to combine. Cook without stirring over medium heat until mixture turns a deep golden brown. Immediately remove from heat.

Microwave Method: In a 2-cup glass measuring cup, combine the sugar, 2 tablespoons water, and salt; stir to combine. Cook on HIGH, uncovered, just until mixture turns pale golden brown, about 4 minutes. Remove from microwave oven and let stand until mixture turns a deep golden brown, about 1 minute.

2. Stirring constantly with a long-handled wooden spoon, very gradually add cream. Be careful of spatters. Mixture will clump and harden.

3. Return pan to medium heat and stir constantly until mixture is smooth.

Microwave Method: Cook on MEDIUM, stirring every 20 seconds, until mixture is smooth, about 1½ minutes.

4. Pour caramel cream into an electric mixer bowl. Cover and chill until very cold—about 1½ hours in the freezer, 3 hours in the refrigerator. May be refrigerated for up to 3 days.

5. Up to 6 hours before serving, beat the cream until stiff peaks form. Cover and refrigerate until ready to use.

♦ TIP ♦

If you accidentally overbeat whipping cream and it begins to turn buttery, gently whisk in additional cream, 1 tablespoon at a time. Do not beat any more than necessary.

♦♦♦♦♦♦♦♦♦♦♦ WHIPPING CREAM—REGULAR OR HEAVY? ♦♦♦♦♦♦♦♦♦♦♦

The term used for cream in this book is "heavy whipping cream" which is the industry-wide description for cream with a milkfat content of between 36 and 40 percent. In some areas, this cream is labeled heavy cream. In many regions, however, the most commonly available cream is 30 to 36 percent milkfat; it is labeled whipping cream. If you live in one of those areas, don't worry—regular whipping cream can be substituted for any recipe in this book that calls for heavy whipping cream.

PAPAYA BAKED ALASKAS

Makes 4 servings

This fruit version of the classic dessert is a sure winner as a summer dinner finale. The coconut in the meringue goes perfectly with the fruit. I use nonsweetened coconut, which is readily available in health-food stores and some gourmet markets. You may need more or fewer berries, depending on the size of the papayas. This dessert can be assembled through Step 2 up to 8 hours in advance, then refrigerated until 30 minutes before the meringue is added. The flavor of the fruit will be much fuller if just slightly chilled.

1½ to 2 cups fresh mixed berries, such as blueberries, raspberries, blackberries, or coarsely chopped strawberries
2 tablespoons Grand Marnier (optional)
2 ripe papayas, cut in half and seeded
4 large egg whites, at room temperature
⅛ teaspoon salt
6 tablespoons sugar
½ teaspoon pure vanilla extract
½ cup shredded coconut, toasted

1. Reserve several of the prettiest berries for garnish. If desired, combine berries with Grand Marnier in a medium bowl; set aside 30 minutes.

2. Position rack in center of oven. Preheat oven to 450°F.

3. If papayas do not sit flat, cut off a thin portion of the bottom of each half. Spoon mixed berries into each papaya half, mounding berries slightly; set aside. Or cover with plastic wrap and refrigerate until 30 minutes before preparing meringue, up to 8 hours in advance.

4. In the large bowl of an electric mixer, beat the egg whites with salt until soft peaks form. Beating constantly, gradually add the sugar, 2 tablespoons at a time. Continue beating until glossy and firm. Beat in vanilla; fold in coconut.

5. Spread a quarter of the meringue mixture over the top of each berry-filled papaya half, making sure to seal all exposed fruit surfaces. Do not cover base of papaya.

Place papayas on a large ungreased baking sheet. Bake 3 to 5 minutes, or until golden brown. Garnish with reserved berries. Serve immediately.

✦✦✦✦✦✦✦✦✦✦✦✦✦✦✦✦✦✦ **SEPARATING EGGS** ✦✦✦✦✦✦✦✦✦✦✦✦✦✦✦✦✦✦

It's easier to separate eggs when they're cold. If you're going to beat the whites, make sure none of the yolk gets into them. The yolk contains fat, which will prevent the whites from reaching their full volume. If a speck or two of yolk gets into the whites, use the corner tip of a paper towel to blot it up. To prevent ruining a bowlful of egg whites, as you crack each egg, transfer the white to one small bowl, the yolk to the other. Then turn the white into the bowl in which it will be beaten.

✦✦

WARM SPICED APPLES WITH CARAMEL BRÛLÉ WHIPPED CREAM

Makes 4 servings

The flavor of this deceptively simple dessert says "comfort" all the way down to the last bite. Don't be surprised if this dessert makes your guests hum with pleasure.

1½ cups Caramel Brûlé Whipped Cream (page 260)
1½ cups apple cider
 ½ cup calvados or other apple brandy, or additional apple cider
 ½ teaspoon ground cinnamon
 ½ teaspoon freshly grated nutmeg
 ½ teaspoon ground allspice
 1 teaspoon pure vanilla extract
 4 tart, medium apples, peeled, cored, and coarsely chopped
 additional freshly grated nutmeg for garnish

1. Prepare Caramel Brûlé Whipped Cream through Step 4 at least 6 hours (or up to 1 day) before the dessert is to be served.
2. In a medium saucepan, combine the cider, calvados, cinnamon, nutmeg, and allspice. Bring to a boil. Reduce heat to medium; add vanilla and apples. Poach apples,

uncovered, turning occasionally, until tender but still slightly crisp, about 10 minutes. If apples are to be reheated just before serving, cook them 1 or 2 minutes less. Cover and refrigerate until ready to serve (up to 1 day in advance).

3. Up to 6 hours before serving apples, beat Caramel Brûlé Whipped Cream until stiff peaks form. Cover and refrigerate until ready to use.

4. If apples have been refrigerated, warm over low heat before serving. Spoon warm (not hot) apples into serving bowls or goblets. If desired, spoon a little of the poaching liquid over apples. Top each serving with Caramel Brûlé Whipped Cream and sprinkle with nutmeg.

◆◆◆◆◆◆◆◆◆◆◆◆◆◆◆ **GRATING FRESH NUTMEG** ◆◆◆◆◆◆◆◆◆◆◆◆◆◆◆

Freshly grated nutmeg is much more pungent than already ground nutmeg. It's wonderful with hundreds of foods, including vegetables, breads, and desserts.

Nutmeg graters and grinders are small tools used to turn the whole nutmeg seed into a coarse powder or flakes. A nutmeg grater has a fine-rasp, slightly curved surface. The grating is accomplished by rubbing the nutmeg across the grater's surface. Many graters store the whole nutmeg in containers attached to the bottom or back of the unit. A nutmeg grinder resembles a pepper grinder except that the cavity is designed specifically to hold a whole nutmeg. When the crank is rotated, the nutmeg is grated.

◆◆

CAMEMBERT-PEAR TART

Makes 8 servings

Fruit-and-cheese fans will love this mélange of sugar-glazed pears and creamy camembert cheese in crisp puff pastry. With a nod to today's busy cook, storebought puff pastry is used. Brie can be substituted if Camembert is not available. The white rind of the cheese can be removed easily in one of two ways. When cold, it can simply be cut off. If the camembert is at room temperature, and therefore soft, cut the round in half and use a spoon to scrape the cheese off the rind.

12 ounces Camembert, at room temperature
1 large egg
1 large egg yolk
2 tablespoons brandy
5 tablespoons butter
¼ cup sugar
1 pound firm, ripe pears, peeled, cored, and cut into ¼-inch slices
2 sheets frozen puff pastry, thawed but still cold (1-pound package)
1 egg mixed with 1 teaspoon water for glaze

1. Remove rind from camembert. In the small bowl of an electric mixer or in a food-processor workbowl fitted with the metal blade, combine the Camembert, egg, egg yolk, and brandy. Beat or process until smooth; refrigerate. Cheese mixture must be thick enough not to run when spread but not hard.

2. In a large skillet, melt the butter. Add the sugar; cook over high heat for 1 minute. Add the pears; cook over medium-high heat until crisp-tender. Transfer pears to a plate to cool.

3. On a floured work surface, roll 1 puff pastry sheet to a 10-inch square; cut out a 10-inch circle. Roll the other pastry sheet to an 11-inch square, cut out an 11-inch circle.

4. Place the 10-inch circle in the center of an ungreased baking sheet. Gently spread the cheese mixture over pastry to within ¾ inch of edge. Spoon cooled pears on top of cheese. Brush ¾-inch border with egg glaze. Do not let the glaze drip onto the baking sheet or baked pastry will stick to sheet.

5. Score the 11-inch pastry circle into 8 equal wedges, cutting only halfway through pastry. Gently lift scored pastry circle and place it on top of pears, lining it up with the bottom pastry. Use the tines of a fork to firmly press edges of pastry together. Brush pastry surface with egg glaze. Use a sharp, pointed knife to make ½-inch-long cuts in a star pattern following the scoring, through the center of the pastry to the pears. Refrigerate at least 20

♦ TIP ♦

Speed the ripening of soft fruits such as avocados, nectarines, peaches, pears, and tomatoes by putting them in a paper bag with an apple.

minutes. Can be made to this point the night before, covered with plastic wrap, and refrigerated.

6. No more than 2 hours before serving, preheat oven to 450°F.

7. Bake tart 10 minutes. Reduce heat to 400°F.; bake an additional 25 to 35 minutes, or until puffed and golden brown. Serve warm or at room temperature.

. . . .

MAPLE–PECAN SHORTBREAD

Makes 32 cookies

If you're not already a fan, I urge you to use pure maple syrup, not only for pancakes and such, but for recipes like this one. Once you've tasted the real thing, it will be almost impossible to return to counterfeit syrups. Be sure to refrigerate pure maple syrup after it's opened to inhibit the growth of mold.

½ **pound (2 sticks) unsalted butter, softened**
½ **cup plus 2 tablespoons pure maple syrup**
1½ **teaspoons pure vanilla extract**
¼ **teaspoon salt**
1⅔ **cups all-purpose flour**
⅓ **cup cornstarch**
1⅓ **cups finely chopped toasted pecans**

1. Preheat oven to 350°F. Set aside an ungreased 13 x 9-inch baking pan.

2. In a large electric mixer bowl, combine the butter, ½ cup of the maple syrup, vanilla, and salt. Beat at medium-low speed until light and fluffy.

3. Add the flour, cornstarch, and 1 cup of the nuts. Stir just until blended. Use a rubber spatula to spread over bottom of baking pan. Sprinkle top of dough with remaining ⅓ cup nuts.

4. Bake 25 minutes. Remove from oven; drizzle top with remaining 2 tablespoons maple syrup. Return to

♦ TIP ♦

A baking sheet should be either cool or at room temperature when the cookie dough is placed on it. Otherwise, the dough will start to melt, adversely affecting the cookies' shape and texture.

oven and bake an additional 20 minutes, or until top is a deep golden brown and cookie begins to pull away from sides of pan.

5. Cut while warm into 32 cookies. Cool in pan. Store in an airtight container.

. . . .

DOUBLE CHOCOLATE FILIGREE COOKIES

Makes about 6 dozen (2- to 2½-inch) cookies

The lily is truly gilded on these dark, rich, lacy cookies with a topping of white-chocolate filigree.

8 tablespoons (1 stick) butter or margarine
1 tablespoon milk
¾ cup packed light brown sugar
3 tablespoons unsweetened cocoa powder, preferably Dutch processed
2 tablespoons all-purpose flour
½ cup regular or quick-cooking (not instant) rolled oats
½ cup chopped walnuts, pecans, or almonds
⅛ teaspoon salt
⅛ teaspoon ground cinnamon
1 teaspoon pure vanilla extract
6 ounces white chocolate, coarsely chopped
1 to 1½ tablespoons vegetable oil

1. Preheat oven to 350°F. Generously grease 2 large baking sheets; set aside.

2. In a medium saucepan over medium heat, combine the butter and milk. Heat until butter melts; remove from heat.

3. Meanwhile, in a food-processor workbowl fitted with the metal blade or in a blender jar, combine the brown sugar, cocoa, flour, oats, nuts, salt, and cinnamon. Process until oats and nuts are finely ground. It may be necessary to stop the blender and push the nuts and oats down several times to make sure they're finely ground. Add to butter mixture; stir to combine. Stir in vanilla.

4. Using a ½-teaspoon measure, drop batter, 2 inches apart, onto prepared baking sheets. If necessary, use the tip of a dinner knife to push the batter out of the measuring spoon.

5. Bake 6 to 7 minutes, or until cookies flatten and look bubbly and lacy. Reverse baking sheets top to bottom and front to back halfway through baking time.

6. Remove from oven. Let stand on baking sheets 1 minute. Use a thin metal pancake turner to gently transfer cookies from baking sheet to a rack to cool. If cookies begin to stick to baking sheet, return to oven 1 minute to reheat and loosen. Repeat Steps 4 through 6 for remaining batter. Allow baking sheets to cool before reusing.

7. Line 2 large baking sheets with wax paper. Place cooled cookies close together on lined baking sheets; set aside.

8. In the top of a double boiler over hot but not boiling water, melt the white chocolate, stirring until smooth. Stir in enough oil to give the mixture a thick drizzling consistency. Do not let it become too thin or the white chocolate won't set properly.

9. Dip the tines of a dinner fork into chocolate; drizzle over cookies in a lacy design. Refrigerate to set chocolate. Store in an airtight container in the refrigerator for up to 2 weeks.

♦ TIP ♦

Store soft and crisp cookies separately. Place each in its own airtight container; store in a cool place. If crisp cookies become soft, recrisp by reheating 5 minutes in a 300°F. oven.

. . . .

BLACK BOTTOM LEMON TORTE

Makes 8 to 10 servings

If you've never tasted chocolate with lemon, you're in for a real treat—it's an elegant and enticing flavor combination.

This dessert is perfect for company dinners because it can be made a day ahead. For an easy shortcut, prepare the lemon mousse by itself and serve it in stemmed glasses, accompanied by thin chocolate wafers.

LEMON MOUSSE:

    1 envelope (1¼ ounces) unflavored gelatin
    ⅓ cup fresh lemon juice
    3 large eggs, separated, at room temperature
    1 cup half-and-half
    1 cup sugar
    ¼ teaspoon salt
  1½ pounds cream cheese, softened
    ½ teaspoon almond extract
    ¼ teaspoon cream of tartar
      Chocolate Leaves or other decorations (page 281) (optional)
    1 lemon slice for garnish (optional)

CHOCOLATE COOKIE CRUST:

   18 Oreo or Hydrox cookies (do not use cookies with double filling)
    3 tablespoons butter, melted

CHOCOLATE GANACHE:

    ¾ cup heavy whipping cream
    8 ounces semisweet chocolate, finely chopped
    1 teaspoon pure vanilla extract

1. In a 1-cup glass measuring cup or a small bowl, stir the gelatin into lemon juice. Set aside 5 minutes to soften.

2. In a small saucepan, lightly beat the egg yolks. Slowly stir in the half-and-half, then the sugar and salt. Cook over medium heat, stirring often, until mixture thickly coats the back of a metal spoon, about 10 minutes.

Remove from heat. Add the gelatin mixture; whisk until dissolved, about 1 minute. Set aside.

3. In the large bowl of an electric mixer, beat the cream cheese and almond extract until perfectly smooth, scraping bowl as necessary. With mixer running at medium speed, slowly pour hot lemon mixture through a fine sieve into cheese mixture. Beat until smooth, scraping sides of bowl as necessary.

4. Refrigerate, uncovered, until mixture begins to mound when spooned on top of itself, about 1½ hours. Stir occasionally while mixture is cooling. If you're in a hurry, chill in freezer for about 45 minutes. Stir often to be sure ice crystals don't form.

5. Preheat oven to 350°F. Lightly oil a 9-inch springform pan; set aside.

6. Prepare crust while mixture is chilling. In a food processor fitted with the metal blade, process cookies until very finely ground. With the machine running, slowly add the butter. Use quick on/off pulses until butter is thoroughly incorporated. Turn mixture into prepared pan. Use the back of spoon to press evenly and firmly over bottom of pan. Bake 10 minutes. Place in refrigerator or freezer to cool quickly.

7. Prepare ganache while crust is baking. Combine cream and chocolate in a 2-cup glass measuring cup. Microwave on HIGH, uncovered, for 1 minute. Stir, then cook on HIGH for 1 more minute. Remove and whisk to combine. Let stand 1 minute, then stir until mixture is smooth. Or combine cream and chocolate in a small saucepan. Heat over medium-low heat, stirring often, until chocolate has melted and mixture is smooth.

8. Stir the vanilla into melted chocolate. Pour over cooled cookie crust; smooth surface. Refrigerate, uncovered, until set, about 30 minutes, or freeze about 15 minutes.

9. When the lemon mixture begins to mound, combine the egg whites with cream of tartar in the small bowl of an electric mixer. Beat until stiff but not dry. Stir a quarter of the whites into the chilled lemon mixture to loosen. Gently fold in remaining whites.

E very sweet has its sour.

—RALPH WALDO EMERSON

10. Spoon lemon filling over chocolate ganache. Cover and refrigerate until set, about 4 hours. If desired, cover with foil and refrigerate overnight.

11. If desired, prepare Chocolate Leaves or other decorations. Or cut a lemon slice from the outer edge to the center. Twist slice to form an S.

12. To remove torte from pan, run a sharp knife between the pan and the torte to loosen. Release and remove side of pan. Use a knife with a long, thin blade to gently loosen the torte from bottom of pan. Then use 2 large metal spatulas to carefully transfer the torte to serving plate. If desired, smooth sides of torte with the dull edge of a dinner knife. Garnish as desired with lemon twist or Chocolate Leaves. May be refrigerated, uncovered, for up to 6 hours.

♦ **VARIATION: Lemon Mousse:** Make the Lemon Mousse as directed, using 4 egg whites instead of 3. Spoon mixture into 6 to 8 stemmed glasses. Top each serving with a dollop of sweetened whipped cream, garnished with a candied violet. Serves 6 to 8.

· · · · · · · · · · ·

TUNNEL-OF-FUDGE CHEESECAKE

Makes 12 to 14 servings

This dessert is a real showstopper. Serve it for your most special occasions and enjoy the raves.

CRUST:

1½ cups Oreo or Hydrox cookie crumbs, including the filling (do not use cookies with double filling), about 22 cookies
3 tablespoons butter, melted

FILLING:

2½ pounds cream cheese, softened
1½ cups sugar
5 large eggs
¼ cup all-purpose flour
½ teaspoon salt
¼ cup heavy whipping cream
3 ounces semisweet chocolate, melted and cooled
½ cup semisweet chocolate chips
1 tablespoon pure vanilla extract

CHOCOLATE SOUR CREAM TOPPING:

3 tablespoons confectioners' sugar
2 teaspoons unsweetened cocoa powder, preferably Dutch process
1 cup sour cream
1 teaspoon pure vanilla extract
2 ounces semisweet chocolate, grated
   Chocolate Leaves or other chocolate decorations (page 281; optional)

1. Position rack in center of oven. Preheat oven to 350°F. Grease a 9-inch springform pan; set aside.

2. In a medium bowl, combine the cookie crumbs and butter. Or place 22 cookies in a food-processor workbowl fitted with the metal blade; process to fine crumbs. Add butter; process 5 to 10 seconds. Turn crumb mixture into prepared pan, being careful not to get crumbs on sides of pan. Using the back of a large spoon, press crumb mixture firmly and evenly over the bottom of the pan. Bake 10 minutes; cool to room temperature before filling.

3. Raise oven temperature to 400°F. In the large bowl of an electric mixer, beat the cream cheese and sugar together until smooth and fluffy. Add the eggs, one at a time, beating well after each addition. Beat in the flour, salt, and cream.

4. Place 2 cups of the cheese mixture in a medium bowl. Stirring constantly, gradually add melted chocolate, blending until well combined. Stir in the chocolate chips; set aside. Stir vanilla into remaining cheese mixture.

5. Pour all but 1½ cups of the light cheese mixture into prepared crust. Spoon chocolate-cheese filling in a 2-inch-wide ring on the light cheese mixture, about 1½ inches from the edge of the pan. Be careful not to get any in center of light mixture. Using the back of a spoon, carefully press chocolate mixture down into light mixture until top is level. Spoon reserved light cheese mixture evenly over all; smooth top.

6. Place cheesecake in center of middle oven rack. Position a 13 x 9-inch baking pan filled halfway with hot water on lower shelf. Bake 15 minutes. Reduce heat to 300°F.; bake an additional 50 minutes. Turn oven off. Let cheesecake cool in oven 1 hour with oven door propped open 1 to 3 inches. Remove to a rack; cool completely. Cover and refrigerate overnight.

7. Run a thin knife around inside edge of pan; remove side of pan. Use a thin knife to loosen crust from the bottom of pan. Using two large metal spatulas, carefully slide cheesecake off pan bottom onto a serving plate. In a medium bowl, combine the topping ingredients except the grated chocolate. Spread over top of cheesecake. Sprinkle the grated chocolate in a 2-inch band around the outer edge of top. Or, decorate top of cheesecake with Chocolate Leaves or other chocolate decorations. Chill at least 1 hour or up to 8 hours before serving.

. . . .

Give me the luxuries of life and I will willingly do without the necessities.
—FRANK LLOYD WRIGHT

CAPPUCCINO POUNDCAKE

Makes 10 to 12 servings

This moist, buttery cake is just as good an after-dinner dessert as it is a coffeecake at breakfast time. A bittersweet chocolate swirl adds a perfect counterpoint to the coffee-flavored cake. Though this poundcake needs little adornment, I suggest accompanying it with Cappuccino Cream (page 276) when serving it as a dessert.

¼ cup coffee-flavored liqueur or whole milk
⅓ cup instant coffee granules or ¼ cup instant espresso coffee
about ¾ cup milk
3 tablespoons unsweetened cocoa powder
⅓ cup confectioners' sugar
¾ pound (3 sticks) butter, softened
2 cups granulated sugar
1 teaspoon pure vanilla extract
½ teaspoon salt
5 large eggs, at room temperature
3 cups all-purpose flour
1 teaspoon baking powder
½ teaspoon baking soda
additional confectioners' sugar for decoration (optional)
2 cups Cappuccino Cream (optional)

1. Preheat oven to 350°F. Generously grease and flour a 10-inch tube pan.

2. In a 1-cup measure, combine the liqueur or milk and instant coffee. Microwave on HIGH for 30 seconds. Remove from oven; stir until coffee dissolves. Or combine the liqueur or milk and instant coffee in a small saucepan. Heat over medium heat, stirring constantly, just until coffee dissolves. Add enough milk to equal 1 cup liquid; set aside.

3. In a small bowl, whisk together the cocoa powder and confectioners' sugar; set aside.

4. In the large bowl of an electric mixer, beat the butter until very soft. Add the granulated sugar, vanilla, and salt; beat until light. Add eggs, one at a time, beating thoroughly after each addition. Scrape sides of bowl as necessary.

◆ TIP ◆

Break up lumps in confectioners' sugar by "sifting" it in a food processor fitted with a metal blade. Create your own superfine sugar by processing granulated sugar until powdery.

5. In a medium bowl, stir together the flour, baking powder, and baking soda. Fold into butter mixture alternately with coffee liquid, a third at a time, stirring just to combine after each addition.

6. Turn half the batter into the prepared pan; smooth surface. Using the back of a kitchen teaspoon, make an indentation ½ inch deep in the batter, circling around the batter halfway between edge of pan and center tube. Spoon cocoa-confectioners' sugar mixture into depression. Carefully spoon remaining batter over top of cocoa mixture. Using the broad side of a dinner knife (neither the top dull edge nor the bottom cutting edge), cut down through the batter to the bottom of the pan, moving the knife in a wide zigzag pattern to create a marbled effect. Use the back of a spoon to smooth surface of batter.

7. Bake 50 to 55 minutes, or until a toothpick inserted in the center of the cake comes out almost clean. A few crumbs clinging to the pick, or the chocolate swirl coating it, are perfectly okay.

8. Remove cake from oven. Cool in pan on rack 15 minutes. Run a knife around center tube and outer edge of pan. Carefully invert onto a rack. Cool to room temperature. If desired, dust lightly with confectioners' sugar. Serve with Cappuccino Cream, if desired.

. . . .

CAPPUCCINO CREAM

Makes about 2 cups

I use this topping for cakes, mousses, and bread puddings. My nephew Barry even loves it on pancakes! Pass it with after-dinner coffee to add a dollop to the cup. Double the recipe to use Cappuccino Cream as a cake filling and frosting.

1 cup heavy whipping cream
1 tablespoon instant espresso coffee powder or
   1½ tablespoons instant coffee granules
1 teaspoon pure vanilla extract
¼ cup confectioners' sugar
2 tablespoons coffee-flavored liqueur

1. In the bowl of an electric mixer, stir together the cream and instant coffee. Refrigerate cream and beaters ½ hour. If using an immersion blender, chill in a deep medium bowl.

2. Stir cream to make sure coffee has dissolved. Beat cream at high speed until the consistency of thick pudding. Add the vanilla and confectioners' sugar; beat until cream forms soft peaks. With mixer running at medium-high speed, gradually drizzle in liqueur, beating until cream is desired consistency.

WHITE CHOCOLATE TRUFFLE TORTE

Makes 12 servings

The sophisticated look of this rich torte belies the simplicity with which it's made, and the fact that it has only five main ingredients.

I like it simply adorned with a dusting of unsweetened cocoa, as with a classic truffle. If you want something showier, garnish the top with some type of chocolate decoration (page 281), such as dark chocolate leaves or curls.

White chocolate can sometimes be temperamental in the melting process. That's why it's important to use a whisk to make sure the final mixture is velvety smooth. If you're not a white chocolate fan, try the dark chocolate variation.

1 **pound white chocolate, finely chopped**
2 **cups heavy whipping cream**
½ **teaspoon salt**
1½ **cups chocolate wafer cookie crumbs from Nabisco brand's Famous Chocolate Wafers (about 23 cookies)**
¼ **cup sugar**
6 **tablespoons butter, melted**
1 **teaspoon unsweetened cocoa**

1. In a heavy medium saucepan, combine the chocolate, cream, and salt. Warm over low heat, using a whisk to stir often, until chocolate has melted and mixture is smooth.

Microwave Method: In a 4-cup glass measure, combine the chocolate, cream, and salt. Cook, uncovered, on HIGH for 2 minutes. Stir well with a whisk. Cook on HIGH for 1 more minute. Use a whisk to stir until chocolate has melted and mixture is smooth.

2. Turn white chocolate mixture into a large electric mixer bowl. Place in freezer or refrigerator and chill, stirring occasionally, until mixture is the texture of a soft pudding—about 1½ hours in freezer, 3 hours in refrigerator.

3. Meanwhile, preheat oven to 350°F. Lightly grease an 11-inch tart pan with a removable bottom or a 10- or 11-inch springform pan; set aside.

4. In a food processor fitted with the metal blade, process cookie crumbs and sugar together until combined. Use quick on/off pulses. With machine running, slowly

Too much of a good thing can be wonderful.
—MAE WEST

add butter. Use quick on/off pulses until butter is thoroughly incorporated.

5. Turn mixture into prepared pan. Use the back of spoon to press evenly and firmly over bottom and up sides of tart pan, or about ¾ inch up sides of springform pan. Bake 10 minutes. Cool completely before filling. Remove cooled crust from pan and place on serving plate.

6. Beat thickened white chocolate mixture at high just until soft peaks form. Turn into crust. Swirl surface decoratively with the back of a spoon. Place cocoa in a fine strainer. Dust top of torte with cocoa. Refrigerate at least 5 hours. May be covered and refrigerated for up to 1 day before serving. Leftovers can be covered and refrigerated for up to 1 week.

♦**VARIATION: Black Magic Truffle Torte:** Substitute semisweet chocolate for white chocolate. Garnish with white Chocolate Leaves or Chocolate Curls (page 281).

. . . .

♦♦♦♦♦♦♦♦♦♦♦♦♦♦♦♦ **WHITE CHOCOLATE** ♦♦♦♦♦♦♦♦♦♦♦♦♦♦♦♦♦

Did you know that white chocolate isn't really chocolate at all? That's because it doesn't contain chocolate liquor—the thick, dark paste left after the cocoa butter is extracted from the nibs. White chocolate is usually made of a mixture of sugar, cocoa butter, milk solids, lecithin, and vanilla. No wonder it doesn't taste like chocolate! Be sure and read the label: If cocoa butter isn't mentioned, it may be white, but it's not white chocolate. Because it has a tendency to scorch and clump when overheated, it must be melted very slowly.

♦♦♦

CHOCOLATE MADNESS

Makes 4 servings

For a showy dessert, serve Chocolate Madness in white Chocolate Cups (page 280). Because this dessert is so rich, the servings are small. It's an easy recipe to double, however, if you have more guests. One caveat: don't substitute milk for the cream, or the dessert won't set properly.

1 **cup heavy whipping cream**
2 **tablespoons instant coffee granules or 1½ tablespoons instant espresso coffee powder**
6 **ounces semisweet chocolate, finely chopped, or semisweet chocolate chips**
¼ **cup Kahlúa or other coffee-flavored liqueur tiny pinch ground cinnamon**
1½ **teaspoons pure vanilla extract**
4 **white or dark Chocolate Cups (optional)**
½ **cup heavy whipping cream, whipped and sweetened to taste, or 1 cup Cappuccino Cream (page 276)**
4 **coffee-bean candies or 2 teaspoons grated chocolate (optional)**

1. In a 2-cup glass measure, combine the cream and instant coffee. Microwave on HIGH for 2 minutes, or just until mixture begins to boil. Or heat in a small saucepan over medium heat.

2. Meanwhile, in a blender jar, combine the chocolate, Kahlúa, and cinnamon. Pour hot cream mixture into blender jar all at once. Cover and process at low speed until chocolate melts and mixture is smooth, 30 to 45 seconds. Add the vanilla; blend 2 seconds to combine.

3. Pour mixture into 4 small (6- to 8-ounce) stemmed glasses or dessert bowls, or cool 30 minutes and pour into chocolate cups. Refrigerate, uncovered, for 2 hours. Cover with foil and continue to refrigerate until set, about 4 hours. Top each serving with a dollop of whipped cream or Cappuccino Cream, and, if desired, a coffee-bean candy or grated chocolate.

♦**VARIATIONS: Mexican Chocolate Madness:** Increase ground cinnamon to ½ teaspoon and add a pinch of ground cloves.

B ring on the dessert. I think I am about to die.
—ANTHELME BRILLAT-SAVARIN (last words)

Irish Cream Madness: Omit the instant coffee. Heat ¾ cup Irish cream liqueur with ½ cup heavy whipping cream instead of 1 cup cream and ¼ cup Kahlúa.

. . . .

CHOCOLATE CUPS

Makes 8 to 12 cups

These showy, edible chocolate cups can be made with either white or dark chocolate. They're easy to prepare, and can be made ahead and refrigerated. Fill them with fruit, mousse, or ice cream for a grande finale!

8 to 10 ounces semisweet, sweet, or white chocolate, melted and cooled to lukewarm

1. Using 16 to 24 fluted foil or paper baking cups, place 1 baking cup inside another, forming a double thickness. Using the back of a regular teaspoon, spread melted chocolate over the bottom and up the sides of paper cups. Push chocolate into ridges; make inside surface as smooth as possible. Chocolate should be about ⅛ inch thick. As each paper baking cup is coated, place in a muffin cup or custard cup to support the sides. Refrigerate 15 minutes, or until chocolate is firmly set.

2. Check chocolate cups to be sure there are no thin spots. If so, dab additional melted chocolate on those places in need of repair. Chill again until set. Gently peel off paper or foil. Be careful not to handle chocolate too much, as the heat of your hands will cause it to melt. Return chocolate cups to refrigerator until ready to fill. May be made a month in advance, covered, and refrigerated.

♦ VARIATIONS: **Harlequin Cups:** Use half white chocolate and half dark chocolate. Spread the melted white chocolate over half of bottom and sides of paper cups. Refrigerate to set. Spread remaining half with melted dark chocolate; refrigerate until set.

Chocolate–Mint Cups: Add 1 teaspoon mint extract to chocolate before melting.

Miniature Chocolate Cups: Use 60 miniature (1½-inch) paper cups. Place 1 cup inside another, forming 30 cups with a double thickness. Proceed as for large cups. The tiny size of these cups makes them particularly vulnerable to the heat of your hands. Remove only 4 to 5 cups from refrigerator at a time; carefully peel off paper. Return to refrigerator while working on remaining cups.

. . . .

CHOCOLATE DECORATIONS FOR DESSERTS

Use dark or white chocolate to create these beautiful garnishes for cakes, pies, puddings, or mousses.

Grated Chocolate: Use a large, thick piece of chocolate for ease in handling. Place grater over a piece of wax paper. Hold one end of the chocolate in a piece of paper towel to prevent the heat of your hands from melting it. Firmly rub chocolate over coarse side of grater. Or place the chocolate in a Mouli rotary grater for fast and easy results. Or use a food processor fitted with either the thin slicing blade or grating disc. Use gentle pressure on the plunger to press chocolate into cutting mechanism. Chocolate processed in a food processor will not be as finely grated as with other methods. Refrigerate grated chocolate until ready to use. Use a spoon to sprinkle it over the dessert.

Chocolate Curls: Use a large, long bar of chocolate. If chocolate is too cold, shavings will be brittle and break. Hold chocolate firmly to warm slightly or place in a warm (90°F.) spot for about 15 minutes. Place a piece of wax paper on the work surface. Holding chocolate in one hand and a swivel-blade vegetable peeler in the other, firmly draw the blade toward you along edge of bar. The pressure you apply will determine the thickness of the curl. Let curls drop onto wax paper. Refrigerate in an airtight container until ready to use. Use a spoon to gently transfer chocolate curls to the dessert.

Chocolate Leaves: Line a large baking sheet with wax paper. Choose 6 to 8 nonpoisonous, firm leaves such as camellia, rose, citrus, or hibiscus, with stems attached. Wash and thoroughly dry leaves. Place on wax paper. Melt 2 ounces chocolate. Using a small metal spatula or the back of a kitchen teaspoon, thickly spread melted chocolate over underside of leaves. Be careful not to let chocolate run over edges of leaves. Use your fingertip to remove any excess chocolate from edges. Place leaves, chocolate-side-up, on prepared baking sheet; refrigerate until chocolate is set. Patch any bare spots with additional chocolate; chill to set. Remove leaf from chocolate by grasping stem and pulling leaf gently away from chocolate. Refrigerate in an airtight container until ready to use.

Chocolate Leaves with Berries: Attach a fresh raspberry or small strawberry to center of chocolate leaf using a tiny dab of melted chocolate as glue.

Chocolate Scrolls: Line a large baking sheet with wax paper. Melt 6 ounces chocolate. Pour onto a smooth work surface, such as marble, formica, or the back of a baking sheet. Use a narrow, metal spreading spatula to spread chocolate about ⅛ inch thick over work surface. Let chocolate cool until firm but not hard. Starting at one end of chocolate and at side closest to you, use a flexible pastry scraper or wide metal spatula tilted at a 45° angle to slowly and firmly move spatula forward. The spatula's edge will lift the chocolate and cause it to roll around itself. Use spatula to gently transfer chocolate scrolls to prepared baking sheet; refrigerate until firm. Refrigerate in airtight container until ready to use.

Chocolate Triangles: Line a large baking sheet with wax paper. Draw an 8- or 9-inch circle on the wax paper. Spread 3 ounces melted chocolate evenly within circle. Refrigerate until almost set. Using a large, sharp knife, cut chocolate circle into 10 to 12 pie-shaped pieces. Refrigerate until completely set. Gently break triangles apart; peel away wax paper, handling chocolate as little as possible. Refrigerate in airtight container until ready to use.

Chocolate Cutouts: Line a large baking sheet with wax paper. Spread 2 ounces melted chocolate $\frac{1}{16}$ to $\frac{1}{8}$ inch thick on the wax paper. Refrigerate until almost set. Using canapé cutters, small cookie cutters, or a pointed knife, cut out desired shapes in chocolate. Refrigerate until completely set. Gently break shapes apart; peel away wax paper, handling chocolate as little as possible. Refrigerate in airtight container until ready to use.

. . . .

◆ ◆ ◆

◆ ◆ ◆

Potpourri

. . . .

I've always disliked having to plow through dozens of recipes in a book when all I want is a sauce or a topping to dress up a dish. That's why I created this Potpourri chapter, chock-full of relishes, salsas, chutneys, jams, toppings—sweet and savory—and a few basics.

Most of the following recipes can be used in a variety of ways. Both the Avocado Salsa and Black Bean Relish, for example, are wonderful atop fajitas, salads, hamburgers, or as an accompaniment to grilled meats. And they're chunky and satisfying enough to be served on their own. The Jalapeño Aioli makes a great dip for French fries and crudités; it's equally wonderful on sandwiches and burgers. Coconut–Citrus Sauce is a true chameleon, changing from sauce to marinade to dip.

There are also recipes created to save you the time, aggravation, and expense of tracking down items that are sometimes hard to find such as sundried tomatoes, mascarpone, and coconut milk. And there's a recipe for one of my very favorite indulgences, Crème Fraîche, with nine flavor variations. May this culinary potpourri please you as much as it does me!

. . . .

CUCUMBER–CORN SALSA

. . . .

Makes about 2 cups

This refreshing salsa is a great adjunct to a variety of dishes including Smoked Corn and Chorizo Burritos (page 63), Grilled Tuna Fajitas (page 194), and Grilled Swordfish (page 191).

about ¾ cup fresh or thawed frozen yellow corn kernels
(1 medium ear corn)
1 large ripe tomato, seeded and diced
⅓ cup diced seeded cucumber
⅓ cup chopped scallions, white and green parts
1 to 2 jalapeño or serrano chili peppers, seeded and minced
1 tablespoon minced cilantro
1 medium clove garlic, minced
2 tablespoons olive oil
1 tablespoon fresh lime juice
salt

In a medium bowl, combine all the ingredients. Cover and refrigerate for at least 3 hours before serving. Taste before serving and add salt if needed.

♦NOTE: The seeds in a cucumber are often bitter. Remove them by cutting the cucumber in half lengthwise, then scraping out the seeds with a regular teaspoon.

. . . .

AVOCADO SALSA

Makes about 2 cups

I could eat this concoction all by itself. It's absolutely wonderful served as a garnish with Black and White Chili (page 147), Black-Bean Breakfast Burritos (page 26), Fajita Salad (page 95), or just plain grilled burgers.

2 tablespoons fresh lime juice
1 tablespoon olive oil
1 medium clove garlic, minced
1 small jalapeño chili pepper, seeded and minced, or
    1 tablespoon minced canned jalapeño pepper
½ teaspoon chili powder
¼ teaspoon salt
4 plum tomatoes, seeded and diced (about ½ pound)
⅓ cup finely chopped jícama
2 tablespoons finely chopped chives or scallion greens
1 to 3 tablespoons minced cilantro
2 medium ripe but firm avocados, peeled, seeded, and diced

◆ TIP ◆

An easy and quick way to cut foods like scallions and chives is to snip them with scissors.

In a medium bowl, whisk together the lime juice, oil, garlic, jalapeño, chili powder, and salt. Stir in the tomatoes, jícama, chives, and cilantro. Add the avocados, stirring only to incorporate. Cover tightly; refrigerate at least 2 hours. May be made a day before serving.

. . . .

BLACK BEAN RELISH

Makes about 2½ cups

Though created to accompany the Black-Bean Polenta Cakes (page 144), this relish is wonderful with any number of dishes. Try it with Fajita Salad (page 95), Grilled Tuna Fajitas (page 194), almost any grilled fish or cold chicken, and folded inside flour tortillas.

¼ cup plus 2 tablespoons olive oil or vegetable oil
2 cups cooked black turtle beans (about ¾ cup uncooked)
½ cup chopped chives or scallion greens
2 medium cloves garlic, minced
2 teaspoons finely grated lemon zest
2 medium tomatoes, seeded and chopped
3 to 4 tablespoons chopped cilantro
2 teaspoons balsamic vinegar
⅛ to ¼ teaspoon cayenne
   salt

1. In a large skillet, heat ¼ cup oil. Over high heat, sauté black beans, chives, garlic, and lemon zest, stirring constantly, for 2 minutes. Remove from heat; stir in tomatoes and cilantro. Turn out onto a plate to cool to room temperature.

2. In a medium bowl, combine the remaining 2 tablespoons oil, vinegar, and cayenne. Add cooled bean mixture; toss to coat. Salt to taste. Cover and refrigerate until 30 minutes before ready to serve.

. . . .

JALAPEÑO AIOLI

Makes about 2 cups

The classic aioli—a garlic mayonnaise from the Provence region of southern France—is a popular accompaniment with meats, vegetables, and the French fish stew *bourride*. This rendition takes a step away from tradition with the addition of jalapeños. It's wonderful with Garlic-grilled Okra (page 175), and a tablespoon or two adds a touch of magic to mashed potatoes, salad dressings, and other cold sauces.

If there's a problem with salmonella in raw eggs in your area (see page 29), use the prepared mayonnaise variation. The Roasted Garlic Aioli variation is much milder than the classic fresh-garlic version.

    4 medium cloves garlic, peeled
    ½ teaspoon salt
    2½ tablespoons white wine vinegar or lemon juice
    2 large egg yolks
    1½ to 2 tablespoons finely chopped jalapeño peppers, fresh
       or canned
    1½ cups olive oil or ¾ cup *each* olive and vegetable oil
    2 tablespoons very hot water (optional)

1. With the machine running, drop the garlic cloves one by one into a food-processor workbowl fitted with metal blade; process until garlic is chopped and clinging to sides of bowl. Scrape down sides of food processor bowl. Or mince the garlic and turn it into a blender jar or medium, deep bowl. Add salt, vinegar, egg yolks, and jalapeño; process, blend, or whisk to combine.

2. In a food processor with the motor running, or with blender at medium-high speed, or whisking constantly by hand, gradually add oil in a very thin drizzle. Process or whisk until all oil is incorporated and mixture is thick. For a lighter aioli, gradually add hot water, processing or whisking until combined.

3. Refrigerate in an airtight container for up to 10 days.

♦ **VARIATIONS: Roasted Garlic Aioli:** Substitute 10 to 12 cloves Roasted Garlic (page 309), pulp squeezed from the skin, for 4 cloves fresh garlic. Omit jalapeños.

> The emotional content of garlic almost equals its culinary value.
> —ARTHUR E. GROSSER

Fennel Aioli: Substitute ¼ cup finely chopped fresh fennel greens for the jalapeños.

Prepared Mayonnaise Aioli: Substitute 1¾ cups prepared mayonnaise for salt, vinegar, egg yolks, and oil. After garlic is chopped in Step 1, add prepared mayonnaise and jalapeños, processing until combined.

. . . .

"SUN"-DRIED TOMATOES

Drying tomatoes in the sun, an age-old process of preservation, gives them an intensely rich, deliciously sweet flavor. Most commercial sundried tomatoes, though, especially those produced in the United States, are not dried in the sun at all—they're dehydrated by oven heat, sometimes combined with hot air. Your own home-dried tomatoes will be better if you use plum tomatoes (also called Roma tomatoes) because their water content is lower than that of most other varieties. The amount of liquid in beefsteaks, for example, is so high that there's little left after drying but skin. Two important tips: Choose tomatoes that are similar in size for even drying and seed tomatoes for faster drying. I prefer to dry tomatoes only until their texture is supple and chewy, somewhat similar to a prune.

There are several ways to store dried tomatoes. My favorite is in oil because there's a bonus—after the tomatoes are gone, the flavored oil can be used for salad dressings, in cooking, or simply to drizzle over thick slices of French bread.

2 **pounds plum (Roma) tomatoes**
 olive oil
 salt

1. Preheat oven to 450°F. Lightly oil a jelly-roll pan or other large, shallow baking pan.
2. Cut the stem portion away from the top of each to-

mato. Cut tomatoes in half lengthwise; seed, if desired. Rub cut edge of tomatoes with olive oil; sprinkle lightly with salt.

3. Set rack on prepared baking pan. Place tomatoes, cut side up, on rack. Put tomatoes in oven; immediately reduce heat to 250°F. Bake for 6 hours, or until tomatoes are dried to your liking. (Drying tomatoes in a convection oven will take about two-thirds the time as a conventional oven.)

Microwave Method: Prepare tomatoes as in Step 2. Line a 10- to 12-inch paper plate with a microwavesafe paper towel. Place 12 tomato halves, cut side up, around edge of plate. If tomatoes have one end that's narrower than the other, point narrow end toward center of plate. Microwave on HIGH for 2 minutes. Open door 1 minute to allow steam to escape. Microwave on DEFROST (30% power) for 30 minutes. Rotate plate a half turn; continue to cook on DEFROST for 30 minutes more, or until dried to your liking. Watch carefully so no burn spots appear. If necessary, remove any tomatoes that are drying faster than others.

4. Cool tomatoes to room temperature. Store in a plastic bag or in an airtight screwtop jar at room temperature for up to 5 days. Or store in refrigerator up to 2 weeks; bring to room temperature before using.

5. To store in oil, generously brush dried tomatoes with distilled white vinegar; let stand 5 minutes. Pat tomatoes dry with paper towels; pack lightly in a screwtop jar. If desired, add dried (not fresh) herbs in between layers of tomatoes. Cover with olive or canola oil; refrigerate for up to 1 month.

. . . .

PUMPKIN-SEED TARTAR SAUCE

Makes 1½ cups

I created this sauce for the Crispy Halibut (page 189), but I've since found that it goes with many kinds of broiled, baked, and fried fish and seafood. It also makes a tangy dip for crudités.

½ cup plain lowfat yogurt
½ cup mayonnaise
1 cup hulled pumpkin seeds, toasted and ground
2 tablespoons minced shallot
1 tablespoon sweet pickle relish
1 teaspoon fresh lemon juice

In a medium bowl, combine all ingredients. Set aside at room temperature for 15 minutes before serving. Or cover and refrigerate for 3 hours; remove from refrigerator 30 minutes before serving.

. . . .

CAJUN TARTAR SAUCE

Makes about 1½ cups

This spicy rendering is great with all manner of seafood, and a must with Hushpuppy-fried Catfish (page 188).

¾ cup mayonnaise
1 tablespoon fresh lemon juice
3 tablespoons finely chopped tomato
2 tablespoons finely chopped green pepper
2 tablespoons finely chopped onion
2 tablespoons finely chopped celery
¼ teaspoon cayenne
¼ teaspoon chili powder
¼ teaspoon dried thyme
   salt and additional cayenne

In a medium bowl, combine the first nine ingredients. Season to taste with salt and additional cayenne. Cover and refrigerate for at least 1 hour before using. May be stored for up to 5 days.

. . . .

CREAMY CREOLE SAUCE

Makes about 2 cups

This sauce adds excitement to everything from fish to chicken to pork. I make a double batch and freeze half of it—it takes just a few minutes to defrost in the microwave and I can instantly jazz up an otherwise bland dish. If the sauce gets too thick for your liking, simply add a little cream, half-and-half, or chicken broth.

2 tablespoons vegetable or olive oil
1 small onion, chopped
½ cup chopped celery
½ cup chopped green pepper
2 large cloves garlic, minced
1 cup chopped canned Italian tomatoes (14-ounce can)
1 cup canned tomato sauce
2 teaspoons minced fresh thyme or ½ teaspoon dried thyme leaves
½ teaspoon cayenne
¼ teaspoon chili powder
¼ teaspoon mace
1 teaspoon minced fresh basil or ¼ teaspoon dried basil
1 tablespoon fresh lemon juice
½ cup homemade chicken stock or canned chicken broth
½ cup heavy whipping cream
  salt and freshly ground pepper

1. In a large saucepan, heat the oil over medium-high heat. Add the onion, celery, and green pepper; sauté for 4 minutes. Add the garlic; sauté for 1 minute.

2. Stir in all the remaining ingredients except the cream and salt and pepper. Cook over medium heat, uncovered, for 20 minutes. Stir occasionally during that time.

3. Stir in the cream. Cook over medium heat, uncovered, for 5 more minutes, stirring often. Salt and pepper to taste. Cover and keep warm over low heat until ready to serve. Sauce may be made up to 3 days in advance and refrigerated. Reheat before serving.

♦ TIP ♦

Adding salt and pepper after a sauce is done allows for reduction and prevents overseasoning.

PLUM BARBECUE SAUCE

Makes about 1⅓ cups

This sauce is a real surprise—first you taste the sweetness, and then the snappy boldness. It's wonderful on everything from roasted pork, to grilled ribs, to broiled or sautéed steaks, even hamburgers. Before it's cooked, the sauce can be used as a meat marinade, as with Plum Delicious Steak (page 211).

The sauce is better if made with dark beer, but lager can be substituted. Forty minutes of cooking means there's not a speck of alcohol left in this sauce; if you prefer, a no- or low-alcohol brew can be substituted.

1½ **cups damson or other plum preserves, large pieces of fruit, finely chopped (12-ounce jar)**
⅓ **cup Worcestershire sauce**
¼ **cup cider vinegar**
1½ **cups dark beer (12-ounce bottle)**
2 **medium cloves garlic, minced**
1 **teaspoon Dijon mustard**
½ **teaspoon Tabasco**

1. Combine all the ingredients in a medium saucepan. Bring to a full rolling boil over high heat. (If using this as a marinade before cooking, combine the ingredients in a pan or bowl large enough to hold meat to be marinated.)

2. Reduce heat to medium-low so that the sauce is boiling very gently. Cook, uncovered, until sauce thickly coats a metal spoon and has reduced to about 1⅓ cups, about 40 minutes.

3. Store sauce in a screwtop jar in the refrigerator for up to 1 month. Reheat over medium-low heat.

. . . .

COCONUT–CITRUS SAUCE

Makes 1¼ cups

Yet another inspiration from my friend, the popular restaurateur Glenn Miwa, this sauce is a real sleeper. It fits my criterion for a winning recipe because it has dozens of uses. Uncooked, it is a good marinade for pork, poultry, as for Tropical Turkey Cutlets (page 232), or fish. Cooked and reduced, hot Coconut–Citrus Sauce adds flavor magic as a sauce for meat or fish. Barely warm, it's a dip for crudités.

When chilled, Coconut–Citrus Sauce takes on the texture of soft sour cream. Dollops of it atop grilled fish and hot vegetables melt like butter to coat and flavor the food. The cold sauce can also be used as a topping for fruit or, thinned with a little milk, as a salad dressing.

1¾   cups coconut milk, homemade (page 299) or canned
  1   tablespoon finely grated lemon zest
1½   cups fresh orange juice
  ½   cup packed mint leaves, minced
  1   tablespoon minced fresh gingerroot
  ½   teaspoon salt

   1. Shake canned coconut milk well before opening. If using this mixture as a marinade merely combine the ingredients in a shallow pan or dish large enough to hold the meat being marinated. Marinate meat as desired.

   2. Otherwise, combine all the ingredients in a medium saucepan. Bring to a full rolling boil over high heat. Reduce heat to medium-low; sauce should be boiling very gently. Cook, uncovered, until sauce coats a metal spoon and has reduced to about 1¼ cups, about 40 minutes.

   3. Cool at room temperature, cover and refrigerate for up to 1 week. Reheat, stirring constantly, over low heat. Or place in a 2-cup glass measuring cup and microwave on MEDIUM-HIGH (70% power) for about 2½ minutes, stirring after 1½ minutes.

CRANAPPLE-
APRICOT
CHUTNEY

Makes about 5 cups

This spicy, colorful chutney complements pork, duck, turkey, chicken, and ham; it's scrumptious on turkey, chicken, or ham sandwiches; and it adds excitement to salad dressings. Serve it warm or at room temperature with meats and hot dishes, cold for sandwiches and salad dressing.

Before measuring the cranberries, be sure to pick out any bruised or shriveled berries, and remove any stems. This recipe doubles easily (just be sure to use a larger pot).

  1 (3-inch) cinnamon stick, broken into 3 pieces
12 allspice berries
  8 cloves
1½ pounds tart apples, peeled, cored, and chopped
    (about 4 to 5 medium apples)
  4 cups fresh cranberries (1 pound)
  1 small onion, chopped
1⅓ cups packed light brown sugar
  1 cup cranapple juice
 ⅔ cup red wine vinegar
 ¾ cup chopped dried apricots
 ⅔ cup dried currants
  1 tablespoon minced fresh gingerroot
  1 tablespoon finely grated orange zest
 ⅛ teaspoon cayenne
  1 cup coarsely chopped toasted walnuts
    salt

Cooking is like love. It should be entered into with abandon or not at all.
—HARRIET VAN HORNE

1. Cut a 6-inch square of double-thickness cheesecloth. Place the cinnamon, allspice, and cloves in center. Bring cheesecloth edges up to form a bag; tie securely with string. Or place the spices in a tea caddy and secure lid.

2. In a large heavy 3-quart pot, combine the spice bag and all the remaining ingredients except the walnuts and salt. Bring mixture to a boil over high heat. Reduce heat to low and simmer, uncovered, until chutney thickens, 20 to 30 minutes. Stir occasionally throughout cooking time. Use a fork to fish out and discard spice bag. Stir in walnuts. Salt to taste.

3. Spoon hot chutney into clean jars (preferably canning jars) with airtight lids. Wipe rim of jar before sealing. Cool to room temperature. Store in refrigerator for up to 4 weeks.

. . . .

ONION-ORANGE MARMALADE

Makes about 4 cups

This condiment adds flavor and flair to roasted and grilled meats and new dimensions to ham sandwiches.

4 tablespoons butter
3 medium leeks, white parts only, cleaned and thinly sliced
3 medium red onions, thinly sliced
2 medium oranges
¼ cup balsamic vinegar
1 tablespoon light brown sugar
1 large clove garlic, minced
4 whole cloves
¼ teaspoon ground allspice
¼ teaspoon freshly grated nutmeg
   salt
   white pepper

♦ TIP ♦

When removing the skin from oranges or other citrus fruits, be sure to take only the thin outer zest or colored portion. The white pith will give your dish a bitter undertaste.

1. In a large heavy skillet, melt the butter over medium heat. Add the leeks and onions. Cook, stirring occasionally, until onions are a deep golden brown, about 20 minutes.

2. Meanwhile, use a citrus zester, vegetable peeler, or small sharp knife to remove the zest from the oranges. If not using a zester, cut zest into tiny slivers. Juice the oranges; you should have ⅔ to ¾ cup juice.

3. Add the orange zest, orange juice, vinegar, brown sugar, garlic, cloves, allspice, nutmeg, ½ teaspoon salt, and ½ teaspoon pepper to the leek-onion mixture; stir to combine. Reduce heat to low and simmer, uncovered, until almost all of the liquid has evaporated and the marmalade is thick, about 30 minutes.

4. Cool to room temperature. Remove the cloves, if desired. Adjust seasoning, if necessary, with additional salt and white pepper.

5. Cover and store in the refrigerator for up to 2 weeks. Let stand at room temperature 1 hour before serving.

· · · · · · · · · ·

SUMMER BERRY SYRUP

Makes about 3½ cups

This topping is just as good cold over ice cream as it is warm over pancakes or waffles. Use any combination of berries you prefer—blueberries and raspberries make a sensational color combination. And, although fresh berries are best, frozen berries make a perfectly respectable substitution.

3 **cups sugar**
½ **teaspoon salt**
1 **cup strawberries, hulled and coarsely chopped**
1 **cup raspberries**
1 **teaspoon pure vanilla extract**

1. In a heavy, medium saucepan, combine 1½ cups water, the sugar, and salt. Bring to a boil, stirring twice. Cover and continue to cook five minutes. Remove cover, cook 5 minutes longer or until syrup reaches 200°F. on a candy thermometer. (If using frozen berries, cook syrup to 210°F.) Stir in berries; cook 2 minutes.

2. Remove from heat; stir in vanilla. Pour into a heatproof serving container. Cool to lukewarm before serving or cool to room temperature, transfer to an airtight container, and refrigerate for up to 2 months.

I f six cooks followed the same recipe, the finished dish would vary six times.

—THEODORA FITZGIBBON

· · · · · · · · · ·

MAPLE CREAM

Makes about 1¼ cups

Originally created as a topping for Mapled Ham Bread Pudding (page 35), this is fantastic over dessert puddings, fresh fruit, such as Morning Blues (page 18), and even pancakes. If you use the crème-fraîche version, make the crème fraîche two days ahead so it has time to thicken in the refrigerator overnight.

1 cup heavy whipping cream or Crème Fraîche (page 301)
3 to 4 tablespoons pure maple syrup

In a small pitcher, stir ingredients together. Cover and refrigerate until ready to use. Stir again just before serving. May be served cold, at room temperature, or slightly warm.

♦VARIATION: **Golden Cream:** Substitute Lyle's Golden Syrup for maple syrup.

. . . .

WHIPPED GINGER CREAM

Makes about 2½ cups

A wonderful topping or spread for dozens of foods including Gingerbread Pancakes (page 22), homemade gingerbread, and fruit compotes. The possibilities are endless.

½ cup heavy whipping cream
 8 ounces cream cheese, at room temperature
⅓ cup packed light brown sugar
 1 teaspoon ground ginger
¼ cup minced crystallized ginger

1. In the small bowl of an electric mixer, beat the cream to firm peaks. Transfer the whipped cream to a small bowl; set aside.
2. In the same small bowl of the mixer, combine the cream cheese, brown sugar, and ground ginger; beat until smooth and the sugar has dissolved.

3. Fold the whipped cream and crystallized ginger into the cheese mixture until thoroughly incorporated. Serve immediately or cover and refrigerate for up to 3 days. Check refrigerated ginger cream for 30 minutes before serving. If too firm, let stand at room temperature 20 to 30 minutes before using.

ABOUT FRESH COCONUT

Fresh coconuts are available year-round, with the peak season being October through December. Choose one that's heavy for its size and that sounds full of liquid when shaken; avoid those with damp "eyes." Whole, unopened coconuts can be stored at room temperature for up to six months, depending on the degree of ripeness.

Drain the liquid from a coconut by piercing 2 of the three eyes with an ice pick. This thin juice can be used as a beverage, though it shouldn't be confused with Coconut Milk (recipe follows). Crack the shell with a hammer and break the meat away, using a knife to peel or scrape away the dark inner skin.

Chunks of coconut meat can be grated or chopped, either in a food processor (use the metal blade) or by hand. One medium coconut will yield three to four cups grated coconut. Tightly covered, grated fresh coconut can be refrigerated for up to four days, frozen for up to six months.

COCONUT MILK

Makes about 2 cups

This fragrant liquid adds a subtle flavor and silky texture to many soups, sauces, and desserts. Coconut milk can also be used to cook rice and pasta.

Though canned unsweetened coconut milk—not to be confused with the sweetened coconut "cream" commonly seen in supermarkets—can be found in ethnic markets and some supermarkets, it's easy to make your own. For those who have neither the time nor the inclination to crack a coconut, dried unsweetened coconut (available in health-food stores and Asian markets) is an easy shortcut. The same coconut can be used twice, resulting in a thinner, lighter-flavored liquid the second time around.

2 cups shredded fresh coconut or dried unsweetened coconut

1. In a medium saucepan, combine 2¾ cups water and the coconut; bring to a boil. Cover and simmer for 10 minutes.

2. Pour into a blender or a food-processor workbowl fitted with the metal blade. Process for 1 minute. To avoid scalding yourself when using the blender, begin at low speed and gradually increase to high; place the pusher in the feed tube of the food processor.

3. Strain liquid through a very fine sieve or a sieve lined with a double thickness of cheesecloth. Cover and refrigerate for up to 5 days.

. . . .

MOCK MASCARPONE

Makes about 2⅓ cups

Hailing from Italy's Lombardy region, buttery-rich mascarpone (pronounced mah-scahr-POH-nay) cheese is ivory-colored and has a delicate texture ranging from that of light crème fraîche to that of softened butter. It's generally blended with herbs or spices and served as an appetizer or used as a topping for fresh fruit. It's an extravagant dressing for baked potatoes and, of course, a must for the Italian dessert, tiramisù.

Because imported mascarpone is so expensive, and relatively hard to find, I decided to create this homemade version. Nothing can duplicate mascarpone's delicate flavor, but this mock version comes close on the texture.

8 ounces cream cheese, softened
4 tablespoons unsalted butter, softened
½ cup Crème Fraîche made with sour cream (opposite)
½ cup heavy whipping cream
1 tablespoon confectioners' sugar

1. In the small bowl of an electric mixer, beat the cream cheese and butter just until soft and thoroughly combined. Do not overbeat, or butter will separate. Transfer to a large bowl. By hand, gently and gradually whisk in the Crème Fraîche.

2. In the same mixer bowl, beat the cream until soft peaks form. Add the confectioners' sugar; continue beating until stiff. Fold the whipped cream, a third at a time, into the cheese mixture. Cover and refrigerate for up to 10 days.

. . . .

CRÈME FRAÎCHE

Makes 1 to 1⅓ cups

This matured, thickened cream (pronounced krehm FRESH) has a slightly tangy, nutty flavor and a velvety-rich texture. It's very widely used in France, where the cream is unpasteurized and therefore contains the "friendly" bacteria necessary to thicken it naturally. Here in America, however, fermenting agents must be added. Commercial crème fraîche is quite expensive, so this homemade version is a godsend. The flavor doesn't exactly duplicate the French original, but it's close.

There are several ways in which to prepare crème fraîche, two of which are offered here. The one made with buttermilk is tangier than the sour-cream version. One isn't necessarily better than the other, it just depends on how you wish to use it. Mock Mascarpone (opposite), for instance, is much closer to the real thing when made with the sour-cream version.

Since crème fraîche doesn't curdle when boiled, it's the ideal thickener for many sauces and soups. Many vegetables (particularly potatoes) benefit from a dollop of it. It's also delicious on fresh fruit, cakes, cobblers, and puddings.

1 cup heavy whipping cream (preferably non-ultrapasteurized), at room temperature
1 tablespoon buttermilk or ½ cup sour cream, very well stirred, at room temperature

1. Combine whipping cream and buttermilk or sour cream in a glass jar with a screw top. Secure lid; shake 15 seconds. Set aside at room temperature for 24 hours, or until very thick. Stir once or twice during that time. Cream will thicken faster if the room is warm. (If ingredients are cold, combine and heat in the microwave on MEDIUM (50% power) about 2 minutes, or until lukewarm.)

2. Stir thickened crème fraîche well. Refrigerate at least 6 hours before using. Cover tightly and store in refrigerator for up to 2 weeks.

♦**VARIATIONS: Extra-Thick Crème Fraîche:** After cream thickens, spoon it into a strainer lined with a double layer of cheesecloth or into a paper-filter-lined coffee cone. Set over a bowl with the bottom of the strainer or coffee cone 2 inches above the bottom of the bowl. Cover bowl and refrigerate for 24 hours.

Whipped Crème Fraîche: Beat crème fraîche until soft peaks form (it won't become stiff).

Sweetened Crème Fraîche: Add 1 to 2 tablespoons confectioners' sugar before shaking the cream in Step 1.

Chocolate Crème Fraîche: In the bottom of a glass jar, combine 2 tablespoons *each* unsweetened cocoa and sugar. Add 2 tablespoons buttermilk; stir until smooth. Stir in cream. Screw on jar lid and shake. Continue as directed.

Vanilla-Flavored Crème Fraîche: Stir 1 to 1½ teaspoons pure vanilla extract into crème fraîche in Step 2, just before refrigerating.

Honeyed Crème Fraîche: Stir 1 to 2 tablespoons honey into crème fraîche in Step 2, just before refrigerating.

Gingered Crème Fraîche: Stir 1½ to 2 tablespoons minced candied ginger or 1 to 2 tablespoons finely chopped crystallized ginger into crème fraîche in Step 2, just before refrigerating.

Spiced Crème Fraîche: Add ¼ teaspoon *each* ground cinnamon and grated nutmeg to the cream mixture before shaking in Step 1.

Herbed Crème Fraîche: Add 1 to 1½ tablespoons finely chopped fresh herbs to crème fraîche in Step 2, just before refrigerating.

Mustard Crème Fraîche: Add 2 tablespoons Dijon-style (or your favorite) mustard and ¼ teaspoon salt to crème fraîche in Step 2, just before refrigerating.

. . . .

COMPOUND BUTTERS

Known in France as *beurre composé*, compound butter is butter that has been combined with various flavorings such as herbs, garlic, wine, spices, and so on. A pat atop meat, fish, or vegetables will slowly melt and flavor the food with which it's paired. Compound butters can also be melted (see Step 4) and brushed on corn-on-the-cob, used to baste meats, or—in the case of sweet compound butters—drizzled over pancakes.

The amount of saturated fat in a compound butter can be reduced slightly by substituting one tablespoon of vegetable oil for one tablespoon of the butter for each stick of butter used. Fragrant oils such as walnut, hazelnut, and sesame add a delicious nuance to like-flavored compound butters. Margarine can be substituted for butter, but be careful not to overbeat it or the margarine will exude water.

Any of the following butters can be made either in a food processor fitted with the metal blade, in an electric mixer, with an immersion blender, or by hand. The standard blender doesn't do a satisfactory job, as it's necessary to keep stopping the motor and pushing the ingredients down into the blades. A word of caution: Whenever combining a liquid or semiliquid substance, such as juice, liqueur, or honey, with butter, add the liquid very gradually, beating constantly, so the mixture doesn't separate.

Method for preparing compound butters (unless otherwise indicated):

1. Using a food processor fitted with metal chopping blade, the small bowl of an electric mixer, or a medium bowl with an immersion blender or by hand, process butter until smooth. Add remaining ingredients; process until incorporated.

2. Pack butter into a crock or mold, or pipe into a serving dish or bowl. Cover and chill until firm. Or spoon the compound butter into a log shape 1 to 2 inches in diameter on a large piece of plastic wrap. Roll the plastic wrap to enclose the butter log, smoothing the sides with your fingers. Twist the ends of the plastic wrap to seal.

3. If possible, refrigerate compound butter at least 6 hours to allow flavors to mingle; it may be refrigerated for up to 1 week. Or double-wrap and freeze for up to 6 months. Let refrigerated butter stand at room temperature 20 to 30 minutes before serving to soften slightly.

4. For melted compound butters, place butter in a microwavesafe bowl. Cover loosely with plastic wrap and cook on HIGH for 1 to 2 minutes, depending on the amount. Or melt the butter in a small saucepan over low heat for 3 to 4 minutes.

SAVORY COMPOUND BUTTERS

TOASTED SESAME BUTTER

Makes about 1 cup

10 **tablespoons butter, softened**
½ **cup toasted sesame seeds, finely ground**
 2 **teaspoons Oriental sesame oil (optional)**
¼ **teaspoon salt (optional)**

♦ **VARIATION: Sunflower-seed Butter:** Substitute ⅔ cup toasted sunflower seeds, finely ground, for sesame seeds. Omit sesame oil.

BLUE CHEESE BUTTER

Makes about 1 cup

8 tablespoons (1 stick) butter, softened
4 ounces Roquefort or blue cheese
1 large shallot, minced

CHEDDAR BUTTER

Makes about ¾ cup

8 tablespoons (1 stick) butter, softened
¾ cup grated cheddar, at room temperature (about 3 ounces)
3 drops Tabasco
⅛ teaspoon salt

AURORE BUTTER

Makes about ¾ cup

8 tablespoons (1 stick) butter, softened
1 tablespoon tomato paste
⅛ teaspoon salt
¼ teaspoon freshly ground pepper

ROASTED GARLIC BUTTER

Makes about 1 cup

½ pound (2 sticks) butter, softened
8 to 10 cloves Roasted Garlic (page 309), pulp squeezed from skin
¼ teaspoon salt

LEMON–DILL BUTTER

Makes about ¾ cup

8 tablespoons (1 stick) butter, softened
3 tablespoons finely chopped fresh dill or 1 tablespoon dried dillweed
¼ teaspoon salt
1 tablespoon fresh lemon juice

Combine butter, dill, and salt. Gradually add lemon juice, beating constantly, until incorporated.

♦ **VARIATION: Lemon-Basil Butter:** Substitute 3 table-spoons finely chopped fresh basil for the dill

GINGER–CHIVE BUTTER

Makes about ¾ cup

8 tablespoons (1 stick) butter, softened
2 teaspoons minced fresh gingerroot
1 tablespoon minced chives
  salt and freshly ground pepper

MUSTARD–TARRAGON BUTTER

Makes about ¾ cup

8 tablespoons (1 stick) butter, softened
¼ cup Dijon-style mustard
2 tablespoons finely chopped fresh tarragon or 2 teaspoons dried tarragon
⅛ teaspoon salt
⅛ teaspoon freshly ground pepper

HERB BUTTER

Makes about ½ cup

8 tablespoons (1 stick) butter, softened
¼ cup finely chopped fresh herbs, such as basil, dill, fennel, oregano, rosemary, thyme, or tarragon, or 1½ tablespoons dried herbs
  salt and freshly ground pepper to taste

SANTA FE BUTTER

Makes about ½ cup

8 tablespoons (1 stick) butter, softened
1 teaspoon minced cilantro
½ teaspoon chili powder
¼ teaspoon crushed red pepper
  salt and freshly ground pepper

CHUTNEY BUTTER

Makes about 1 cup

12 tablespoons (1½ sticks) butter, salted
⅓ cup Major Grey chutney, large pieces of fruit finely
    chopped
¼ teaspoon curry powder

. . . .

SWEET COMPOUND BUTTERS

GINGER–PEACHY BUTTER

Makes about 1 cup

8 tablespoons (1 stick) butter, softened
¼ cup confectioners' sugar
½ to 1 teaspoon minced fresh gingerroot or crystallized
    ginger
    pinch salt
½ medium peach, peeled and minced (¼ cup)

Process all the ingredients except peaches. Fold in peaches. (Nectarine or apricot may be substituted for peaches.)

HONEY BUTTER

Makes about ¾ cup

8 tablespoons (1 stick) butter, softened
⅓ cup honey
¼ teaspoon pure vanilla extract

♦VARIATIONS: **Cinnamon–Honey Butter:** Add ½ to ¾ teaspoon ground cinnamon to Honey Butter.

Honey–Berry Butter: Fold ½ cup minced fresh blueberries or strawberries, blotted dry on paper towels, into Honey Butter.

Citrus–Honey Butter: Make Honey Butter recipe, increasing butter to ⅔ cup and adding 2 tablespoons fresh lemon, lime, or orange juice and 2 teaspoons finely grated lemon, lime, or orange zest.

MOLASSES BUTTER

Makes about 1¼ cups

2 **sticks butter, softened**
2 **tablespoons light or dark brown sugar**
2 **tablespoons molasses**
1 **teaspoon pure vanilla extract**
   pinch salt

Cream butter and brown sugar together. Slowly drizzle in molasses and vanilla, beating constantly until thoroughly incorporated.

♦**VARIATION: Maple Butter:** Substitute 3 tablespoons pure maple syrup for 2 tablespoons molasses. If desired, stir in 2 tablespoons minced toasted pecans.

AMARETTO BUTTER

Makes about 1½ cups

2½ **sticks butter, softened**
 3 **tablespoons honey**
 ¼ **teaspoon finely grated orange zest**
 ¼ **teaspoon almond extract**
 ¼ **cup Amaretto**

Process the butter, honey, orange peel, and almond extract together until well combined. Slowly add the Amaretto, beating constantly until thoroughly incorporated.

♦**VARIATION: Frangelico Butter:** Substitute ¼ cup Frangelico for Amaretto. Omit almond extract.

. . . .

♦ TIP ♦

Create butter curls with a butter curler; butter balls with a melon baller; butter molds with decorative butter or candy molds; or use a pastry bag with a large star tip to pipe butter into glass bowls.

ROASTED GARLIC

Makes 4 to 6 servings

When garlic is roasted, it becomes buttery-soft and golden, its flavor slightly sweet and nutty. Even garlic haters have been seduced by roasted garlic's wonderful flavor and texture. There are many uses for it. The most popular in my house is to squeeze the soft garlic out of the skin and spread it like butter over thick slices of French bread that have been drizzled with olive oil. (Squeeze from the pointed end, so the garlic pops out of the root end.) I also use Roasted Garlic in soups, sauces, and salad dressings, on baked potatoes and in mashed potatoes, on focaccia (page 57), and to spread over meats—both before and after cooking.

I've given you both the oven and microwave directions in this recipe. My preference, though it takes a few minutes longer, is oven-roasting. The result is softer garlic that is easier to spread. And I like to separate the cloves before roasting—the skins turn golden all over and the cooked cloves are easier to handle.

3 heads garlic
3 teaspoons olive oil

1. From the tip end of each head of garlic, **gently** rub off the outer layers of papery skin. Separate the cloves, but leave their skins attached. Or leave the heads intact.

2. Preheat oven to 400°F.

3. Place individual cloves (or garlic heads, root end down) in a medium baking dish or pan; drizzle with oil. Cover with foil. Bake about 25 to 30 minutes, or until soft when pierced with a metal skewer or the tip of a pointed knife.

Microwave Method: Place garlic in a small, covered baking dish; do not drizzle with oil. Cover; microwave on HIGH for 5 to 7 minutes, or until tender. Drizzle with oil. Let stand, covered, 5 minutes.

4. Baking time may vary with either method, depending on the size of the garlic. When done, remove from oven and cool to room temperature.

5. Refrigerate leftover cloves in an airtight jar for up to 10 days. To use as a spread, bring to room temperature.

Garlic is the ketchup of intellectuals.

—ANONYMOUS

ROASTED GARLIC OIL

Makes about 1 cup

This mild, fragrant oil adds a touch of culinary magic when brushed on meats, breads, and vegetables. It's great for salad dressings and stir-frying.

8 medium cloves Roasted Garlic (page 309)
1 cup olive or vegetable oil

1. Squeeze garlic from skins into a small bowl. Use a fork to mash garlic. Add about 2 tablespoons of oil, mashing and stirring the garlic to blend. Gradually add remaining oil; stirring well to blend. Transfer to a screwtop jar. Refrigerate for up to 2 weeks.

2. If olive oil was used, let stand at room temperature 30 minutes before using. Or, reliquify in microwave oven on HIGH for 20 to 30 seconds.

✦✦✦✦✦✦✦✦✦✦ QUICK-PEELING METHOD FOR GARLIC ✦✦✦✦✦✦✦✦✦✦

The time-honored method of peeling garlic is to place the flat side of a chef's knife on top of a garlic clove and rap the blade sharply with your fist to break the skin for easy removal. This method is good for peeling a few cloves at a time. If too much pressure is used, however, the clove can easily be smashed.

The following methods are good for peeling large amounts of garlic, as for soup or Caramelized Garlic Cloves (opposite). Because the garlic is heated in both methods, it is partially cooked and therefore milder in flavor.

Stovetop Method: Separate head of garlic into individual, unpeeled cloves. Drop cloves into boiling water to cover; cook 2 minutes. Turn into colander; rinse with cold water. Let stand until cool enough to handle, then peel.

Microwave Method: Place whole head of garlic on a paper plate. Microwave on HIGH for about 1 minute, rotating plate at 30 seconds. (Time will vary according to the size of the head.) Let rest in microwave oven 1 minute. Remove; let stand until cool enough to handle, then peel.

CARAMELIZED GARLIC CLOVES

Makes 4 to 6 servings

Caramelized garlic can be used in any way suitable for Roasted Garlic (page 309). I prefer the latter for spreading on bread, but caramelized garlic can be used in all manner of foods and makes a spectacular presentation when sprinkled over such meats as rack of lamb. I've given you three methods by which garlic can be caramelized—each one delivering slightly different results. Because of its caramelized coating, the garlic is slightly sweeter, the texture a bit firmer.

3 **heads garlic**
3 **tablespoons sugar**
2 **tablespoons olive or canola oil**

1. Quick-peel the garlic cloves (opposite).

2. In a skillet, combine the sugar and oil. Heat over medium heat until the sugar melts. Add the garlic cloves; stir to coat with oil mixture. Cook over low heat 20 to 25 minutes, or until garlic is soft and golden-brown.

Oven Method: Preheat oven to 250°F. In a heavy oven-proof pan, combine the garlic with sugar and oil, making sure cloves are well coated. Bake, uncovered, for 1 hour 15 minutes, or until soft and golden.

Microwave Method: In a covered, microwavesafe container, combine the sugar and oil. Microwave on HIGH for 30 seconds. Add the garlic cloves; stir to coat. Cover and microwave on MEDIUM (50% power) for 3 to 4 minutes, or until cloves are soft. Rotate container after 2 minutes. Remove from oven; let stand 10 minutes.

3. Refrigerate leftover cloves in an airtight jar for up to 2 weeks.

If the soup had been as
  warm as the claret . . .
If the claret had been as old
  as the chicken . . .
If the chicken had been as
  fat as our host . . .
It would have been a
  splendid meal.
  —DONALD MCCULLOUGH

Ingredient Substitutions and Equivalent Charts

	FAHRENHEIT	CELSIUS			FAHRENHEIT	CELSIUS
Water Freezes	32°	0°			160°	71.1°
	40°	4.4°			170°	76.7°
	50°	10°			180°	82.2°
	60°	15.6°			190°	87.8°
	70°	21.1°			200°	93.3°
	80°	26.7°		Water Boils	212°	100°
	90°	32.2°			250°	121°
	100°	37.8°			300°	149°
	110°	43.3°			350°	177°
	120°	48.9°			400°	205°
	130°	54.4°			450°	233°
	140°	60°			500°	260°
	150°	65.6°				

✦✦✦✦✦✦✦✦✦✦✦✦✦✦✦ OVEN TEMPERATURE EQUIVALENTS ✦✦✦✦✦✦✦✦✦✦✦✦✦✦✦

DESCRIPTION	FAHRENHEIT	CELSIUS
Very slow	250°–300°	121°–149°
Slow	300°–325°	149°–163°
Moderate	350°–375°	177°–190°
Very hot	450°–475°	233°–246°
Extremely hot	500°–525°	260°–274°

✦✦✦✦✦✦✦✦✦✦✦✦✦ COMMON MEASUREMENTS AND EQUIVALENTS ✦✦✦✦✦✦✦✦✦✦✦✦✦

½ teaspoon	=	30 drops
1 teaspoon	=	⅓ tablespoon or 60 drops
3 teaspoons	=	1 tablespoon
½ tablespoon	=	1½ teaspoons
1 tablespoon	=	3 teaspoons or ½ fluid ounce
2 tablespoons	=	⅛ cup or 1 fluid ounce
3 tablespoons	=	1½ fluid ounces or 1 jigger
4 tablespoons	=	¼ cup or 2 fluid ounces
5⅓ tablespoons	=	⅓ cup or 5 tablespoons + 1 teaspoon
8 tablespoons	=	½ cup or 4 fluid ounces
10⅔ tablespoons	=	⅔ cup or 10 tablespoons + 2 teaspoons
12 tablespoons	=	¾ cup or 6 fluid ounces
16 tablespoons	=	1 cup or 8 fluid ounces or ½ pint
⅛ cup	=	2 tablespoons or 1 fluid ounce
¼ cup	=	4 tablespoons or 2 fluid ounces
⅓ cup	=	5 tablespoons + 1 teaspoon
⅜ cup	=	¼ cup + 2 tablespoons
½ cup	=	8 tablespoons or 4 fluid ounces
⅝ cup	=	½ cup + 2 tablespoons
¾ cup	=	12 tablespoons or 6 fluid ounces

✦✦✦✦✦✦✦✦ COMMON MEASUREMENTS AND EQUIVALENTS *(continued)* ✦✦✦✦✦✦✦✦

⅞ cup   =   ¾ cup + 2 tablespoons

1 cup   =   16 tablespoons or 8 fluid ounces or ½ pint

2 cups   =   16 fluid ounces or 1 pint

1 pint   =   2 cups or 16 fluid ounces

1 quart   =   2 pints or 4 cups or 32 fluid ounces

1 gallon   =   4 quarts or 8 pints or 16 cups or 128 fluid ounces

✦✦✦✦✦✦✦✦✦✦✦✦✦✦✦✦✦ CONVERTING TO METRIC ✦✦✦✦✦✦✦✦✦✦✦✦✦✦✦✦✦✦✦

When converting to or from metric, be sure to convert *all* measurements. Otherwise, the proportions of the ingredients could be critically imbalanced.

WHEN THIS IS KNOWN	MULTIPLY IT BY	TO GET
teaspoons	4.93	milliliters
tablespoons	14.79	milliliters
fluid ounces	29.57	milliliters
cups	236.59	milliliters
cups	.236	liters
pints	473.18	milliliters
pints	.473	liters
quarts	946.36	milliliters
quarts	.946	liters
gallons	3.785	liters
ounces	28.35	grams
pounds	.454	kilograms
inches	2.54	centimeters
Fahrenheit	subtract 32, multiply by 5, divide by 9	Celsius (Centigrade)

✦✦✦✦✦✦✦✦✦✦✦✦✦✦✦✦✦✦✦✦ CONVERTING FROM METRIC ✦✦✦✦✦✦✦✦✦✦✦✦✦✦✦✦✦✦✦✦

WHEN THIS IS KNOWN	DIVIDE IT BY	TO GET
milliliters	4.93	teaspoons
milliliters	14.79	tablespoons
milliliters	29.57	fluid ounces
milliliters	236.59	cups
liters	.236	cups
milliliters	473.18	pints
liters	.473	pints
milliliters	946.36	quarts
liters	.946	quarts
liters	3.785	gallons
grams	28.35	ounces
kilograms	.454	pounds
centimeters	2.54	inches
Celsius (Centigrade)	multiply by 9, divide by 5, add 32	Fahrenheit

✦✦✦✦✦✦✦✦✦✦✦✦✦✦✦✦✦✦✦✦✦✦ EMERGENCY INGREDIENT SUBSTITUTIONS ✦✦✦✦✦✦✦✦✦✦✦✦✦✦✦✦✦✦✦✦✦✦✦

Although I don't recommend making a habit of substituting ingredients, there are times when it is necessary. The following substitutions can be used in most recipes with satisfactory results.

IF THE RECIPE CALLS FOR:		SUBSTITUTE:
Baking powder, double acting–1 teaspoon	=	¼ teaspoon baking soda plus ⅝ teaspoon cream of tartar *or* ¼ teaspoon baking soda plus ½ cup buttermilk or sour milk (reduce liquid in recipe by ½ cup) *or* ¼ teaspoon baking soda plus ⅜ cup molasses (reduce liquid in recipe by ¼ cup; adjust sweetener).
Beef broth. See Broth		
Bread crumbs, dry–1 cup	=	¾ cup cracker crumbs
Broth, chicken or beef–1 cup	=	1 bouillon cube or 1 teaspoon granules mixed with 1 cup boiling water
Butter–1 cup (2 sticks; 16 tablespoons; 8 ounces)	=	1 cup margarine *or* ⅞ cup vegetable oil, lard, or vegetable shortening *or* ¾ cup strained bacon fat *or* ¾ cup strained chicken fat
Buttermilk or sour milk–1 cup	=	1 cup plain yogurt or 1 tablespoon vinegar or lemon juice plus enough milk to equal 1 cup (let stand 5 minutes) *or* 1¾ teaspoons cream of tartar plus 1 cup milk
Chicken broth. See Broth		
Chocolate, semisweet–1 ounce	=	½ ounce unsweetened chocolate plus 1 tablespoon granulated sugar
Chocolate, unsweetened–1 ounce	=	3 tablespoons unsweetened cocoa plus 1 tablespoon butter or margarine *or* 3 tablespoons carob powder plus 2 tablespoons water
Coconut, grated–1 cup	=	1⅓ cups flaked coconut
Coconut milk, fresh–1 cup	=	3 tablespoons canned cream of coconut plus enough hot water or lowfat milk to equal 1 cup
Cornstarch–1 tablespoon	=	2 tablespoons all-purpose flour *or* 2 teaspoons arrowroot

IF THE RECIPE CALLS FOR:		SUBSTITUTE:
Corn syrup, dark–1 cup	=	¾ cup light corn syrup plus ¼ cup light molasses
Corn syrup, light or dark–1 cup	=	1¼ cups granulated or packed brown sugar plus ¼ cup liquid*
Cream, light (20 percent fat)–1 cup	=	3 tablespoons butter plus enough whole milk to equal 1 cup
Cream, sour–1 cup	=	1 cup plain yogurt *or* ¾ cup sour milk, buttermilk, or plain yogurt plus ⅓ cup butter *or* 1 tablespoon lemon juice plus enough evaporated whole milk to equal 1 cup**
Cream, whipping (30–40 percent fat)–1 cup	=	¾ cup whole milk plus ¼ to ⅓ cup butter
Egg, whole–1 large egg	=	2 large egg yolks plus 1 tablespoon cold water *or* 3½ tablespoons thawed frozen egg *or* ¼ cup egg substitute (imitation egg)
Egg white–1 large white	=	2 tablespoons thawed frozen egg white
Egg yolk–2 large yolks	=	1 large egg (for thickening)
–1 large yolk	=	3½ teaspoons thawed frozen yolk
Flour–2 tablespoons all-purpose flour	=	1 tablespoon cornstarch, potato starch, or rice starch *or* 4 teaspoons arrowroot *or* 2 tablespoons quick-cooking tapioca (for thickening)
Flour–1 cup sifted all-purpose	=	1 cup minus 2 tablespoons unsifted all-purpose flour
Flour–1 cup sifted cake flour	=	1 cup minus 2 tablespoons sifted all-purpose flour
Flour–1 cup sifted self-rising flour	=	1 cup sifted all-purpose flour plus 1½ teaspoons baking powder and ⅛ teaspoon salt
Garlic–1 small clove	=	½ teaspoon minced garlic *or* ⅛ teaspoon garlic powder
Gingerroot, fresh–1 tablespoon finely chopped	=	⅛ teaspoon ground ginger

* Use whatever liquid the recipe calls for.
** Based on how the ingredients interact in the recipe and not on exact flavor or proportion of sweetness.

IF THE RECIPE CALLS FOR:		SUBSTITUTE:
Half-and-half (10 to 12 percent fat)–1 cup	=	1½ tablespoons butter plus enough whole milk to equal 1 cup *or* ½ cup light cream plus ½ cup whole milk
Herbs, fresh–1 tablespoon finely chopped	=	1 teaspoon dried crumbled herbs
Honey–1 cup	=	1¼ cups granulated sugar plus ¼ cup liquid*
Lemon juice–1 teaspoon	=	½ teaspoon vinegar
Milk, nonfat–1 cup	=	⅓ cup powdered nonfat milk plus ¾ cup water
Milk, sour–1 cup	=	1 tablespoon lemon juice or white vinegar plus milk to equal 1 cup
Milk, whole–1 cup	=	1 cup nonfat milk plus 2 tablespoons butter or margarine *or* ½ cup evaporated whole milk plus ½ cup water *or* ⅞ cup water plus ¼ cup powdered whole milk *or* ⅞ cup water plus ¼ cup powdered nonfat milk plus 2½ teaspoons butter or margarine *or* 1 cup soy milk
Mustard, prepared–1 teaspoon	=	1 teaspoon powdered mustard plus 1 teaspoon water
Sour cream. See Cream, sour		
Sugar, confectioners'–1 cup	=	½ cup + 1 tablespoon granulated sugar
Sugar, granulated–1 cup	=	1¾ cups confectioners' sugar *or* 1 cup packed light brown sugar *or* 1 cup superfine sugar
Sugar, light brown–1 cup	=	½ cup dark brown sugar plus ½ cup granulated sugar
Tomato juice–1 cup	=	½ cup tomato sauce plus ½ cup water
Tomato sauce–1 cup	=	⅜ cup tomato paste plus ½ cup water
Vinegar–1 teaspoon	=	2 teaspoons lemon juice**
Yeast, active dry–¼ ounce envelope	=	1 scant tablespoon active dry yeast *or* 1 (.06-ounce) cake compressed fresh yeast

* Use whatever liquid the recipe calls for.
** Based on how the ingredients interact in the recipe and not on exact flavor or proportion of sweetness.

✦✦✦✦✦✦✦✦✦✦ COMPARATIVE BAKING-PAN SIZES ✦✦✦✦✦✦✦✦✦✦

The following table will help determine substitutions of pans of similar approximate sizes. It's important to note that adjustments in baking times will be necessary when pan sizes are changed.

COMMON PAN SIZE	APPROXIMATE VOLUME

Square and Rectangular Pans

8″ x 8″ x 1½″ square	6 cups
8″ x 8″ x 2″ square	8 cups
9″ x 9″ x 1½″ square	8 cups
9″ x 9″ x 2″ square	10 cups
11″ x 7″ x 2″ rectangular	6 cups
13″ x 9″ x 2″ rectangular	15 cups
8″ x 4″ x 2½″ loaf	4 cups
8½″ x 4½″ x 2½″ loaf	6 cups
9″ x 5″ x 3″ loaf	8 cups

Round Pans

1¾″ x ¾″ mini muffin cup	⅛ cup
2¾″ x 1⅛″ muffin cup	¼ cup
2¾″ x 1⅜″ muffin cup	scant ½ cup
3″ x 1¼″ giant muffin cup	⅝ cup
8″ x 1¼″ pie plate	3 cups
9″ x 1½″ pie plate	4 cups
9″ x 2″ pie plate (deep-dish)	6 cups
10″ x 1½″ pie plate	4½ cups
11″ x 1″ tart pan	4 cups
8″ x 1½″ cake	4 cups
8″ x 2″ cake	7 cups
9″ x 1½″ cake	6 cups
9″ x 2″ cake	8½ cups

COMMON PAN SIZE	APPROXIMATE VOLUME
10″ x 2″ cake	10¾ cups
9″ x 3″ bundt	9 cups
10″ x 3½″ bundt	12 cups
8″ x 3″ tube	9 cups
9″ x 3″ tube	10 cups
10″ x 4″ tube	16 cups
9½″ x 2½″ springform	10 cups
10″ x 2½″ springform	12 cups

INDEX